A Century of Labor-Management Relations at McCormick and International Harvester

A Century of Labor-Management Relations at McCormick and International Harvester

Robert Ozanne

THE UNIVERSITY OF WISCONSIN PRESS
Madison Milwaukee London
1967

Published by the University of Wisconsin Press
Madison, Milwaukee, and London
U.S.A.: Box 1379, Madison, Wisconsin 53701
U.K.: 26–28 Hallam Street, London, W.1

Printed in the United States of America by
George Banta Company, Inc., Menasha, Wisconsin
Library of Congress Catalog Card Number 67-25939

Preface

This book is a detailed account of labor-management relations in the International Harvester Company and its McCormick predecessors throughout the century from 1860 to 1960.

American labor history frequently has been largely a chronicle of the rise and fall of unions, based on information skillfully gleaned from newspaper reports of strikes too big to be ignored, from court records, from government investigations, and from union records—which, except for convention proceedings, are notable for their scanty coverage of important events.

Knowledge of the evolution of management's practices in labor relations has been even more limited, since decision-making in this area has been universally carried on behind closed doors. The elaborate business histories, despite their access to corporate records, have failed to penetrate the decision-making process. We find ourselves today with many unanswered questions.

What was the nature of early factory unionism? What were the unions' bargaining goals and tactics? What impact did the early unions have on management practices? What has been the evolution of specialized personnel departments in industry? How did corporate welfarism and company unionism originate? What differing points of view has management taken over labor relations policies?

Even where skillful historians have deduced answers to these questions, they have been unable to document their conclusions adequately.

Economists who seek today to trace the causes of wage movement are seriously handicapped by lack of historical statistics. The rough statistics available, generally from census and other government studies, are quite divorced from the institutional labor and management settings which might give them full meaning.

The McCormick Collection, at the State Historical Society of Wisconsin in Madison, includes the records of the McCormick Harvesting Machine Company, the International Harvester Company, and the personal and business correspondence of members of the McCormick family. These papers make it possible to follow labor-management relations continuously over a hundred-year period. The collection abounds in detail on management deliberations over employee and trade union problems that confronted the company almost from its inception. In addition it contains complete payroll records for over a century. Thus the economist is provided with that essential combination: information on both management's labor policy and detailed wage movement.

The conclusions of this study, insofar as they can be generalized, indicate a far earlier and greater impact of the union on management-labor relations, personnel policies, and wage policies than has hitherto been suspected.

A work which is still in preparation will analyze wage movements on the basis of study of these payroll books. In combination the two volumes will present a picture of the institutional labor relations setting together with a detailed analysis of wage practice and theory.

The author and the public are greatly indebted to the McCormick family for making available such complete and candid corporate and family records, and to the International Harvester Company for expending much effort in locating additional wage and labor relations information. Many officials of both the United Auto Workers and the International Harvester Company submitted to prolonged hours of interviews in order to fill in gaps in the written records. The International Union of Molders, Blacksmiths, and Allied Workers kindly contributed its early records, reaching back to 1863.

Financial support for the research was provided by both the Graduate School and the Extension Division of the University of Wisconsin. Mrs. Herbert Kellar, curator of the McCormick Collection, gave generously of her time and her detailed knowledge of the McCormick family and the Harvester companies. Mrs. Charles Lloyd skillfully did endless typing and retyping. I should also like to thank the Employee Relations Department of the International Harvester Company for providing the photographs of the McCormick family and the McCormick Works which appear in the book.

The editors of *Labor History* have given permission to make free use of materials from my article "Union-Management Relations: McCormick Harvesting Machine Company, 1862–1886," which appeared in the Spring 1963 issue.

R. O.

Madison, Wisconsin
September, 1966

Contents

List of Illustrations

List of Tables

Introduction

In 1831 a farmer, Cyrus Hall McCormick, built and operated a horse-powered reaper in Rockbridge County in western Virginia. The United States Patent Office gave him a patent on this device in 1834. After an unsuccessful venture in iron smelting, McCormick in 1839 turned his attention again to the reaper. He enlisted his father and brothers in manufacturing a small number of reapers in the blacksmith shop on the family farm and licensed various machine shops to manufacture and sell others. With little capital but with big ideas and the blueprints of his reaper, Cyrus McCormick moved in 1847 to Chicago, where in partnership with Charles M. Gray he built his own factory.

This historic plant, known as the McCormick Works, was to produce agricultural machinery continuously for the next 113 years;[1] and throughout various changes of company name—McCormick and Ogden, C. H. McCormick Company, C. H. and L. J. McCormick Brothers, C. H. McCormick and Brothers, McCormick Harvesting Machine Company—was to remain until 1902 the sole plant of the firm. By then this plant was producing 35 percent of America's harvesting machinery. In that year its owners, the sons of the inventor, merged their firm with their four leading competitors to form International Harvester Company. At birth the new trust produced 85 percent of the country's harvesting machinery. In recent years the firm has ranked in sales among the top twenty of America's manufacturing corporations.

The account in this book of a century of labor-management relations traces events at the McCormick Works. Events at other plants are introduced after 1902 when the formation of International Harvester created a multiplant firm. Chapter 7, "Employee Representation," is based on the firm's steel plant, Wisconsin Steel. While wage rates differed somewhat from plant to plant and especially from city to city, the fundamentals of labor relations policies of International Harvester were companywide. Thus a description of events in one plant had broad though not necessarily universal applicability.

Whether the reapers were made in the farm blacksmithy, in the first small factory, or in the many plants of the worldwide International Harvester Company, the McCormick family—at least through 1951—was personally involved in management of the enterprise and shaped the labor relations decisions. The inventor, C. H. McCormick I, with the assistance of two brothers, William and Leander, directed the business until his death in 1884. His son Cyrus H. McCormick II was president from then until 1918. Like his father, Cyrus II had the assistance of his two younger brothers, Harold and Stanley. Harold became a vice president in 1902 and was president from 1918 through 1922. In 1922 Alex Legge became the first non-McCormick president, and Cyrus H. McCormick III was a vice president. Another vice president, Fowler McCormick, son of Harold, succeeded Legge in the presidency in 1941 and directed the company for the next eleven years. Among the decision-makers of the McCormick family one woman must be named: Nettie Fowler McCormick, widow of the inventor, who on several occasions significantly influenced company labor policy.

As the McCormick Works grew from 23 workers in 1847 to over 9,000 in World War II, it inevitably drew into its work force members of all the diverse immigrant groups which crossed America. The first employees were of English extraction. Soon the Irish took over the hot, heavy jobs, such as those in the foundry. Swedes furnished the skilled woodworkers. Germans predominated in the toolroom and pattern shop. The progressive breakdown of work into its simpler components called for ever-increasing quantities of semiskilled and common labor. To meet this need the McCormick Works utilized every new labor source which came to Chicago. Each group slowly progressed up the occupational ladder, the Irish relinquishing the foundry to the Poles, who after World War I turned over much of this onerous work to Negroes.

McCormick Works employees might well be called "union prone."

Beginning as early as 1862, the workers of this plant at one time or another affiliated with every brand of unionism known to America: craft unionism, the shorter hours movement of the National Labor Union, the mass unionism of the Knights of Labor, the anarchism of the Black International, the AF of L, the CIO, company unionism, and Communist-line unionism. By 1919 the McCormick Works was considered by the company its most "radical" plant.

Among the foremen and skilled workmen at the McCormick Works was a group of long-tenure families. Such was the Hinchley family, four generations of whom spent their lives as blue-collar workers in the McCormick Works. In their 103 years of service the Hinchleys witnessed firsthand the evolution of labor relations. From great-grandfather to great-grandson, they saw the work week fall from 60 hours to 40 plus paid vacations. Great-grandfather John by 1858 received 11 cents an hour as a skilled planer operator. Edward Jr. when he retired as a patternmaker in 1961 was making $3.78 an hour plus valuable fringe benefits. John's and James's security in old age was their ability to get their children jobs at the McCormick Works. Edward and Edward Jr. retired on pensions.

All the Hinchleys suffered chronic seasonal and cyclical unemployment, though as patternmakers Edward and Edward Jr. worked in the plant's most stable department. Every Hinchley was familiar with work interruptions due to strikes. There is no evidence of any Hinchley assuming union leadership. In fact they appear to have avoided it, possibly a factor in the family's long tenure. In the violent strikes of 1886 James is listed in company records among those trustworthy employees who were issued revolvers, presumably to aid their ingress and egress during the strike. After the passage of the Wagner Act, Edward Jr. became an enthusiastic member of the AF of L Pattern Makers' League.

For some years obsolete, the McCormick Works was closed in 1961. Two years later, bulldozers leveled the historic site—which might better have been preserved as an agricultural and industrial museum. In this one plant can be traced key elements of the complex labor-management relations story in America's transition from an agricultural to a highly industrialized economy.

A Century of Labor-Management Relations at McCormick and International Harvester

1

Prelude to Haymarket, 1862–1886

The Company and the First Union

The 1930's are so frequently referred to as the period of unionization of the mass production industries that we are apt to overlook the fact that the iron and metalworking industries had been organized—though on a craft basis—almost six decades earlier. By 1865 the Sons of Vulcan had a trade agreement with associated employers in the Pittsburgh area. The molders were so effectively organized by 1863 that the proprietors of iron foundries, in an effort to restrict union influence, met in Chicago to set maximum wage rates for the entire territory west of Buffalo.[1] The downfall about the turn of the century of this early unionism in steel manufacturing has been well chronicled,[2] but relatively little has been written on the nature of the widespread unionism which existed in other manufacturing from 1860 to 1900. By use of the McCormick Collection's extraordinarily detailed records it is possible to trace the development, sometimes day by day, of labor-management relations in one historic plant.

From the time it was built, in 1848, McCormick's Chicago reaper "manufactory" was essentially a modern factory. Even the original machinery—lathes for turning wood and iron, boring machines, saws, mortices, planers, and grindstones—was steam driven. As early as 1849, 123 employees were turning out 1,500 reapers a year. By 1884, 1,400 employees produced 55,000 machines.

Production was geared to the fall harvesting season. Work on the next year's models began in August or September, with employment expanding slowly to a peak in March–July. Brief shutdowns were not uncommon in late August or early September. Employees worked a ten-hour day, though piecework molders not infrequently stayed overtime to complete the pouring of hot metal. Workers were paid weekly and in cash.

The climate for unionism appears to have been more permissive in the new reaper factory than in the workshops of an earlier merchant-capitalist era. Wider profit margins resulting from new production methods, the marketing of a new product, the expanding grain belt, and some patent protection gave the company a certain latitude when faced with wage demands of a unionized work force.

A foundry strike in September 1862, probably occasioned by the Civil War inflation, is the first concrete evidence of unions in the McCormick Works. Citywide Local 23 of the National Union of Iron Molders, to which McCormick molders belonged, was chartered in Chicago in March 1860; and the company's molders may have been affiliated as early as that date or may have belonged to a local molders' union even earlier. The evidence available at this time indicates a union only in the foundry department. Bargaining relationships between Chicago Molders' Local 23 and the McCormick Company were continuous from 1862 through 1886, but settlements directly covered only skilled workmen in the foundry, approximately 10 percent of the work force. Studies of McCormick Company payrolls and correspondence indicate that part of the bargaining gains of this small band of skilled molders were passed along to the unskilled foundry workers (equal in number to the molders), and usually to the entire plant, within a week or two. Workers in the rest of the plant were the skilled machinists and woodworkers, semiskilled machine operators, and common labor. Unionism in these groups was sporadic, generally in conjunction with some unusual upheaval such as the great eight-hour strike of 1867. In the mid-'80's, at the McCormick plant as elsewhere, all levels of workmen swarmed into unions in a surge foreshadowing that of the 1930's.

Molders' Local 23 bargained in the early 'seventies for about thirty machinery foundries and one stove shop in Chicago. As the stove industry moved west, the proportion of stove molders grew. In 1878 the machinery molders broke off to form a separate local, No. 233. A third local, of bench molders, No. 239, was organized in 1882. The monthly reports of Locals 23 and 233 to the national union indicate that the bargaining relationships at McCormick were frequently part of a citywide bargaining pattern for molders.[3] Since other cities were similarly organized, the picture of union-management relations revealed at McCormick's was probably duplicated in many respects in other large Northern cities.

Civil War inflation stimulated vigorous union activity. Correspondence of McCormick executives indicates not less than six strikes from the fall of 1862 through 1864. The nature of the union demands and the company attitude are shown in the following excerpts from the McCormick correspondence of 1863 and 1864. Note the tandem relationship between foundry strikes and wages in the entire plant:

> We have a strike of molders again *every* man of them have struck and work is standing they demanded 12½ pr ct added to wages paid which had been raised by last springs strike 25 pr cent they have been making from 2.75 to $5 pr day if admitted every other division of the business will follow suit . . .[4]
>
> . . . our moulders are now going on their fourth strike for an advance of wages since last fall. They now want 25 percent more!!! Manufacturers will have to shut up shop if things go much farther in this line. There is no help for this state of things. . . . We wish we could help it but we are powerless.[5]

The above correspondence very clearly indicates that at an early stage in its history the company was faced with an effective union which, at least during the tight Civil War labor market, had a real impact on company wage policy. In fact the payroll ledgers show that McCormick wages during 1862–65 more than kept pace with the spiraling cost of living; by contrast, real wages for manufacturing employees nationally fell 26 percent from 1862 to 1865.[6]

Collective bargaining practices of this period differed considerably from those of today. Wage settlements were oral and of no set duration. Union rules that appear to have been successfully enforced included having skilled foundry work performed exclusively by the journeymen molders; one helper per journeyman; and payment of the minimum, locally determined union-wage scale. Piecework was permitted by the union, and was the method of payment to molders in the McCormick foundry. Union shops for journeymen molders were demanded, but it is not clear how often they were achieved. Bargaining lacked much of the give-and-take of today's drawn-out negotiations. One side or the other opened "bargaining" by unilateral action: the employer generally by effecting a wage cut, the union by presenting a citywide ultimatum to all foundry employers calling for a wage increase by a certain date. Managements that failed to comply were generally struck, though compromises were sometimes achieved. Because of the rapidly growing use of iron, the molders' possession of an irreplaceable skill, and union rules that restricted the work load, molders across the nation, even apart from the Civil War, achieved impressive wage gains.[7]

The 1867 Movement for an Eight-Hour Day

Molders' Local No. 23 did not evaporate in the recession that followed the Civil War. On the contrary, for the next twenty years the Molders were the catalyst in all union activity at McCormick's, acting either alone or in concert with other unions which sporadically rose and fell within the plant. On May 1, 1867, Local 23 was a leader in what may have been the original May Day labor demonstration, nineteen years before the historians' usual bench mark of May Day, 1886. As a harmless gesture to the mushrooming post-Civil War labor movement, the Illinois legislature, in March 1867, passed a law declaring eight hours to be the "legal work day in the State of Illinois." Chicago trade unionists, spurred on by Richard Trevellick, a gifted orator-organizer from the National Labor Union, determined to breathe life into this eight-hour law. With careful organization and extensive publicity they designated May 1, 1867, for a demonstration and inauguration of the eight-hour law.

On Wednesday, May 1, despite united employer opposition, 10,000 trade union workers abandoned their jobs and paraded all day through downtown Chicago. The *Chicago Times* called it the "largest procession ever seen on the streets of Chicago."[8] Strikes followed, as employers stood firm against the eight-hour day. Riots occurred throughout the city when unemployed workers from other cities converged on Chicago to take the ten-hour jobs that were going begging.

When its employers opposed the eight-hour day, Molders' Local 23 struck all but eight of the city's foundries. Though generally unsuccessful, it had the distinction of being on strike long after the rest of the city had gone back to work at the ten-hour schedule. At the McCormick plant, however, the outcome was quite different. On Wednesday management was forced to shut down the entire plant while the workmen were on parade. On Thursday the plant stayed open for the regular ten-hour shift—but the entire body of workmen left after eight hours. They repeated their early departure on Friday and Saturday. On Monday both sides compromised, the union agreeing to the ten-hour day in return for a plantwide 10 percent pay boost for both dayworkers and pieceworkers.

Some measure of the degree to which the union upset normal company procedures in arriving at the new wage is revealed by the McCormick payroll books, which indicate that this was the first increase ever given in the middle of the payroll week, the first across-the-board raise, and the first percentage raise in the company's history. Management's feelings were voiced by plant superintendent and partner Leander McCormick as he poured out to his brother Cyrus his plans to free the company from union control:

> I mentioned our troubles with Eight hour men to you and I have thought . . . whether it would not be well . . . to employ an agent to send us [emigrants] as I have seen that [there] are large numbers arriving, If we could get say 20 to 30 & pay prices pd. to our present men heretofore and make an arrangement with them for say a couple years or part of them say 20 at least, and I have thought that we ought to employ a foreman as we have no confidence in Green [foundry foreman] . . . The union is controlling our shop complete is *our situation* and we ought at whatever cost to hire men outside of it I would suppose that there are agencys among them on arrival & if so by paying such person a few dollars for each man sent us *—or that comes to us* so much is just what I have thought of . . .[9]

The letter demonstrates two basic facts of union-management relations at the McCormick Company at this time: the union was a powerful force; and the company had a real desire to curb or destroy it. There is no evidence of the company's ever carrying out Leander McCormick's plan for using contract immigrants to smash the union.

By the fall of 1867 the strike for an eight-hour day was clearly a failure. The last of the shops in Chicago had returned to ten-hour operations. At this point the McCormick Company rescinded the 10 percent across-the-board increase which had been paid since early in May in lieu of the eight-hour day.

Prosperity, the Long Depression, Revival

Defeat in the struggle for the eight-hour day weakened Molders' Local 23 as well as other Chicago unions. Reviving prosperity in

1869 rebuilt union strength. Local 23 was active enough during the prosperous period of 1869–73 to conduct two strikes against the Bouton Company, one of Chicago's leading foundries. Though the first strike was won by the union in 1872 after dragging on for two years, the company broke with the local and replaced its entire force with nonunion molders. The Bouton Company also blacklisted its striking molders, with the cooperation of fellow employers in Chicago. Pinned to the McCormick payroll ledger for 1872 are the names of the Bouton strikers—an indication that the reaper firm among others was aiding in the blacklist. A comparison of union membership as listed in the Molders' *Journal* for this period with the McCormick payroll ledgers shows that most of the molders at McCormick's were union members. The year 1873 was a wage peak at the McCormick Works not reached again in money wages until 1913, though reached in real terms in 1882.

The depression that began in 1873 gave the McCormick Company a chance to loosen the union bonds. In late August the company closed its foundry for a month, though the rest of the plant continued to operate. Upon the foundry's reopening, wages were slashed up to 20 percent.[10] Curtailment of operations after the machines for the year's harvest had been produced was not uncommon; but from the complete shutdown of the foundry alone followed by a drastic wage cut one can infer that the company hoped hungry workers would be less apt to strike. The Molders struck—but at the end of the second month accepted the wage cut and went back to their jobs. Having beaten the Molders, the company a week later cut wages in the rest of the plant to correspond with the foundry cuts. This was the first of five successive wage cuts in the course of the long depression of 1873–79. The cost of living tumbled, but wages fell even faster.

What was the effect of loss of the 1873 strike and the successive wage cuts on Molders' Local 23 and on its membership in the McCormick foundry? While most American trade unions collapsed in the depression, Molders' Local 23, despite heavy losses, survived as a going organization. Throughout the depression it applied rearguard wage pressures, though it was too weak to block the successive wage cuts. In 1876, for example, Local 23's secretary warned the McCormick Company against initiating further wage cuts:

> We have reliable information that the foreman of your foundry has been going to various foundries in the city and inciting the proprietors and superintendents of their shops to reduce the wages paid to molders.

Knowing your reputation for fair dealing with your employees, we can hardly believe that you sanction the afore mentioned action on the part of your foreman.

We have no desire to provoke any breach of the present peaceful relations existing between Employers and Employees; but if the above course is persisted in, it will prove anything but satisfactory to one of the parties.[11]

The company replied:

In answer to your threatening note of November 6 would simply say that we never interfere with the business of others nor allow our employees to do so for us. While at the same time we propose to have the same privilege for ourselves. Our foreman has not, nor have we consulted anyone about wages or do we intend to.[12]

Not only did Molders' Local 23 remain alive and active but after four years of depression it was also in condition to spawn a second local. In 1878 McCormick members of Local 23 took the lead in organizing the sister local, No. 233, for machinery molders. Local 23 thereafter became primarily a stove molders' local.

The new local, No. 233, whose officers were regularly McCormick foundrymen, carried on the bargaining tactics that had been learned in Local 23. During the upswing years 1879–82 the rescission of several depression wage cuts was achieved. Collective bargaining negotiations with employers or with employers' associations were still very limited. In early April 1881, for instance, Local 233 announced to its employers that on April 19 wages were to be raised 25 cents a day for dayworkers and 15 percent for pieceworkers. Most shops, including McCormick's, granted an acceptable increase; three refused and were promptly struck. Within a week two of the three holdouts conceded; but the third, Crane Brothers, engaged in a long battle. McCormick's union men and other working unionists were assessed to help the men on strike.[13]

The Strike of 1885

In the years following 1880, McCormick management experienced substantial turnover. Partner Leander McCormick, who had superintended the Works since its origin in 1848, walked off the job in consequence of a long-smoldering quarrel with brother Cyrus. He was replaced by Cyrus H. McCormick II, the twenty-one-year-old eldest son of President Cyrus H. McCormick. To fill the post, young Cyrus was pulled out of Princeton after completing only his second year. The man who actually directed the foremen and workmen was the new assistant superintendent, George B. Averill, formerly foundry foreman, who, deservedly or not, became particularly unpopular among the workmen. The third member of the new management team was E. K. Butler, an aggressive sales agent from rural Illinois who became general manager, though he did not officially receive the title until 1883. Replacing Averill in the key post of foundry foreman was the ex-president of Molders' Local 233, William H. Ward. This was not the gesture of friendship toward unionism it might seem, since Ward had been expelled from his union office and membership in November 1880 "for trying to wreck our union."[14]

With youthful enthusiasm Cyrus McCormick II described in his diary on September 7, 1881, the installation of the new management team: "Went to the Works this morning and announced to the heads of all the departments the new order of things viz:—I to be Superintendent of the Works and Mr. Averill as the Asst. Supt. Everything will I think work well under the new regime." So far as relations between management and labor were concerned the prophecy was too optimistic. Except for Assistant Superintendent Averill, who had been McCormick foundry foreman since the conclusion of the 1873 strike, the management team entrusted with the direction of 1,200 restless factory workers lacked previous firsthand experience with so large an industrial work force. By contrast, Leander McCormick had worked side by side with the older employees. His leaving, together with the retirement of veteran superintendent John Hamilton, destroyed the personal contact which had formerly characterized the Works. The size of the plant now made it inevitable that the workmen would henceforth deal only with hired managers. Most of young McCormick's time was spent at the downtown office, miles removed from the plant on the southwest side of Chicago.

A letter of January 1883 to President McCormick from a disgruntled worker, signed "Many Employees," points up the depersonalizing process in the rapidly expanding factory:

> . . . It only pains us to relate to you . . . that a good many of our old hands is not here this season and if Mr. Evarts is kept another season a good many more will leave . . . we pray for you to . . . remove this man . . . we are treated as though we were dogs. . . . he has cut the wages down so low they are living on nothing but bread. . . . we can't talk to him about

wages if we do he will tell us to go out side of the gate. . . . he discharged old John the other day he has been here 17 years. . . . there is Mr. Church who left us last Saturday he went around and shook hands with every old hand in the shop . . . this brought tears to many mens eyes. He has been here 19 years and has got along with them all until he came to Mr. Evarts the present superintendent. . . . he claims he can run the shop a great deal cheaper than it has ever been run this he may do but he is starvng the men to do it and if he knew that you was getting a letter from us and who we were every man would be discharged. . . .[15]

The improved accounting practices of the 1880's helped to make McCormick management increasingly conscious of the union's role. While manufacturing costs per machine had been previously calculated, 1881 marks the first time that the accountants broke down the per machine cost into material costs and labor costs. With this refinement, it became known that labor accounted for $2.32 of the $3.00 increase in harvesting machine production costs from 1880 to 1881.[16] A new "hard line" on wages was instituted forthwith. When the molders came around for their 1882 raise, with a petition for a 10 percent increase signed by 98 molders, the company was ready to fight. Assistant Superintendent Averill went to the union meeting to discuss the wage demand. He spoke of the "suicidal course"[17] they were pursuing and temporarily talked them out of their wage demand. In April the molders again threatened a strike. Averill talked them out of it.[18]

In 1884 President McCormick died. He was succeeded by Cyrus H. McCormick II. Young Cyrus' eager management team was now in complete control of the enterprise. During the depression of 1884–85 the new management unilaterally instituted a wage cut of 15 percent for pieceworkers and 10 percent for dayworkers, unwittingly stumbling into what was shortly to become the bitterest labor-management struggle in the company's history. The motive for the wage cut appears to have been merely normal economizing on the part of a cost-conscious management. Wage cutting had been an accepted and widely practiced tactic in the depression of the 'seventies; its resumption with the onset of the business slump of 1884 was hardly unexpected. The management decision-making process in this fateful wage cut is described very simply in the young president's diary entries:

[Dec. 6, 1884] At works from 10 a.m. to 5 p.m. . . . Talked with Averill about a reduction of 10% in the Wages at the Works. He favors the plan. Read Emersons Essay on "Friendship." It is like a nut full of sweet meat.

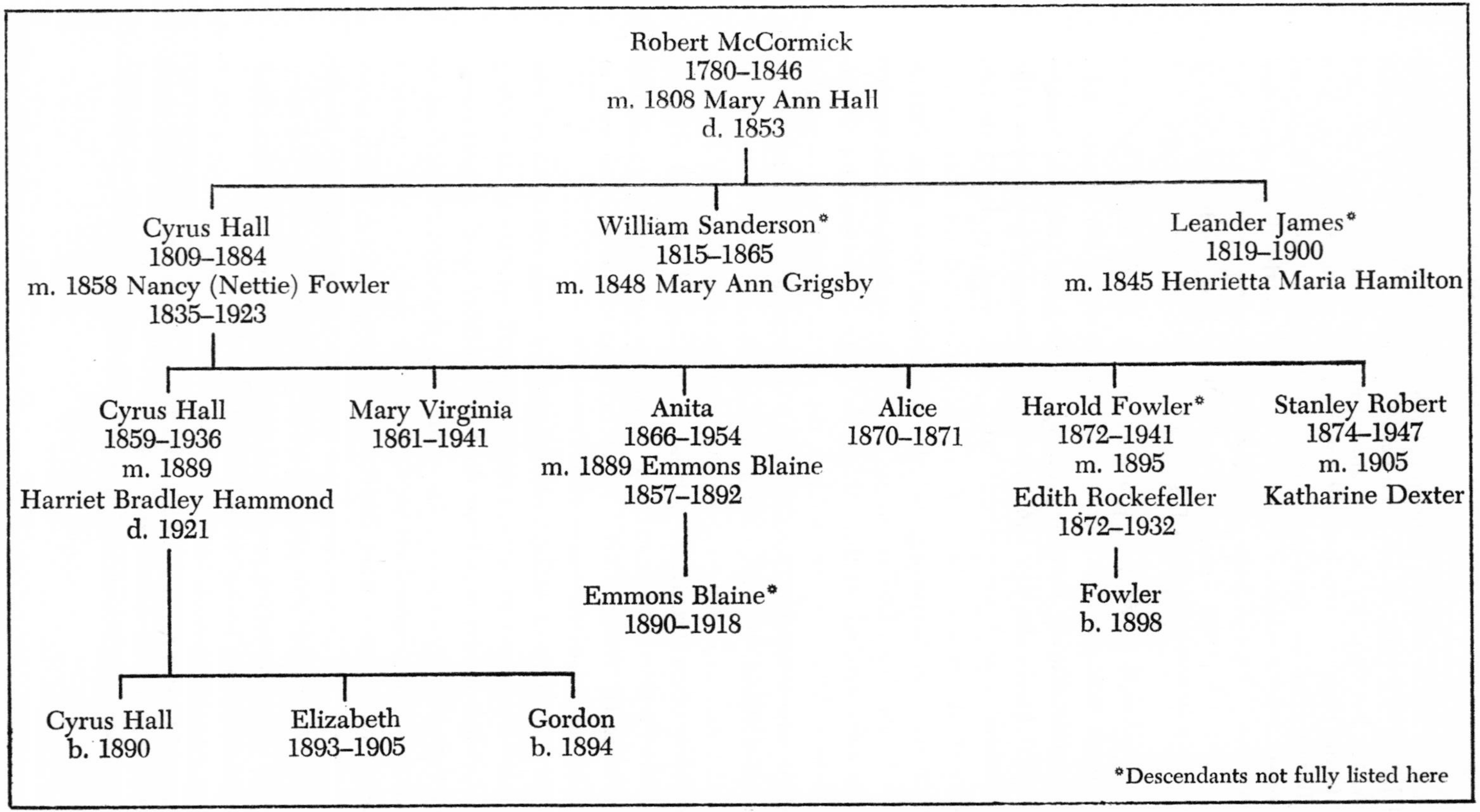

Robert McCormick
1780–1846
m. 1808 Mary Ann Hall
d. 1853
Cyrus Hall
1809–1884
m. 1858 Nancy (Nettie) Fowler
1835–1923
William Sanderson*
1815–1865
m. 1848 Mary Ann Grigsby
Leander James*
1819–1900
m. 1845 Henrietta Maria Hamilton
Cyrus Hall
1859–1936
m. 1889
Harriet Bradley Hammond
d. 1921
Mary Virginia
1861–1941
Anita
1866–1954
m. 1889 Emmons Blaine
1857–1892
Alice
1870–1871
Harold Fowler*
1872–1941
m. 1895
Edith Rockefeller
1872–1932
Stanley Robert
1874–1947
m. 1905
Katharine Dexter
Emmons Blaine*
1890–1918
Fowler
b. 1898
Cyrus Hall
b. 1890
Elizabeth
1893–1905
Gordon
b. 1894
*Descendants not fully listed here

The McCormick Family

On December 9 and 10 President McCormick enlarged upon and implemented the cut:

EKB [General Manager Butler] and I drove to the works at 10. Went carefully over the Wages each man is getting today both piece work and day work. Decided to cut down 10% on the day workmen and 15% on the piece-men—I am back at 3 o'clock.

Office at 9:30. E. K. Butler went to the Works according to arrangement yesterday and talked to the Foremen of the different Departments about reducing wages. He told them we must reduce 10% on all day workmen and 15% on all piece work commencing next Saturday. They all agreed.

Subsequent to the strike that ensued, President McCormick, elaborating on the motive for the cut, wrote that he was merely following the lead of other Chicago employers who were cutting wages because of the business recession, and claimed, ". . . we were the last people in the city almost to make this reduction."[19] It is certain that the decision to cut wages was not forced upon young McCormick by economic conditions of his own company. In November the accountants had brought in the year's financial statement, a new profit record showing 71 percent net on the stated capital investment of $2,500,000.[20] Pricing prospects for the firm's production for the coming year looked good. On November 20 the annual price-fixing meeting of the leading reaper manufacturers had been held and list prices set between $200 and $225 on the harvester binder.[21] The claim of being mere followers in city-wide wage cuts is open to question. The payroll ledgers of the McCormick Company and its chief competitor, the Deering Company, reveal that the McCormick cut preceded Deering's by an entire month.[22]

The truth seems to be that in cutting wages young McCormick made a crucial decision with little understanding of the issues or possible consequences. Nothing at Princeton or in his four years as understudy to his father had given him any insight into the feelings or temper of the 1,400 men who labored in his factory.

Molders' Local 233 was a disciplined organization. It did not react rashly to the December wage cut but bided its time. Three months later, on March 16, 1885, at the peak of the spring production rush, in accordance with the bargaining custom of that time, the union delivered its ultimatum: "We the undersigned Molders in your employ do hereby demand that you discontinue the reduction of 15% on our wages to take effect March 20, 1885 hoping to receive an answer by the above date we remain, Yours etc."[23] Ninety-one members of the Molders'

Union signed the petition. Not being members of that union, 1,200 workers in the reaper department and 90 laborers in the foundry did not sign.

If the wage cut had originally been made without much forethought, it was now reconsidered in the face of the impending strike—and reaffirmed. General Manager Butler summed up: ". . . we all agree that it would not answer for us to meet the demand made by the molders; to do so would result in a like demand from every branch of the Shop; . . . . Mr. Averill and myself both feel confident that should they do so [strike], we would be able to bring them to terms in ample time to finish our wants. . . . We shall discharge a number of men in our wood department altogether."[24] At this time when mature counsel was so badly needed, the strategy was being formulated by a general manager whose background in sales had hardly equipped him to deal with unions.

Even after the Molders' strike had begun, the company considered it an opportune occasion for teaching the men a much-needed lesson as well as for further depressing wages. According to Butler:

> We have treated the matter indifferently with all our men, for the reason that those who were nonunion men went out with the others and we did not think best to offer any nonunion men work until they sought it themselves, and then not to take even those back without some little punishment in the way of a further small reduction in their wages . . . in the long run it will provide benefit to us as a lesson to our men generally. We could never have a difficulty of this kind at a more opportune time; hence we can hardly fail of success. . . .
>
> My reason for feeling so . . . is that we have many men employed who have been with us for years without a lesson of this kind. . . .
>
> . . . Discharging a number of men has had a good effect upon the strikers that went out, as well as upon all the mechanics who have been retained.[25]

As soon as the foundrymen went on strike, the company rushed construction of barracks inside the plant gates to house strikebreakers and began actively recruiting nonunion molders. Telegrams and letters went out to McCormick dealers in all Midwestern cities. Illustrative are:

> To J. F. Utley, Agent, Sterling, Illinois:
>
> Molders at works out on strike. Can you get some good nonunion moulders to come. We guarantee protection, provide accomodations [sic] inside our yard. If so how many.[26]

To J. B. Field, Milwaukee, Wisconsin:
. . . see if you can arrange to get some [nonunion molders] . . . say not to exceed thirty. . . . You understand that they must be non-union men, and in order to prevent trouble we would want them to agree to board inside the shop yards for a time, we agreeing to give them comfortable quarters at moderate prices, and protect them from the strikers. You can explain to the men that when our men went out of the shop they were receiving on an average of $3.07 per day. . . .[27]

These invitations did not sound any more attractive in 1885 than they do today. Typical results can be gleaned from such messages as the following telegrams:

To Tom Braden, Agent, Des Moines, Iowa:
Out of the lot of men you sent us yesterday but two of them showed up in Chicago, Mr. C. Allen and his brother, the balance having deserted on the way. We find it is not safe to ship these critters at our expense unless nailed up in a box car or chained. Therefore you need not send us any more at present. We were unable to get the Messrs. Allen inside our gate today, and presume that before we shall be able to do so they will also disappear.[28]

To J. F. Utley, Agent, Sterling, Illinois:
The gentleman you sent in to us as a Molder, Mr. Jas. McBride, did not remain over an hour or two until he packed his valise and skipped. We took special pains to get him into the Works by his riding with Mr. McCormick in his buggy. We can hardly imagine his purpose in coming at our expense and taking the course which he did. If you are able to do so try and collect back his Rail Road fare.[29]

Although over a thousand reaper workers entered the gates daily, the Molders' pickets kept strikebreaking molders from gaining admittance to the foundry. But Friday night, April 3, the company succeeded in slipping twenty-five scab molders into the plant by means of the company tug.[30] So difficult was it to procure strikebreaking molders that most of these twenty-five were enticed away by a $5 weekly bonus from another struck Chicago shop, the Cribben and Sexton Company.

As soon as the striking Molders discovered they had been outmaneuvered and that nonunion molders were performing their work, they set about to induce the mass of reaper workers to join in the strike. At this critical moment when both union and company were bidding for the loyalty of the reaper workers, Cyrus McCormick appeared at the commencement exercises of Chicago's Presbyterian Theological Seminary and, oblivious to public and worker reaction, announced a gift of $100,000, bringing recent McCormick family contributions to the Seminary to $450,000.[31] Rumors immediately circulated that the wage cut was to pay for the donation. Union speakers and even newspapers never mentioned the one without referring to the other.

In addition to this public relations handicap, the company faced other obstacles in getting reaper workers to continue working. Retired General Manager C. W. Spring, Jr., explained: "There is no doubt that $^{10}/_{12}{}^{\text{ths}}$ of the men wanted to continue work at what we were paying them, but the fighting Irish element of the $^{2}/_{12}{}^{\text{ths}}$ were ready to knock down and beat and abuse the Germans, Swedes, and Norwegians that were quiet and wanted to work. They forced them, drove them back, would not let them enter the yard, and any that made the attempt to go in after being warned were set upon and beaten unmercifully and not a Police man would stir a hand to protect them or hinder the outrage."[32]

The crucial battle at the plant gate occurred on a Tuesday morning, which also happened to be an election day. The police were scattered across the city ensuring an "honest" election. Pinkerton men proved unequal to the task of keeping the plant approaches free of pickets. On that and subsequent days would-be scabs riding trolleys and McCormick omnibuses were beaten, as were the drivers, until no one could be found to drive or ride. Even a busload of Pinkerton men was attacked; detectives were beaten; a bus was burned, and a case of twenty Winchester rifles, intended for protection of the strikebreaking molders, imprisoned within the plant, was seized by the strikers. The police detail in this area was under the charge of Captain O'Donnell, an experienced and highly respected officer. Substantial police protection was provided, though not in sufficient force to satisfy the company; the police lapses in diligence were most noticeable when they were called on to protect the Pinkerton men from the strikers.

President McCormick appealed to Mayor Carter Harrison for more adequate police protection. As it happened, at the last election young Cyrus McCormick II, in the interest of reform politics, had shut down the plant on election day so the workers might all have the opportunity to vote this same Carter Harrison out of office. Now the mayor praised the union committee and proposed that Mr. McCormick consult with it, declaring, "I hope you will come to some agreement which results in the good of all."[33] President McCormick noted with skepticism that two of the gentlemen whom the mayor praised were "the prime movers in all the disturbance."[34]

After returning from Mayor Harrison's office, however, McCormick heeded his advice and for the first time met with a delegation of twenty-five workers. He expressed to them the official company attitude: "I told them that we should be glad to treat with them individually, but could not do so as a body, and explained to them why the reduction had been made on account of the business depression, and treating them politely and pleasantly, but they went away without of course accomplishing anything."[35]

For several days the situation, from the company standpoint, grew steadily worse. The switchmen's union refused to run cars in or out of the plant. The Pinkerton men were driven from the scene. The company, defeated in its attempt to open the plant, refused to meet again with the union committee. Chicago capitalists became thoroughly alarmed lest this rising tide of union defiance start a general conflagration. At this juncture, Philip D. Armour, capitalist elder and head of the well-known meat-packing firm, tactfully notified young McCormick that he would like to talk with him. In a friendly way, Armour discussed several strikes which he had experienced. He bluntly told the young executive that the public was holding him to blame since there had been no such occurrence in his father's time. Armour then advised him to settle the strike even if it meant paying the men what they asked, since the situation was developing into "open war."[36]

McCormick acted with dispatch. To Superintendent Averill he assigned the task of meeting with the union committee. With McCormick at the other end of the telephone, Averill tried to limit the wage restoration to 10 percent. The union refused. With Armour's advice ringing in his ear, McCormick gave Averill the order to settle: 15 percent for pieceworkers, and scabs dismissed.[37] The union had won a glorious, though, as it turned out, short-lived, triumph.

The company absorbed its defeat with a minimum of dislocation. Apart from the family, there were no stockholders. Only the president's mother, Nettie Fowler McCormick, demanded a full accounting. Though in Philadelphia during the strike, she would not be put off with bland assurances. She was the largest stockholder; her specific questions had to be answered. Below are Mrs. McCormick's queries and her son's answers:

1. What did the strike cost us? Calculating simply in dollars and cents, we expended $2829.19 in providing other molders &c. This does not count the time lost in stoppage of business.

2. Stoppage of Works? The Works were shut down for six working days. [Not counting the additional two weeks for the foundry.]
3. Spoiling melting iron? $546.61. This amount was paid the scab molders who went into the foundry temporarily and their work was of no account. We did not lose any iron which was melting, as the shutting down was done after the cupolas were all emptied.
4. Work badly done because strikers' mind and attention was not on their business? This cannot be calculated directly and I cannot set a figure upon that.
5. Killing horses? Nothing.
6. Burning Bus? $325.
7. Paying Pinkerton's men? $618.75.
8. Settling bills accruing from violence? Nothing.
9. Surgeon's bill? Nothing.
10. Police? Nothing.
11. Night service protection? $100.[38]

The chief omission is the fact that the company's profits, in great part because of the strike, fell from $1,776,506 in 1884 to $841,007 in 1885.[39]

What was the impact of the strike on the twenty-five-year-old chief executive who was to guide the policies of the company for the next half century? He had executed vigorously one after another of the generally ill-chosen proposals arrived at by his management team. He had faced personal danger on the picket line calmly. When his efforts to win the strike had failed, Cyrus McCormick was not too proud to follow the wise advice of an outsider, conceding this battle to the union while quietly resolving to destroy it at the first opportunity. Despite his apparent calm, the strike had been a harrowing experience which, as later events demonstrated, endowed him with a lifelong distrust of unions.

Before and during the strike McCormick had relied on the advice of his subordinates. Now he determined to give careful study to the company's labor problems. As he wrote his mother: "The whole question of these labor troubles is a vast and important one and throws new light upon a department of our manufacturing interests which we have not hitherto studied with sufficient depth and understanding. I trust, however, that we will be able to improve as time goes on."[40]

He methodically analyzed the causes of the company defeat and listed them for his mother thus: the lack of police support, which enabled the union to intimidate the loyal workers; the unfortunate timing of his gift to the seminary; the desertion of his fellow employers, who rescinded their wage cuts at the first signs of trouble; the refusal of the switchmen's union to ship cars in or out of the plant.

The gulf between second-generation executive and industrial worker was so great that Cyrus McCormick II relied upon Pinkerton operators to learn about his employees. Here is a Pinkerton analysis of the behavior of McCormick employees:

> The assault on the Pinkerton police on three occasions during the strike . . . was urged and participated in by Irishmen, who are employed at McCormick's as Molders and helpers and these Irishmen are nearly all members of the ancient order of Hibernians, who have a most bitter enmity against the Agency since the hanging of the Molly Maguires in Pennsylvania. . . . The police patrolling in the section of the city where the McCormick's factory is located are nearly if not all Irishmen and belong to this order.
>
> . . . . .
>
> . . . Mr. McCormick has a nest of dangerous, vicious men in his employ, and he will have lots of trouble to get rid of them. They are also instigated by agents of the International Working Men's Association, known as socialists. Parsons of this anarchist society has been among McCormick's employees, advocating besides, how to make dynamite. . . .[41]

On the matter of the wage reduction McCormick did grudgingly admit to a minor error: "The main trouble seemed to be, not that we reduced the mechanics, but that the laborers, who number only a few in our work, were reduced the 10%, and as of course laborers get less than other branches of trade these figures were heralded around in the papers and some capital was made of it."[42] This evaluation shows some understanding of public relations but little feeling for the lot of his workmen. The defeat taught young President McCormick only to recognize the tactical errors which had aided the union's cause; and he resolved to correct them.

The sole person in the McCormick enterprise who showed any real appreciation of the causes of the strike was Cyrus' mother, Nettie F. McCormick. Her analysis of the strike from the distance of Philadelphia was more accurate than that of her son and other officers at the scene in Chicago. "And I can see," she wrote, "that the course pursued . . . was all a miscalculation of what a man can do with employees. . . . That doing was all wrong."[43] Though isolated from the factory, Mrs. McCormick alone expressed sympathy for the ordinary workman.

> We have had a week of trial and anxiety . . . a great "strike" and all the resulting derangement of our relations—old and pleasant as they were—with

our workmen. Trouble has come to hundreds of families in consequence, hatred and fierce passions have been aroused; . . . .

. . . If the wages had not been reduced *twice* . . . well, we came out by a concession of that which, if never required in the beginning, would have saved a vast deal of discredit. . . . What a sore heart I have carried these days.[44]

The Strike of 1886

On the several occasions that Cyrus McCormick II analyzed the company's loss of the strike, he always concluded with a confident prediction. Thus: "I do not think we will have a similar trouble again, because we will take measures to prevent it"; and "I do not think we will be troubled by the same thing again if we take proper steps to weed out the bad element among the men."[45]

The "weeding out" process was soon begun on a grand scale. Within two weeks of the end of the strike, plans were under way to dispense with the entire force of molders. This was to be accomplished by a bold plan for mechanizing the foundry. By April 24, 1885, Superintendent Averill was already in Indianapolis negotiating with a machinery producer for the installation of enough pneumatic molding machines to displace all the company's skilled molders. The estimated cost of the installed machines was $500,000.[46]

In August the foundry was shut down for two months while the molding machines were installed. Upon its reopening, common labor was used to operate the machines. Of the ninety-one Molders who had signed the petition requesting a wage restoration in March 1885, not one was on the payroll for the beginning of the 1886 season. Molders' Union leaders Myles McPadden and Pat Enright had already been fired in June and July, despite the company's promise that men would not be discriminated against on the basis of union activity.

As the 1886 showdown approached, it looked as though Cyrus McCormick's careful plans would produce a company victory. By utilizing the latest technology, McCormick had eliminated the men who had been the key to the union victory of the previous year. Changes in the police force gave promise of more adequate police support than was available in the 1885 strike. In personal charge in the vicinity of the McCormick Works was newly appointed Inspector Bonfield. In contrast to Captain O'Donnell's humane handling of the 1885 McCormick strike, Bonfield, then a captain, had distinguished himself on the occasion of the 1885 streetcar strike by opening a path for strikebreaking motormen, literally clubbing his way across the entire city at the head of a police detail. For this service he was promoted to the inspectorship of the force. Already famous for his slogan on that occasion, "Clubs today spare bullets tomorrow," Bonfield was to go down in history for his ill-fated dispersal order to the dwindling and bedraggled Haymarket audience.[47] The response was the Haymarket bomb.

Though the union was seemingly outmaneuvered by the displacement of the molders, its cause was not hopeless. Molders' leader Myles McPadden was a veteran trade unionist; before spending three years in McCormick's foundry he had had a career in union leadership in both St. Louis and Pittsburgh. When the company's mechanization of the foundry left him a general without troops, he proceeded to raise a new army. Enlisting the aid of two other unions, the resourceful McPadden successfully organized every department of the reaper plant by February of 1886. He put skilled machinists, blacksmiths, and patternmakers into the United Metalworkers' Union, a militant group affiliated with Chicago's anarchist-led Central Labor Union. The mass of the workers joined District Assembly 57 of the Knights of Labor, McPadden himself being both a Knight and a Molder. According to the *Chicago Mail*, out of 1,381 production workers, union membership could be estimated roughly as follows: Knights of Labor, 750, Metalworkers' Union, 250, Molders' Union 10, nonunion, 300.[48] Thus, while the company at great expense was replacing its skilled union molders with molding machines and nonunion laborers, the overwhelming mass of reaper workers was enrolling in new unions.

By mid-February 1886 it was touch-and-go on whether the newfangled molding machines would replace the molders after all. The expensive pneumatic squeezers turned out poor castings, and required taking on enormous numbers of common laborers. In 1885, using skilled molders and no machines, the peak foundry labor costs were $3,000 a week. A year later, when machines had displaced the skilled molders, foundry labor costs were over $8,000 a week. Most of the increase was the cost of unskilled labor. Fifteen molders, including five nonunion men, who were willing to violate the union's rule against supervising more than one helper, were also hired, in early 1886, when it became evident that the molding machines could not produce certain types of castings.

On February 12, 1886, a union committee representing Metalworkers, Knights of Labor, and Molders called upon the McCormick Company. Its demands were as follows:

> that the wages of all laboring men [common labor] be advanced from \$1.25 to \$1.50 a day. Second, That all vice hands be advanced to \$2.00 per day, and that blacksmith helpers be advanced to \$1.75. Third, That time the men should spend in the water closet be not limited as heretofore. . . . Fourth, That, in as much as the molding machines are a failure, the preference should be given the old hands . . . . the scabs in the foundry must be discharged, and a pledge given that no man would be discharged for serving on the committee or for taking part in the strike, or because of any position held in the Order.[49]

The McCormick Company's response was quite different from that of the previous year. It immediately granted the extensive wage demands. It conceded extra time in the water closets. In fact, it gave way on all but one of the union demands—the discharge of the five nonunion molders.[50] A joint mass meeting of members of the three unions rejected the McCormick offer and voted to strike on the morning of February 16, 1886. Before the strike could begin, the company declared a lockout and shut down the plant "indefinitely."

At the end of two weeks the company was prepared for reopening. In addition to recruiting a force of strikebreakers during the lockout, it had organized a core of 82 loyal workers, each armed with a revolver purchased through company channels.[51] On the positive side, and as a further concession to the workers, the company had quietly dismissed its unpopular superintendent, George Averill. Now, in contrast to the 1885 strike, the McCormick management and the city police were in perfect rapport. Symbolic of the changed relationship, hot meals were served to police on company premises at company expense and with Cyrus McCormick II personally pouring the coffee. On reopening day, March 1, 400 city police under the command of Inspector Bonfield crumpled union picket lines and opened a wide path for all who wished to work.

Despite elaborate preparations, only a fraction of the normal work force entered the plant that day. The company claimed 350[52] out of 1,400 workmen; the union said it counted only 161.[53] A check of the payroll ledgers indicates that only 160 production workers and foremen were paid for working on March 1.[54] As the days wore on, more and more workmen, mostly unskilled, were successfully recruited. Unskilled workmen were available in abundance, though replacement of skilled metalworkers was extremely slow.

The company continued its recruitment from all sources. President McCormick wrote to a company agent in Rockford: "We would like 4 or 5 firstclass beam makers, a few metal pattern makers and a few firstrate machinists for lathe and vise work; also few good blacksmiths helpers; . . . Our reason for suggesting that you help us in this way is that some of our best workmen have not yet returned, ..."[55] Many of these men never did return.

Lack of skilled workmen crippled production severely. In 1886 the company produced only 38,000 machines as compared with 55,000 in 1884 and 60,000 in 1887, the two closest nonstrike years. However, the unions' ability to withhold skilled labor was insufficient to force company recognition of the union. Though the strike was never officially called off, over the months the company gradually replaced the skilled strikers and production slowly improved.

With the strike of February 16 still in progress at McCormick's, the eight-hour-day strikes convulsed Chicago on May 1. Half of the newly recruited McCormick work force joined this strike movement. The desperate management granted the eight-hour day with pay for ten hours.[56]

On Monday afternoon, May 3, an eight-hour-day mass meeting was held by 6,000 members of the Lumber Shovers' Union. Though completely unconnected with the McCormick Company or its union, the Lumber Shovers by pure chance met on Black Road, a short distance from the McCormick plant. Because of this proximity, an undetermined number of McCormick unionists who were still carrying on the strike voted on February 16 were on the fringes of the Lumber Shovers crowd listening to a talk by anarchist August Spies of the Central Labor Union. At 3:30 P.M. the McCormick plant bell tolled, signifying the end of the second eight-hour day. At this signal, unprovoked by Spies, a group of several hundred presumed McCormick strikers pulled out of the audience and moved to attack the nonunion workers who were at that moment leaving the nearby McCormick factory. They drove the departing workmen back into the plant and began smashing plant windows. A special detail of 200 police arrived and attacked the assailants with clubs and revolvers, killing two and wounding several.[57]

Upon hearing the shots, the Lumber Shovers dispersed. August Spies rushed toward the McCormick plant, witnessing the tail end of the police rout of the McCormick Works attackers. He hurried back to his office and wrote the famous circular calling for a mass meeting in Haymarket Square the next night to protest the police brutality to McCormick strikers. Spies had good reason to be concerned with the fate of the McCormick strikers. These men were members of the Metalworkers' Union, affiliated with Spies's Chicago Central Labor Union. He and his fellow anarchists had often addressed McCormick workers during their unsuccessful strike in February and March.

The protest meeting on May 4 at Haymarket Square was poorly attended. Mayor Carter Harrison put in an appearance but left as the peaceful crowd dwindled. Soon after, a police detail under the command of Inspector Bonfield and Lieutenant Ward ordered the crowd to disperse. Someone threw a bomb that killed seven policemen. In the weeks that followed, an antiunion wave of repression swept over Chicago and many parts of the country. Though the court did not discover the bomb thrower, four Chicago anarchist leaders were hanged. The severe police repression of unions weakened the union movement; by fall the McCormick Company felt free to revoke the eight-hour day.

The McCormick strikers' direct involvement in the attack on the McCormick Works and in the Haymarket bomb incident may be less than is implied by an outline of events. A search of the McCormick Works payrolls for two years prior to May 1886 fails to reveal the names of any of those killed or injured by the police in the plant attack of May 3; the name of only one of the fourteen additional persons arrested by police on this occasion appears. This payroll examination is not conclusive as to the degree of participation of ex-McCormick employees in the attack on the plant. Clever workers may have given false names to avoid the much-feared blacklists of that period. Moreover, newspaper reporters were careless about ascertaining the correct spelling of workers' names. It remains doubtful, however, that many ex-McCormick employees were involved in the attack on the plant, though some may have incited and led it. There can be no doubt that the company's ruthless actions toward unions in the strikes of 1885 and early 1886 had aroused substantial resentment among its employees, certainly enough to have inspired such an attack.

The Haymarket affair made a deep impression on all Chicago capitalists, perhaps especially on Cyrus McCormick II because of its connection with his striking workers. The result, however, was merely to reaffirm the strong antiunion attitude he had acquired during the strike of 1885. The company victory in the strike of 1886, in contrast to its defeat in 1885, must have given him confidence in his ability to outflank unionism. In any event, it confirmed his belief that, when faced with overwhelming odds, retreat does not mean loss of the war. Time and again in the next fifty years Cyrus McCormick II was to make concessions to workers while withholding that essential to union survival—recognition of the union and of the workers' right to participate in union activity without discrimination.

This destruction of the unions after twenty-five years of continuous relationship made the McCormick Company a precursor by six years of the Carnegie Steel Company—whose action at Homestead in 1892 ended long years of bargaining with the Amalgamated Association of Iron, Steel, and Tin Plate Workers—and a precursor of the Steel Trust which in 1901 followed up Carnegie's victory.

Causes Underlying the Destruction of Unionism at McCormick's

After a quarter of a century of substantial accomplishment, how could the Molders' Union be destroyed at the McCormick Company?

The first answer to this question is that, despite a twenty-five-year relationship with the union, McCormick management at no point philosophically accepted unionism as a desirable means for dealing with its employees. The labor-management relationship was never more than the meeting of opposing power blocks.

While there was a cyclical variation in this power relationship from 1860 to 1886 favoring the union in prosperity and the company in recessions, there was also a secular trend favoring management. The steady expansion of the firm's profits from $300,000 in 1871 to $1,776,000 in 1884 gave the company a variety of powerful means with which to combat the union. Meanwhile the unions' prime weapon, the ability to withhold the workers' labor at peak spring production rushes, had declined because the introduction of machinery made the molders' skill obsolete.

To defeat the union in 1886 took, first of all, enough capital to equip the entire foundry with pneumatic molding machines, which involved the risky capital investment of $500,000 in new and untried machines; second, willingness and ability to absorb huge losses in sales resulting from an indefinite period of plant closure at the peak of the production season; and third, the substantial cost of acceding to union wage demands so that the public relations battle could be fought on the closed shop issue rather than on the wage issue, as in 1885. And finally, the company undertook the not inconsiderable expense of recruiting large numbers of new workers, of breaking in new hands, of paying for meals for police and for detective protection, and of some destruction of property.

The cost to the company of mechanization and of strike interruptions in production is partially shown in Table 1, which compares foundry labor costs as a percent of total labor costs before and after the introduction of the molding machines. The significant rise from 18.8 percent in 1884 to 31.0 percent in 1886 occurred despite (or actually because of) the mechanization of the foundry. That production of harvesting machines fell off substantially in 1886 appears to have been due both to the shortcomings of the molding machines and to strike interruptions. The drop in profits of over a million dollars in 1886, as compared with 1884, is a good indication that a company with fewer financial resources could not have broken the union. It was the enormous prosperity of the years 1879–84 that gave the McCormick Company the strength for that.

TABLE 1

Foundry Labor Costs as a Percent of Total Labor Costs, Machines Manufactured, Net Profits, 1884 and 1886

	1884	*1886*
Foundry labor cost as a percent* of total labor cost (typical weeks at peak production)	18.8%	31.0%
Machines manufactured†	54,841	37,712
Annual net profit‡	$1,776,506	$679,924

* Based on payroll ledgers, McC.H.M.Co. records in the State Historical Society of Wisconsin.
† Company memorandum [undated], McC.H.M.Co., NFMcC papers, Subject File.
‡ Financial statements, McC.H.M.Co., CHMcC II papers, unindexed material.

The motive behind the company's decision to mechanize its foundry is significant. It has been generally recognized that mechanization weakened unions through lessening the skill requirements of the worker. It has been assumed that this deleterious effect on unions was an incidental by-product, and that the main purpose of the labor-saving machinery was cost cutting. In the case of the molding machines for the McCormick foundry, the main purpose was clearly to destroy the union. If it had been cost saving, surely the company would first have bought one or two machines for experimental purposes, then added others if these proved economical. Instead its original purchase covered the complete needs of the foundry. The new machines proved unsatisfactory and were abandoned after three years; the company later sued the manufacturer in an attempt to recover its investment. However, the machines did turn out enough castings to serve their purpose of smashing the union.

The changed attitude of the Chicago police force was also a crucial factor in the McCormick victory. It is unlikely that the company would have taken on the union again in 1886 had it not been sure of full police support. There is no evidence to show what part, if any, the company itself may have played in bringing this change about, but after the experience of 1885 it could not have been indifferent to the problem. Mayor Carter Harrison, whom Cyrus McCormick II had opposed prior to 1885, was henceforth supported by the McCormicks.

Labor's failures have sometimes been attributed to the divisiveness of craft unionism. Theoretically, such criticisms are unassailable. In the McCormick situation, however, the solidarity which accompanied craft unionism was surprising. As we have seen, in 1885 91 Molders out of 1,400 workers struck against plantwide wage cuts. When, after ten days of strike the company was finally able to bring in 25 strikebreakers, the entire plant joined the Molders. Yet this plantwide solidarity received its severest test in 1886, when the company granted to all workers the union demands for wage increases and grievance settlements and denied only the demand for the dismissal of five nonunion molders. It looked as though the Molders' Union alone stood to gain by the strike, yet the entire plant went out in support of it.

Craft unionism, regardless of size, can be a very effective bargaining instrument as long as the craft skill is actually irreplaceable. From 1862 through 1885 a small band of skilled Molders successfully led the collective bargaining battles of all the McCormick workmen. When in 1886 the company attacked the craft union's source of strength—the skill of its molders—by installing automatic machinery, the Molders' leadership countered by organizing all workers, both skilled and unskilled, in the plant. But even this full-fledged industrial unionism of 1886 could not prevent the quick replacement of the unskilled strikers. Thus the outcome of the 1886 strike still hinged upon the actions of the skilled workmen and the company's ability to replace them. With the molders already replaced by machines, the issue revolved around the skilled machinists, blacksmiths, and patternmakers. These skilled men remained on strike and were able to cripple production for many months, but in time they too were replaced.

Success before 1886 had made the skilled molders somewhat overconfident; the company referred to them as "arrogant." Their overconfidence prevented a realistic approach to the problem of mechanization. When the molding machines began to break down in the early part of 1886, the company was forced to hire a few skilled molders. Lacking the vision of the typographers who in the 1890's successfully secured the work on the newly invented linotypes for union members, the molders asked only that they not be required to operate the machines. Shortsighted as the attitude was, it did not affect the outcome of the immediate struggle.

However, the basic reason for the union defeat at McCormick was simply that the resources of the large corporations—economic, technological, and political—were growing too fast to be matched at the time by trade unionism of whatever form.

To what ideology did the union leaders of this period of 1862–86 adhere? Did it influence the outcome of the struggle? Evidence is scanty, but it points to pure bread-and-butter unionism, at least until 1885. The bargaining demands of Molders' Locals 23 and 233 always centered on wages and hours. The violent strikes of 1885 and 1886 added only the issue of union security.

The case for a socialist or anarchist ideology is confined to the last two years, 1885–86. During these years McCormick workers were addressed on several occasions by the famous Chicago anarchist leaders, Albert Parson, Michael Schwab, and August Spies.[58] The United Metalworkers' Union—which in 1885 and 1886 enrolled the McCormick blacksmiths, machinists, and patternmakers—was affiliated with the anarchist-led Central Labor Union. This affiliation did not mean acceptance of anarchism; the bargaining demands were confined to bread-and-butter shop issues. On one occasion, when a joint meeting of the Metalworkers, Molders, and Knights of Labor was held, Knights leaders objected to appearing on the platform with "socialists." But there is no reason to believe that the socialist or anarchist fringe had any effect on the company's implacable opposition to unionism: prior to the Haymarket bomb McCormick management appears to have been as much upset by Irishmen as by anarchists. The management decision to smash the union had been made twelve months before Haymarket.

2

The Origin of Welfarism

Factory Betterment

After the widespread strikes of 1886, thoughtful firms experimented with new approaches, in some cases idealistic efforts to harmonize employer and employee interests, more often merely indirect means of warding off unions. These included bonuses, profit sharing, piece-rate pay systems, factory "betterment," safety, ventilation, recreation, clubhouses, foreman training, systems of worker suggestions, apprentice training, pensions, and mutual funds for sickness and accidents.

The McCormicks until 1901 tried none of these new approaches. Though the discharge of union activists in the labor disputes of 1885 and 1886 had given the company a respite of several years from union wage pressures, the fear engendered by strikes in other Chicago plants kept the McCormicks' antiunionism strong. In 1890 a strike of workers at the nearby Chicago Malleable Iron Company had threatened to engulf the McCormick plant. At the first news of possible trouble, Nettie McCormick, nervous ever since the 1885–86 disorders, telegraphed Manager Butler urging "granting the eight hour day."[1] Her fears were exaggerated and the danger passed.

The Pullman strike of 1894 again reinforced the McCormicks' fear of organized labor. Nettie McCormick, vacationing in Bar Harbor, Maine, read reports of burning boxcars and the importation of federal troops and envisioned near anarchy in Chicago. She wrote her son Cyrus:

Every half day's mails and papers are sought, these last two days hoping for news of the military getting the upper hand, but the troops seem a pitiful handful in the presence of 75,000 rioters, stretched over a radius so great that it would need the presence of soldiers in a hundred places at the same moment to quell the riots. . . .

. . . I am fearing for your personal safety . . . . And for the *Works*, lest they be fired in so many places that Captain Crowley cannot handle the matter! . . . I suppose you and Mr. Butler would have Mr. Utley take a hundred of the trustworthy of our working men and make guardsmen and watchmen of them!

. . . Will you not hire some persons to guard all of our houses? . . . Any wretch may . . . throw burning oil rags in and set fires . . . *easily.*[2]

Cyrus McCormick II recognized the exaggerations in her information but he fully shared her anxiety: "I secured a watchman for our houses, ... I had the police and fire call near your bedroom door tested and put in order, ... at the works every proper precaution was also taken. We have secured extra watchmen, ..."[3]

While his own men had "worked on quietly and without the least friction through all this trouble," Cyrus felt much like a general who, though his own troops were not fighting at the moment, was deeply concerned with the fate of the troops guarding his flank. He congratulated President Grover Cleveland for sending federal troops to Chicago, assuring him of "my personal appreciation of your good judgment in this calamitous situation."[4] He participated in planning the strategy to defeat the enemy, as in this letter to the Rev. Thomas C. Hall: "I found by the papers yesterday morning that the meeting in regard to which I wrote you had been postponed, ... The purpose of Bishop Fallows and Dr. Hensen may have been worthy enough in trying to do something to abate the dreadful condition of things here, but their method of giving an invitation to Debs, et al. to give their views on the present difficulties, would be simply an opportunity to fan the flame which has already reached such dreadful proportions."[5]

Even though the machines the company was making could not be sold at that time, Cyrus deliberately kept his own men at work, "Because we thought it was far better that they should be employed and out of the streets rather than be floating around and liable to be drawn into crowds and mobs."[6] And his feeling against Eugene Debs could not have been more bitter if Debs's followers had burned reapers instead of boxcars. He wrote his mother: "The grand sympathetic strike, which was expected to do so much, has been a fizzle; and Sovereign, King of the Knights of Labor, seems to have lost his grip. Debs and his Lieutenants may now devote their attention to the Grand Jury, which has indicted them."[7] And "the last squeak has been issued by Debs in this morning's papers, from the headquarters of the A.R.U. in the County Jail. There was no necessity of his going to jail whatever but he did so in order to pose as a martyr . . . ."[8]

While the McCormicks were afraid to "fan the flame," their general manager, Butler, in a rational rather than emotional expression of class feeling, almost hoped the threatened sympathetic trade and labor union strike would occur. He explained to Mrs. McCormick: "If all the workers go out with the proclamation of the President and the protection of the Federal and State forces with us and the situation well in hand it will for a few years to come destroy in Chicago the power of said organized labor. . . . I most hope they will all do their work now. With the idle labor at hand and the protection assured plenty will soon be found to take places of any who may go out. We may never have in Chicago such protection as we have at this moment. Hence now is the time to fight it out."[9]

The time "to fight it out" did not come in 1894, but once again the McCormicks had seen organized labor as a violent group to be feared and consequently destroyed.

In 1901 an odd thaw became noticeable in the McCormicks' attitude toward their workers. President McCormick in an unprecedented move employed a woman social worker to begin among the employees what was then called "betterment work." And at midyear a proposal for a substantial gift of stock to employees was discussed within the close-knit family circle.

What was the origin and purpose of these unusual moves? The motives in employing a woman social worker are readily discerned. Up to 1901 the company's nearly five thousand factory employees were men. That year the firm began its own twine production in a newly constructed plant adjacent to the McCormick Works, employing four hundred women. If the McCormicks had not been overly solicitous of their employees' welfare in the past, having this many women employees with primarily male supervisors aroused their concern. Now in jeopardy were not only the morality and health of the new women employees but the McCormick clan members' Presbyterian consciences and the proud McCormick name, known for substantial gifts to religious education as well as for the reaper. Safeguarding these stakes called for a major innovation in industrial relations, the employment of a genteel woman social worker. Such a woman was Gertrude Beeks, "social secretary" of the McCormick Works as of February 1901.

When approached by Cyrus McCormick in 1900, Miss Beeks, then aged thirty-three, was a full-time employee of the Civic Federation of Chicago, an organization devoted to governmental reform. She was also president of the National Association of Women Stenographers. President McCormick probably learned of her from the pioneer Chicago social worker and friend of the McCormick family, Jane Addams. At any rate, after Miss Beeks's first six months on the job Jane Addams advised him that Gertrude Beeks could "superintend the work of men as well as girls."[10]

Miss Beeks's job assignment was loosely defined as "betterment work." When, after she had been quietly at work for a year, Chicago newspapers learned of her activity, the *Tribune* interpreted its purpose as follows:

> GIRL AN ANGEL OF PEACE. M'CORMICK COMPANY HIRES ANTI-STRIKE "SOCIAL AGENT."
>
> Firm Employs Miss Gertrude Beeks to Aid in Solving the Problem of Capital and Labor—She Wins Women by Placing Plenty of Mirrors in Their Dressing Room—Has Many Duties Involving Welfare of the Workers.
>
> With a view of solving the serious problem of the relations of capital and labor, the McCormick Harvesting Company is experimenting with what is known as a "social agent"
>
> . . . . .
>
> The success of Miss Beeks's work is said to be shown best by the freedom from labor disturbances which the big harvester plant has enjoyed since she entered on her novel duties.[11]

While this was not a wholly accurate description of Miss Beek's job, it contained much truth. Theoretically her work was entirely separate from wages, hours, and labor relations. Her primary concerns were health, sanitation, and recreation.

To bring to the McCormick Works the best information about welfare practices, the company sent Miss Beeks during 1901 and 1902 on four extensive factory inspection tours. She went from coast to coast visiting and studying some two dozen firms which were noted for pioneering in employee welfare or betterment work. Miss Beeks's detailed notes[12] of these visits give a candid description of personnel practices among progressive American firms of the time. Because of the confidential nature of her investigations, she frequently was told the motives behind the welfare practices, which were often to build dams against a feared flood of unionism.

At the J. B. Stetson Company a Christmas gift and bonus plan was in effect. A recent effort to unionize, she learned, had been nipped by a strategic increase in the bonus. The Plymouth Cordage Company management reported that its welfare program brought contentment despite poor wages. The Enterprise Manufacturing Company operated the only nonunion foundry in Philadelphia, as a result of winning a nine months' strike of the Molders—"one of the best investments ever made by the company."[13] Now its welfare activities enabled it to attract molders in spite of its antiunion policy. Several companies had profit-sharing plans in operation. The Willamette Iron and Steel Works gave 25 percent of its net profits to the employees annually—a policy adopted just after a machinists' strike.[14]

One of the more elaborate welfare programs was that of the H. J. Heinz Company. Here Miss Beeks was told that the company's motive was not to prevent strikes, not to get appreciation from the employees, but to hold employees' loyalty by "love-HEART power." The secret of the company's success, she was informed, was that they "Do not employ a single union man."[15]

Her visit to the National Cash Register Company at Dayton, Ohio, had the most impact on Miss Beeks. In terms of program and philosophy this company was the most progressive of all those she saw. Miss Beeks was impressed with the high status given here to labor relations work. The company's Labor Bureau was responsible not only for welfare work but also for wage administration, a marriage which did not take place at Harvester till the 1920's. The head of the Labor Bureau, C. U. Carpenter, was a member of the Board of Directors of the company.

Carpenter explained to Miss Beeks his belief that welfare work was destined to fail unless accompanied by a fair wage structure. Despite its welfare work National Cash Register had had a serious strike a year and a half earlier because of wage inequalities. Carpenter felt the strike had been good for the company. There had been no unions at National Cash Register three and a half years earlier. At the time of Miss Beeks's visit the company recognized 29 unions.[16]

One of Carpenter's pioneering reforms was to begin the transfer of the foreman's authority over dismissal to the central personnel department. To curb arbitrary dismissals, workers were permitted to appeal over the foreman to the Labor Bureau. Carpenter also instituted classes in human relations for the foremen, which he himself instructed.

The company certainly received its money's worth when Miss Beeks returned to the McCormick plant from her tours. Employed initially to do betterment work among the Twine Mill girls, she soon made the entire McCormick Works her bailiwick. One of her first acts was to have the firm dig new wells and supply pure drinking water to all departments of the factory. When Samuel Gompers later heard of this move, which was advertised as a welfare achievement, he was extremely caustic in his criticism of welfare work; but the truth is that bad water from the city mains had been a common cause of illness among the workers. Cyrus McCormick II's diary for March 8, 1882, reads, in part, "200 men sick from impure water."[17] Fans to carry out twine lint, sanitary toilets, lunchrooms, and hot coffee also were introduced by Miss Beeks.

Miss Beeks ran Sunday outings to refresh the tired employees who worked six days a week; she organized a choral group and staged an operetta; when the firm would not finance a library for the employees, she persuaded the owners to contribute as individuals; she encouraged the McCormick family to set up a summer camp for workers' wives and children, near Chicago so the men could join their families each night. Her proposed annual budget called for $7,000 to establish a bank to lend money "at a minimum rate," "to provide for destitute cases" and "avoid the money shark."[18] This budget also included $4,496 for a "Christmas Remembrance," a subscription to the *Ladies' Home Journal* for the women in the mill and to the *Saturday Evening Post* for the men in the Works. Sensing that some of her suggestions would be resented by the plant superintendent, F. A. Flather, she would sometimes appeal directly to Stanley McCormick, youngest brother of Cyrus H. McCormick II and now comptroller of the firm, as in her report in December 1902:

> It might be regarded as a matter of interference on my part for *me* to take up the following with Mr. Flather and I would strongly urge that these matters be given serious thought.
>
> Under the present plan of increasing the facilities cannot the basement core room be abandoned?
>
> Cannot arrangements be made at once for providing water and flushes in the men's toilet rooms, . . . ?[19]

Miss Beeks was very concerned that welfare programs should not be given to the workers in lieu of fair wages. So while the scope of her authority was limited to factory betterment work and specifically excluded any control over wages and hours, she never lost an opportunity to call attention to shortcomings in the company's total industrial relations program. In her December 1902 report to Stanley McCormick she declared, "I cannot say enough to emphasize the necessity of a fair wage scale. With our present system of cutting piece-workers, the men feel there is no chance for an ambitious man as they can make only so much any way." In this same report she was merciless in her criticism of the company's treatment of its office workers:

> Is it necessary to patronize the employment bureaus in employing office men at the Works? These employment bureaus are a great evil and usually supply a low grade. It may be, however, that the salaries offered by this Company to beginners would not secure a better grade, especially considering the long hours, with barely enough time to snatch a bite to eat, no time for recreation . . . A mere existence these fellows have, too tired when they reach home at night to read or have any pleasure to speak of. It has been brought very forcibly to my attention that more work could be accomplished with shorter hours and a better class of men. Then, too, I understand that it is the policy of the Company to keep a good man where he is, rather than promote him to a better position if one is open, the idea being that it is easier to put an outsider in the open position than to teach two men new work, the result being that the Company continually loses good men whenever they find an opening elsewhere.

After a year and a half of this teeming activity, Miss Beeks resigned, ostensibly because of poor health. Actually, not only poor health but also poor rapport between Miss Beeks and the non-family executives, particularly Flather, superintendent of the Works, caused her resignation. Stanley McCormick reported Miss Beeks's feelings at the time of her resignation: "She said that she did not see how she could work under Mr. Flather, and she felt that his influence on Mr. Wood [assistant superintendent] had made the latter more unfriendly to her work than previously. She considered Mr. F. unfriendly to the general idea of her work, although professing to be friendly, and said she could not work under those circumstances, . . . "[20]

The typical "up from the ranks" executives' hostility to "welfare work" was inevitable. Any plant superintendent intent upon running a quiet operation would need the greatest empathy for welfarism to welcome this innovator who investigated every facet of his operation, called for drastic changes, and sent his costs skyward. Instead, such executives appreciated only cost cutting. In addition, their very status and the respect of the men under them were jeopardized by having a woman telling them how to run the plant. To these usual causes of conflict was added the fact that Miss Beeks, supposedly their subordinate, had direct access to the McCormick brothers who hired her and were personally interested in her work. This ultimate humiliation made her their mortal enemy. Miss Beeks left the firm in December 1902—though she returned six months later in response to worker demand for extension of her reforms to the Deering Works and served there in 1903–4.[21]

The Stock Gift

More startling than the hiring of Miss Beeks, and more complicated in its causes, was the next burst of sunshine in McCormick labor relations, a $1,500,000 stock gift from the McCormick's to their employees. The probable origin of this profit-sharing plan lay with the youngest of the McCormick brothers, Stanley.[22] Where did Stanley get the idea? A few profit-sharing plans existed at this time, but most of them were based upon the future earnings of the company and were reserved for key executives and sales personnel. Stanley McCormick's plan was unusual in that it began with an outright stock gift of $1,500,000 to all classes of employees, including factory laborers. The gift stock was redeemable in cash at par after three years. In the course of more than two years of discussion, mid-1901 to November 1903, when the plan was completed, it underwent many changes, but it retained these two features of Stanley's early proposals.

Stanley McCormick, the youngest of Cyrus McCormick I's three sons, was graduated from Princeton with the class of 1895. Four years later he was superintendent of the family's huge Chicago reaper plant with 4,000 employees. A number of influences were at work to make Stanley receptive to new ideas. The depression of the 'nineties and the Pullman strike focused new attention on the problems of capital and labor. As second-generation industrialists the McCormick brothers had good college educations and leisure in which to become acquainted with the cultural, religious, and sociological currents of their time. Jane Addams was a visitor at the McCormick home. Stanley's sister, Anita McCormick Blaine, took a deep interest in children's education and was a friend and financial supporter of John Dewey and Col. Francis Parker, both of whom were then experimenting with educational reform in Chicago.

At the time that Stanley McCormick was superintendent of the reaper plant (1899–1901), the State of Illinois employed as a factory inspector a wealthy young reformer, William English Walling. The two became fast friends. Another of Stanley's liberal acquaintances at this time was the social worker–theologian at the University of Chicago, Prof. Graham Taylor, who, like Jane Addams, pioneered in social and educational work among Chicago's slum dwellers and founded the West Side settlement house called Chicago Commons. Professor Taylor relates in his autobiography Stanley's deep interest in improving conditions of the firm's workmen:

> Stanley McCormick was entering very seriously upon his responsibilities at the International Harvester Company's McCormick Works when we were taking up our residence at Chicago Commons. When showing me the great plant one day, he expressed his deep desire to make its working conditions promote the welfare of its thousands of employees, for whose interests he personally cared. This led him to seek an interview with me. The interview forecast the great promise of his early years until continued illness withheld its fulfillment. His family has continued his annual contributions to some of the social agencies in which he was most personally interested.[23]

Stanley McCormick apparently sold his idea of a stock gift for the employees to the rest of the family.[24] His brothers Cyrus and Harold saw in it an opportunity to capture the loyalty of key executives. Recently several had been caught in conflict-of-interest situations and dismissed. Cyrus substantially sweetened the stock distribution formula in favor of the executives. His aim was the conventional one of using stock distribution to ensure future service. Indeed Cyrus, who was closer to the business than his younger brothers, wished to cut the manual workers from the stock distribution altogether. When he was outvoted by the family on this, he proposed a differential service requirement which would give stock to top executives regardless of years of service and would progressively increase the years-of-service requirement for lesser employees up to twenty years for manual workers. Again Harold and Anita sided with their more liberal younger brother Stanley and saw to it that workmen of five years' experience shared in the distribution.[25]

A further motive in the minds of the McCormick family in setting up the stock distribution plan may have arisen from their plans for merger of their company with four others to form the International Harvester trust. As the plans for merger took shape from 1901 through October 1902 when the merger became effective, a struggle for control arose among the executives of the two leading firms involved, the Deering and McCormick companies. The McCormicks were determined to control the new trust and to ensure that after the merger former McCormick employees would remain loyal to the McCormick family. This struggle for control was to go on for ten years after the formal merger.

While Stanley McCormick's idea of the stock distribution appears to have been chiefly altruistic, the mundane motives that arose eventually all but displaced the original one. The very decision to give stock rather than cash probably appealed to the family as safeguarding McCormick voting control in the new trust. The larger proportion of the stock which was given to key executives, even when they had less than the minimum years of service, points up the heavy intrusion of non-altruistic motivation. Eventually the impact of the labor dispute of 1903 twisted the plan so as to all but destroy the original altruism.

The early discussions of the gift to employees proceeded in a desultory manner through 1901 and 1902, since trips to Europe and visits to Stanley McCormick's New Mexico ranch made it difficult to assemble a family quorum. On November 18, 1902, the figure of $1,000,000 was set as an upper limit for stock distribution. Events soon occurred which forced the family to make quick decisions on the lagging plan.

On April 27, 1903, a strike broke out at the Chicago Deering Works of the International Harvester Company. The next day Deering strikers picketed the McCormick Works in an effort to spread the strike. This strike activity served as a shot in the arm to the stock distribution planners. Alex Legge, assistant manager of domestic sales, urged that the long-debated but still vague plan be announced "today . . . so as to get the benefit of the act before strike might be called."[26] Accordingly, at 5:30 P.M. on April 28 a special plant meeting was held of McCormick Works workmen with service of five years and more. While Deering strikers picketed outside, Stanley and Harold McCormick made one of their rare plant tours and personally promised minimum gifts of $100 or one share of stock as a reward for faithful service.[27] Other executives described to incredulous workers the long-time interest of the McCormick family in worker welfare. The same day top company executives met and decided to "fight to the end on the [labor] issue now drawn."[28] McCormick Works union leaders were being systematically dismissed.[29]

The next day the loyalties of McCormick workers were still wavering; more were joining the strike. The previous day's $100 minimum offer, restricted to five-year men, had covered only 700 of 4,000 production workers. President Cyrus H. McCormick II therefore proposed to the executive committee a bonus plan of $25 minimum to men who had been with the company for only a year. Action was deferred, but that evening the McCormick family approved liberalizing the stock or bonus plan to include less-than-five-year employees. On Thursday, April 30, in a desperate effort to keep the employees at work, Stanley and Harold McCormick again visited the plant and told groups of employees that "less than five-year men . . . would be remembered by some plan of bonus or stock purchase."[30]

Although the strike of Deering workers continued, the McCormick workers did not join. Cash and stock dangling daily before their eyes plus the systematic dismissal of union leaders had apparently turned the tide.

The liberalizations in the profit-sharing plan offered during the strike increased the cost to the McCormick family of the stock offer from $1,000,000 to $1,500,000. At the end of the strike the family at a stockholders' meeting on May 18, 1903, confirmed the $1,500,000 figure, including a pension system for older employees and stock for employees of three and four years' experience.[31] Apparently the offer made during the strike to include "less than five-year men" was now to be interpreted as limited to three- and four-year men.

Despite the rapid progress made in the stock distribution plan during the several weeks of the Deering strike, the family's earlier lassitude toward it returned when the strike was over. Six months after the end of the strike McCormick Works employees had heard no further official mention of the stock distribution and had nothing to show for their "faithful service." The McCormicks, however, heard of rumors circulating among the workers that the announcement had been simply "buncombe with the intention of keeping the men at work during the strike."[32] This finally brought forth on November 8, 1903, an official announcement of the stock distribution plan. A production employee's share was to equal 5 percent of his aggregate salary during his total employment with the company. The promise of April 30, 1903, made personally by Harold and Stanley McCormick, that workers of less than five years' standing would be included by some plan of bonus or stock purchase was not mentioned in the announcement. Another four months passed before workmen received their certificates, valued at an average of $300 each for nearly 700 production workers. This was a substantial gift, in some cases about equal to a worker's annual income.

Yet even in the actual stock distribution, antiunionism intruded in such a way as to twist the originally generous plan into an instrument of thought and action control for years to come. Twenty union officials and activists who met the five-year requirement for length of service failed to qualify as "faithful" employees and were omitted from the stock distribution, several losing between $400 and $500 worth of stock.[33]

The cases of these twenty union activists were reviewed on three subsequent occasions. The first review was made in December 1904. The excluded men were put in four separate categories based on the intensity of their union activity. Group A contained names of men who entered the company as small boys and served it well. They were considered as having been "led into trouble by other employees." Group B was similar to Group A except that these men had entered service of the company after they were well along in life and their cases did "not warrant quite as much consideration as those shown under Group A." Group C, like Group A, included men who entered the service of the company as boys but were more active in the union, " in fact every one of them held an office in the local organization." Group D was reserved for unpardonable offenders. It contained but one name. His crime? "He started the circulation of a petition for the purpose of organizing a department, the toolroom, and making demands on the Company for which he was properly discharged." The 1904 review denied the stock benefits to all of these men.[34]

In another review of these cases in July 1905 Stanley McCormick recommended that all men except the one man in Group D be forgiven in order not to prolong the recollection of the "troublesome days." This recommendation was not followed. In late 1907 the last review of the case was conducted. In a letter to Cyrus and Harold McCormick John Chapman, agent in charge of stock distribution, again recited the union activities of the men. After further discussing Stanley McCormick's desire to pay the men their stock, Chapman concluded, ". . . we do not recommend that they be given stock now."[35] President Cyrus McCormick II concurred in this recommendation.[36]

John Dewey and the McCormick Institute

The search for milder fare than unionism for their workers, which had led the McCormicks to factory betterment and stock gifts, also spawned the McCormick Institute. Cyrus McCormick's diary for May 14, 1903, in the midst of the Deering Works strike, contains this entry: "Lunch with Bruere who wishes to become interested in betterment work at the McCormick Works." At the conclusion of the strike Henry Bruere, a young man with two years of welfare experience, was engaged by the McCormicks personally to make a survey of working conditions in the plant and to determine the best form of men's club or institute for the McCormick employees. During the summer of 1903 Bruere toured the East visiting and consulting. Among those he saw were Samuel Gompers and the officers of the International Association of Machinists. According to Bruere, their only concern was lest the McCormick educational activities "increase the number of apprentices over the number desired by the unions."[37] In late August 1903 Bruere was transferred to the payroll of the International Harvester Company. By his account the firm's notion of his duties was vague.[38] One suggestion which hints at company unionism was that he should take employment in the shops with a view to developing "an employees association." Stanley McCormick suggested a men's club similar to one with which Bruere had been connected in Boston.

Bruere rejected these suggestions. He considered "the proposition to form a benevolent employees Association, or a mere Social Club, whereof, by some magic, I would secure the leadership, mere sentimental idealism. . . . men organize and hang together for some selfish end, for the sake of a principle or for idle good fellowship. There was no suitable, inspiring principle forthcoming . . . ." He regarded "the attempt to hold a Workingmen's Social Club to high ideals, . . . [as] at best quixotic."[39]

Instead, Bruere proposed the establishment of a McCormick Institute based on the principle that "It is important, therefore, that every man be given an opportunity to prepare himself for some higher quality of work than the lowering of a lever and the occasional adjustment of a jig."[40] To this end the Institute would offer elementary courses in arithmetic, English (notices were sent out in five different languages), and technical drawing. Upon this educational foundation, whose nature would exclude the "undesirable element," clubs for "debating, base-ball, singing" would be organized.

The McCormick Institute was to be only a first step in the development of a "People's Institute." Bruere, an admirer of the University of Chicago's educational philosopher, John Dewey, was shocked by the conflict between the individual's need for imaginative self-expression and the confluence of forces—i.e., factory work, elementary education, parental and religious controls—which developed only "passivity, . . .

submissive obedience, honesty, and fear of punishment."[41] The purpose of the People's Institute would be to counteract these stultifying forces, to give the individual a "free opportunity for self-development—to broaden his life and render his environment happier, ..."[42] There would be lectures and concerts, theatricals and dancing. The Institute would be open to all persons employed in the McCormick area of Chicago. Its influence would be "steadily directed towards local improvement, purer politics and richer social life."

Bruere felt very strongly that even the McCormick Institute should be "an independent institution rather than the integral part of an industrial organization." To have the Institute be the creature of one company would have only the advantage of "the cultivation of men's loyalty to that company. But so cultivated, loyalty to the company is likely to stand in the way of the healthiest development of the employees." In his fight for the independence of the Institute Bruere interjected one plea motived by an ulterior purpose: "If the Institute were independent, other employers might be interested in contributing to its support and, in that way, the movement against industrial warfare extended." Bruere evidently failed to realize that "the cultivation of men's loyalty" was just what the Harvester Company had in mind. His request to establish an independent institute was denied.

John Dewey actively supported Bruere's educational institute plans by counseling with him, by visiting the factory, and by writing a letter to the Harvester president's influential mother, Nettie McCormick:

I have been much interested in talking over with Mr. Bruere his educational plans in connection with the Reaper Works. He had been good enough to come over here twice and talk to me about the possibilities of the educational work, and last Tuesday I spent the day with him on the ground. After investigating, I am sure that Mr. Bruere's ideas regarding the development of education work are thoroughly sound and feasible. I also feel like congratulating all concerned upon their having Mr. Bruere to undertake this sort of work. His purposes and methods are wholly in the right direction, and I am sure that his temperament and executive qualities fit him unusually well to carry them out. The Manual Training work for the boys and the cooking and household economy for the girls are clearly the points at which to begin this educational work.

In case it is undertaken I shall have great interest in following its development and shall be glad to cooperate and advise in every way in my power. The School of Education is so much indebted to the McCormick family, through the great generosity of Mrs. Blaine, that it will give me unusual pleasure to do anything that I can in the way of even a very small return.[43]

Though the McCormick Institute never metamorphosed into the People's Institute, it did provide technical training for one to two hundred of the 5,000 McCormick workers each year for many years. Many of the McCormick foremen and some of the skilled workmen came from these classes. However, the Institute failed to have much impact on the average worker. Circumstances had conspired to give it a foreboding send-off. Early classes were conducted in the basement of the McCormick Twine Mill. In 1903 an imposing brick clubhouse was planned; and when declining company profits in 1904 caused the company to curtail its welfare expenditures and withdraw its support of the proposed clubhouse, Stanley McCormick personally donated the money for the building. Unfortunately this came at a time of severe unemployment among McCormick workers. Also, a Harvester union contract was abrogated, the work week lengthened, and wage rates slashed. Counseled Miss Beeks, who was now back at her post as welfare director of the National Civic Federation, which had moved to New York, writing to Cyrus McCormick II: "it would be a great blow to welfare work for you to put up a $40,000 building at the same time that you cut wages or increase hours."[44] Nevertheless the imposing brick walls of the Institute rose directly across the street from the plant, in striking contrast to the surrounding squalor. Workers were again alienated from clubhouse activity when during the strikes of World War I scabs evaded the picket lines via an underground tunnel connecting the plant and clubhouse. In the 'twenties the clubhouse became the home of a supervisors' club.

Though the Institute existed in this limited fashion for many years, Bruere himself survived only two years of corporate in-fighting. In almost a re-run of Miss Beeks's difficulties, enmity developed between Bruere and the non-family executives. They resented his well-financed, McCormick-blessed project. He flaunted his McCormick family support and condescendingly ordered the executives about with such directives as "You will turn over to me, then, all the Sociological work in the factory . . . ."[45] Miss Beeks, who had herself suffered so much from jealous officials, was ruthless in attacking Bruere and his "expensive fad."[46] In more reasoned tone she advised Cyrus McCormick II: "When the body is in healthful condition through provision for physical comfort and recreative efforts, it becomes possible to think more about education; but, in my opinion, the time has not yet arrived."[47]

3

Union Resurgence

The Strike of 1903

While Miss Beeks was still carrying on betterment work at the McCormick Works and Stanley McCormick was urging the family to adopt profit sharing, unionization was again moving forward in the company's Chicago plant. The revival of unions during 1902–4 was part of a national union upsurge. As the long depression of 1893–98 gradually gave way to prosperity, unionism nationally quadrupled, from 500,000 members in 1898 to over 2,000,000 in 1904. Chicago, as in 1886, was in the thick of the labor "troubles," witnessing during the period major strikes of foundrymen, patternmakers, machinists, streetcar operators, teamsters, building trades workers, and meat packers.

Vainly McCormick officials struggled to isolate their employees from the temper of the times. In 1900 Chicago contractors locked out the building trades unionists in the midst of construction of a new McCormick Twine Mill. At the same time the International Association of Machinists called a citywide strike for the nine-hour day and other concessions. Nonunion labor under the direction of the McCormick building supervisor completed the Twine Mill almost on schedule, and the machinist strike merely slowed production in the McCormick toolrooms. Indication of continued restlessness is the fact that a year later a labor spy reported to President McCormick on a union meeting of the McCormick machinists.[1]

The formation of the International Harvester trust seems to have given added impetus to combinations among the workers. As one Deering worker expressed it to Gertrude Beeks, "If William Deering had kept the business, the trouble would not have come, but people say 'The Company has gone into a Trust; why should we not combine?' "[2]

Since at least the 1880's the handful of quasi-competitive companies that manufactured harvesting machines had dreamed of combination. Price-fixing agreements regularly broke down for lack of enforceable production quotas, and the demands for real combination became more insistent. Patent pools in the early 'eighties gave way to a full-blown plan for an American harvester trust in 1890. Mutual distrust and the high profits of the two leading companies, McCormick and Deering, prevented fruition of this plan.

The successful formation of the United States Steel Corporation in 1900 pointed the way for the harvester industry. In October 1902 the McCormick Harvesting Machine Company merged with four other producers of harvesting machinery—the Deering, Champion, Plano, and Milwaukee companies—to form the International Harvester Corporation.[3] Three large plants—which became divisions—of the new trust were in Chicago: the Deering and Plano plants as well as the McCormick Works. Thus International Harvester came to own the Wisconsin Steel Works, a Chicago steel mill of the Deering Company on whose records Chapter 7 of this book, "Employee Representation," is chiefly based. The McCormick and Deering families together controlled about 80 percent of the stock of the trust and dominated the management, although four of the five combining companies were represented on the Board of Directors.[4] Major labor policies such as changes in wages, hours, or union relations were decided by an executive committee composed primarily of the McCormick and Deering families plus George W. Perkins, representative of the Morgan banking firm which had handled the merger. The committee's decisions applied to all three Chicago plants, yet during the early months of the merger the relationships between workers and management in each plant retained some characteristics peculiar to the particular plant, such as the stock gift from McCormick family funds to workers at McCormick Works. At the time of the merger none of the three plants recognized unions in any form.

The new trust was extremely sensitive to the workers' efforts to combine. McCormick Division payroll records show that union officials and activists were dismissed from the McCormick Works beginning in October 1902. Still the pace of unionization was so threatening that the executive committee of International Harvester met four times during

December 1902 and January 1903 to discuss the "labor situation." On January 9, 1903, this committee decided "to take no action yet showing timidity."[5] But a week later extensive wage increases were given in the most restless departments of the three Chicago plants.

The McCormick Division of International Harvester sought to checkmate its growing unions by forestalling any support they might receive from the Chicago Federation of Labor. In an unprecedented bid for the goodwill of the Federation, the company wrote to Federation President William G. Schardt:

> We are informed by the papers that a labor trouble is being suggested at our works. We have no unanswered grievances from any of our men. Won't your federation look into this matter for us?
>
> International Harvester Company
> McCormick Division (per A. E. Mayer)[6]

This candid approach produced a vital measure of goodwill for the McCormick Division which proved crucial in later weeks. The Federation's investigating committee heard strikers outside the McCormick gates complain of the company's discrimination against unionists. Inside the plant it heard Flather, assistant general manager, declare that he had never discriminated for or against union men.[7] Though O'Donnell of the Metalworkers, on hearing this report at the Federation meeting, scoffed at the remarks of the McCormick superintendent and said there had been discrimination, the committee concluded, "We see no reason to doubt his [Flather's] word."[8] The committee also reported that wages and working conditions in the plant were good.[9]

While labor unrest simmered at the McCormick Works, a full-blown strike erupted at the Deering plant. On April 27, 1903, F. A. Francke, shop steward for the Metalworkers, went to the office of Deering Works manager B. A. Kennedy, and asked him to sign an agreement with the Metalworkers. Francke was kept in the office talking the matter over for about two hours. His tools were brought to the office, he was paid, and summarily discharged. Within a few hours, 2,000 men had followed him out of the plant. By April 30 the majority of the departments were seriously hampered, and the Deering management announced that since it could not continue to run the works with the diminished force the plant would close until further notice.[10]

The Chicago Federation of Labor, considering whether or not to support the Deering strike, submitted the following demands of the Deering strikers to the company: a 20 percent wage increase, a general nine-hour day, improved sanitary conditions, union recognition, and reinstatement of those discharged for union activity. Management refused the demands and cavalierly told the Federation leaders that "if they would order the strikers back to work the company would inform 'its employes' what concessions it was willing to make."[11] The Federation's shock and anger at this attitude were expressed by strike leader M. J. Deutsch, Federation official who was coordinating the activities of the ten striking Deering unions, in his report of the Federation's conference with E. A. S. Clarke, Harvester general manager of manufacturing:

> At first we could not understand what Mr. Clarke meant, . . . for the proposition was so preposterous. He made himself clear by telling us that he could not see why the employees should be organized. This remark of his settled it, and now we will fight.
>
> . . . we have the employees thoroughly organized, even to the window washers, and since the company wants war it can have it.[12]

With the Deering plant closed, the Deering strikers carried the war to International Harvester's McCormick Works. "If the McCormick employees continue to work," noted the *Chicago Record-Herald*, "it is believed the Deering strike will fail. Both plants are divisions of the same combine, and during the slack summer season the work of the Deering factory could be accomplished by the other."[13] In spite of the picketing, mass meetings, and desperate pleas for help by their fellow workers at Deering, the McCormick workers refused to strike.

Several factors held them at their jobs. Primary among these was the stock distribution plan. The promise of substantial cash and stock gifts served as a bribe they could not afford to ignore. "Checked by Hope of Rewards," headlined the *Chicago Tribune:*

> The McCormick employees gave as their reason for not joining the strike that they have always been well treated and that the McCormick family is about to reward all its workmen, who have been employed five years. The plans have not been fully completed, but the lowest sums to be given will be $100 and from that up to between $3,000 and $4,000. There are 1,100 who are eligible and the total sum will be in the hundreds of thousands of dollars. All will be paid in cash. The employees know of these plans and consequently are unwilling to strike.[14]

As might be expected, pressure from McCormick foremen was another factor in holding the McCormick workers in line. The following speech, delivered personally to the foremen by President Cyrus H. McCormick II, indicates the careful calculation in the company effort and, further, the use of the stock gift as an antistrike weapon:

Foremen of the McCormick Division of the International Harvester Company: I congratulate you upon the fact that all of your rooms are running this morning. It is through your watchful care of all of your forces that this is possible. I know that no appeal is necessary to enlist your continued enthusiasm, but for a few days I want to ask you to use all of your efforts in one direction, and that is to keep all of your men that have not been laid off, at work. If any man stays out, use every means to get him in, talk with each man in your room and tell him that you appreciate the fact that McCormick men are so loyal and not affected by excitement. We shall keep a daily record of all workmen who stay with us from now on and we shall then have figures that will give you all the credit that I know you will all deserve.

Now fellow officials, let us have as high a percentage as possible of the workers who are now here in each of your departments, stay at their work, until all neighboring clouds have rolled away. Then, gentlemen, we shall compare our first and last record and all of you faithful foremen will have my full appreciation, and better still, some kind of substantial recognition from the Messrs. McCormick, as well as their appreciation.

P.S.—Should any man be threatened we would like you to spare no effort in getting the details of the threat and the men who made it and the time when made.[15]

Besides the deterring forces within the plant, several external forces restrained a walkout by the McCormick workers. The Chicago Federation of Labor was one of these. Unlike the Deering strikers, who viewed the McCormick Works as an integral and similar part of International Harvester, the Federation considered the McCormick plant separate from and superior to the Deering plant in its labor policy. While Deering strikers were begging the McCormick workers to join their strike, President Schardt of the Federation and Deutsch, Building Trades leader in the Federation and the Federation adviser to the Deering unions, were asking these McCormick workers not to strike. "I do not want the employees at McCormick to strike," said Deutsch. "I will advise against a strike. But I will advise them to organize themselves into unions. The company has said it does not discriminate against union workers. I know it does. But if it will allow its employes to unionize there will be no trouble."[16] The Federation ordered the

Deering pickets withdrawn from the McCormick Works.[17] Deutsch's incongruous attitude toward the McCormick plant is difficult to explain, unless the International Harvester Company had already indicated sympathy with the demands of the Building Trades that future plant construction be carried out with union contractors. At some point such a demand was granted, as this clause was included in the written contract which concluded the strike.

Another restraint upon the McCormick workers, particularly upon the Twine Mill girls, was the ambivalent attitude of Jane Addams, who found herself an adviser to the Deering strikers and a friend of the McCormick management. At the time of the strike she was well acquainted with the McCormick family, which had contributed to her social work for some years. She had given President Cyrus McCormick II advice on the betterment work at the McCormick plant and had placed one of the Hull House social workers, Mary Thaon, on the McCormick payroll as a betterment supervisor in the new Twine Mill. She had even given McCormick advice on the merits of unionism. He recorded in his diary for January 20, 1901: "Miss Jane Addams took tea with us. She believes in pure unionism for working men with good leadership."

Now, in 1903, Miss Addams, in response to an appeal from the Chicago Federation of Labor, agreed to serve as an adviser to the striking Deering Twine Mill girls. At their union meeting she urged the Deering girls: " 'The men will support the women and you as women should not forget that you must support the men.' . . . union men are chivalrous and I believe in them. They are aiding their leaders in making Chicago the best city in the world for the workers."[18]

However, like the Chicago Federation of Labor, Miss Addams regarded the McCormick Works as a separate concern. While her advisees were supporting their striking union men by urging the McCormick Twine Mill girls to join the strike, Jane Addams, escorted by McCormick office manager George S. Steele, toured the new McCormick Twine Mill. Instead of encouraging the McCormick girls to join their striking sisters, she reported that she was "well pleased with it."[19] She then went to a meeting of the Deering girls and told them that, so far as possible, she would watch over their union and aid in directing it.

Undoubtedly, there was a difference between working conditions at the Deering and McCormick twine mills. Conditions in the Deering Twine Mill were described by the president of the Twine Mill union:

. . . our work shop is filthy and our toilet rooms need a garden hose and barrels of soap. We are not allowed to sit down during working hours, no matter if we are ill.

. . . . .

We are not even given help to clean our machines and sometimes we are forced to do that dirty work in our lunch hour.[20]

The McCormick Twine Mill was new and more sanitary. As a result of Miss Beeks's betterment program it had attractive lunchrooms, mirrors in washrooms, rest rooms, and noon dances.

However, Miss Addams had failed to recognize the vital role of the twine mills in the Deering strike. As the *Chicago Tribune* explained: "Should the war be of long duration the strikers declare that the work of harvesting throughout the country will be seriously injured. They assert that while the local companies have a surplus of machines on hand they will be unable to run out enough twine to meet the demand. On this account they base their hope of success on the fight the twine girls are making."[21]

Since wages were the same in both the Deering and McCormick twine mills and the stock gift plan applied to neither, it was probably the newness of the McCormick mill, the work of Miss Beeks, and the approval of McCormick plant conditions by Miss Addams that kept the McCormick girls from joining the strike.

In spite of holding the McCormick Works in line, the trust was softened by the month-long Deering strike. In his diary Cyrus H. McCormick II expressed the changing attitude of his associates as follows: ". . . we must modify to some extent the stand heretofore taken of entire independence of the union question. . . . We must decide to abstain positively from any discrimination against unions."[22] The official wording of the company's earlier policy toward unionism was that it "neither discriminates for nor against unions." In practice this policy had resulted in systematic dismissals of union activists. Under the new policy of positive abstention from discrimination, negotiations were carried on directly with President Schardt of the Chicago Federation of Labor.

Though they lost their battle to induce the McCormick workers to join the strike, the Deering strikers stubbornly refused to go back to work. The Federation recommended acceptance of an International Harvester proposal which promised the right to organize, freedom from discrimination against unionists, and arbitration of wages and hours.[23] This the strikers rejected. Not until the nine-hour day with ten hours' pay was included in the company offer did the strikers agree to a settlement. The strike ended on May 14, 1903.

The final signed contract that ended the strike was in the form of a letter from the union to the company. This comprehensive agreement, carrying the signature of E. A. S. Clarke as general manager of manufacturing for the International Harvester Company, represented a major company capitulation. The agreement was to run for almost sixteen months, ending September 15, 1904, and covered not only the Deering plant where the strike occurred but the company's two other major Chicago plants, the McCormick and Plano Works. Forcing the company for the first time in history to put its signature to an agreement was an unprecedented victory for the striking unions. The rank-and-file Deering plant workers had proved themselves more militant than the officers of the Chicago Federation of Labor who had directed the strike and negotiated with the Harvester Company. The union signatures to the agreement were:

WM. G. SCHARDT, *Pres. C. F. of Labor,*
M. J. DEUTSCH, *Secy. B. M. T. Council,*
J. J. KEPPLER, *I. A. of Machinists,*
JOS. W. MORTON, *Steam Power Council,*
MISS E. D. LANAGAN, *Twine Workers' Union,*
J. H. PAYNE, *Box Makers,*
C. B. MYERS, *M.P.B.P. & B.W.U. of N.A.,*
MARK PIERCE, *Int. Union Steam Engineer,*
F. L. RIORDON, *Int. Brotherhood Firemen,*
J. J. O'DONNELL, *United Metalworkers,*
CHAS. KIRKPATRICK, *United Metalworkers,*
N. J. DONNELY, *Freight Handlers,*
A. W. LEMME, *Iron Moulders.*

The terms of the agreement, which are summarized below, testified to the strength of the union victory.

1. No discrimination against union members or grievance committeemen.
2. Old employees, including union officers, to be given preference in employment.
3. Inauguration of overtime pay at time and one-quarter on week days and double time on Sundays and holidays.
4. Foremen forbidden to use obscene language.

5. Clean toilets, seats for employees, and fans for ventilation.
6. Establishment of the nine-hour day at wages now paid for ten hours.
7. When the company puts up new buildings it should do so by contract or under the rules now existing between the Carpenters' and Builders' Association of Chicago and the Carpenters' Council.[24]

The increase in straight hourly wage rate gained by moving to the nine-hour day was 11 percent, which had to be added to the substantial wage increases previously awarded in the winter and spring of 1903 in the vain hope of staving off unionization. Especially humiliating to the company was the public admission of unsatisfactory sanitary and health conditions. Provisions 4 and 5 were in response to an employee demand that the company do for the Deering workers "what Miss Beeks had done at the McCormicks."[25]

Breaking with the Union

Once before, at the conclusion of the 1885 strike, Cyrus McCormick II had capitulated to the unions. His concessions at that time represented no softening attitude toward unionism but were regarded by the company as only a temporary truce in the war against unionism. The 1885 verbal agreement was openly breached by the company, first through discharges of union leaders, and, following the fall shutdown of 1885, by the discharge of all union molders.

The formal wages and hours provisions of the 1903 labor agreement were scrupulously observed. In accordance with the contract provisions on working conditions, Miss Beeks, who had resigned six months earlier from the McCormick Works, was rushed back from New York to extend her welfare program to the Deering plant. She did not agree to stay permanently; she returned only to make a survey and recommendations for an extended new welfare program.

After five weeks of observation, Miss Beeks reported the results of her survey to E. A. S. Clarke in his capacity as general manager of the Deering Division.[26] Most striking to her was the contrast between the "feeling of coercion and oppression" among the Deering workers and the attitude of James and Charles Deering, who were "so desirous of having conditions as they should be, and really pained to know that there had been any cause for dissatisfaction." "Finding the heads of the institution so very well intentioned," she continued, "I could not understand why complaints had not been made in the past which would keep the Company informed of these needs, but I found among the rank and file, . . . that they would not have the 'nerve' to complain, . . . they feared they would be made examples of should any of them make any requests." She suggested that "conditions would be better if Messrs. James and Charles Deering, . . . [and] yourself would occasionally make visits to the various departments," instead of relying upon the reports of "subordinates." She went on to tell Mr. Clarke what he would find on such visits:

"I spent one night from 2 o'clock until about 4:30 in the workrooms [in the twine mill], and feel that this night work is really very undesirable for women. Some of them were in fair condition, but others very tired. I found one girl sound asleep in the toilet room." Work rules aggravated rather than assuaged their weariness. "In the spinning room the girls say that while they were not allowed to sit down before the strike, there is no objection made now if they lean up against the bobbins.

"The preparation girls would like higher stools. They claim when they sit on a bench, the foreman will come along and kick it under the machine and tell them to get up, also that if they do not tell them to get up, they give them a meaning look." Not only was night work physically wearing, it was demoralizing as well: "It appears that some parents will not allow their girls to work at night. . . . There is no doubt but that the tone of the mill is lowered through the night work, and that girls seeking work go elsewhere rather than endanger their reputations here."

Miss Beeks hoped that the company would do away with night work and "not await the time when the law must step in to prevent women from working at night . . . ."

One of the greatest desires of the men at Deering, Miss Beeks found, was for a place to wash up. "In the cutter bar department I saw a pail of water which was very dirty and was informed that it had been used by the men at the noontime, but that it would be freshly filled before quitting time. It seemed to me rather pathetic. The foreman in the department stated that if he could get a place to wash up he would feel that he had the earth. The foreman of the grinding room exclaimed that the '. . . men would carry him around on their shoulders if he could get a place for them to wash up.' " In recommending washing facilities

Miss Beeks warned, "In order to avoid the stealing of soap, the powdered soap holders that are made for rough use in factories should be installed."

She was less practical and more philosophical when she recommended small hand towels to replace the disease-spreading roller towels in the office women's toilet room. "The Company may have some towels stolen, even with this class of young women, but such things are taken in the very best clubs." Miss Beeks particularly stressed the need for a rest room for these women office workers: "I understand it is only lately that they have even had a chair in the toilet room, and they claim they had to 'fight' to get that. . . . At present, when ill, they have to lie down on the toilet room floor."

Miss Beeks concerned herself not only with the 1903 contract demand for improved physical facilities but also with its stipulation that there should be no discrimination against union members. She reported to Mr. Clarke: "You should know, also, that the girls [Twine Mill employees] accuse some of the foremen of advising them not to belong to the Union." She found discrimination against the union prevalent throughout the Works, and recommended foremen's meetings in which the company should "make it understood that an agreement with the labor unions must be lived up to to the letter." "I understand now that it is difficult to force the foremen not to discriminate, as they are so prejudiced against unions, but trouble will come surely if this is not insisted upon."

The company did not heed her warning. Though International Harvester had ostensibly accepted the contract with the union, it had by no means come to accept unionism in its plants. The executive committee planned continued guerrilla warfare against the unions. Meeting in July of 1903, it issued a directive forbidding any kind of meeting, including social and recreational events, which would "commingle" the working force of the three Chicago plants. This directive ended even the popular interplant athletic activities by limiting them to those "which will be attended by employes in the adjacent factory only, ..."[27] We have already noted the omission of union leaders from the substantial stock gifts to McCormick Works employees.

Hostile company actions such as these, combined with the worsening economic situation, robbed the union of its bargaining power. The depression of 1903–4 hit the agricultural implements business, and employment was slack.[28] Despite all the supposed advantages of combination, the trust's earnings in the first year fell precipitously. The annual statement in October 1903 showed a meager $4,000,000 profit compared to the $10,000,000 combined profits of the constituent companies in the last year of cut-throat competition. Even this figure appears to have been an optimistic view of the balance sheet, for when the Federal Trade Commission in 1913 published its study of the International Harvester trust it put the true earnings of the trust in its first year as $796,822, less than one-tenth of the pre-merger earnings.[29]

Cyrus McCormick II was particularly sensitive to this financial shortcoming of the new trust because two of the nation's most powerful capitalists were attentively watching its progress. Most embarrassing was the attitude of J. P. Morgan. The Morgan firm had taken its payment for handling the merger in the form of stock of the new corporation. At the outset no one of the five companies that combined had a controlling stock interest in the new trust. To prevent struggles for control and debilitating internal fighting, an impartial moderator was needed. The McCormicks picked George W. Perkins, Morgan partner, for this role. All parties reluctantly agreed for a period of ten years, 1902–12, to give Perkins power to name corporate executives, fix salaries and titles, and try to weld the separate dynastic companies into a single corporation.[30] Hence legally the Morgan trustee, Perkins, could select or remove officers of the International Harvester Company, including President McCormick. Mr. Morgan's opinion therefore could not be taken lightly.[31] When only a 3 percent dividend was declared (though not earned), J. P. Morgan personally chided Cyrus McCormick and urged him to declare an additional 3 percent stock dividend.[32]

The McCormicks were also beholden to John D. Rockefeller, who loaned the $4,500,000 in cash that enabled the McCormick family to raise their stock holdings in the new trust above the crucial 50 percent mark. Rockefeller's primary motive was not pecuniary but stemmed from his daughter Edith's marriage to Harold McCormick. Nevertheless, Mr. Rockefeller asked for and received regular reports on the financial condition of the new company. Little wonder that Cyrus McCormick at this point determined upon some economies in the operation of the new enterprise.

In the early summer of 1904, well before the September 15 expiration date of the union contract, Harvester's general manager of manufacturing, E. A. S. Clarke, was ordered to make a careful study of the union-management relations in Chicago and particularly at the three Chicago Works—McCormick, Deering, and Plano. Clarke's report and recommendations for action were completed and sent to President

Cyrus McCormick II on August 19, 1904. This gave the seven-man executive committee of the Board of Directors a scant month before the expiration of the union contract to arrive at and implement a decision. In this time the report was dissected and debated in nine prolonged meetings of company executives.

The Clarke report, excerpted below, is a classic of management's thinking on labor relations in the period.[33]

. . . I know of no case where the employers have taken a firm stand with their help and a strike has resulted, in which the employers have not won. . . .

The condition of the International Harvester Company seems to be about as follows: We have spent during the past year in the three Chicago plants about $400,000 more in wages than we would have spent under the old arrangement. Of this amount about $125,000 was due to the agreement made with the Chicago Federation of Labor, the balance being the result of what we gave ourselves in the hope of staving off trouble. This $400,000 in a full year of manufacture would have been practically doubled. The condition as regards our business is that we will have a considerable carry-over of machines and twine and a very small estimated manufacture for next year. Therefore, as regards the condition of our business, it would seem that we are in a more favorable position today to have a fight with Labor, if necessary, than we have been for some time past or are likely to be in for a long time to come.

The general situation as regards supply of labor is that the supply exceeds the demand and there are a great many men out of employment and ready for work. The labor unions in general are not financially strong; they have spent a large amount of their resources fighting strikes up to date. It is not believed that they want to have any serious fight. I therefore believe that the time . . . is more favorable than it is likely to be in a long time for a fight with Labor, ...

My recommendation, therefore, is that on the expiration of our contract with the Federation of Labor on September 15 next, we go back to a sixty hour week with sixty hours' pay . . . . [The current union contract called for 54 hours' work for 60 hours' pay.]

I would readjust [cut] all piece work rates that needed equalization by September 15, ... As regards day workers, in cases where we are paying excessive rates I would gradually let out the high priced men and hire new men to do the same work at lower rates, if possible.

As regards overtime, I would go back to the practice which formerly obtained [before the union contract] . . . .

. . . . .

. . . We consider it probable that we shall have trouble with machinists, pattern makers, and some of the other skilled trades, but no such trouble as cannot be overcome in reasonable time and without serious expense; and no matter what the trouble or the expense may be, we believe that it will be very much less than the $400,000 which we have paid out during the past year and would pay out in another year, not to mention the weakening of our position toward our employes if we do not take some firm stand. . . . We do not anticipate a strike of the general rank and file of workmen, but think it entirely probable that we may have a strike of certain of the skilled trades. To successfully fight this strike it may be necessary to import non-union men and strikebreakers; it may be necessary to board and lodge these men inside our works; it may be necessary to practically put our works in a stage of siege; to take every possible precaution to defend them against violence or attempts at incendiarism or dynamiting. We must assume that our plants will be picketed; that we shall have to have police protection; we may have to employ men to protect the plants and escort workers to and from work; that there may be violence, slugging, rioting, even loss of life; we may have to organize an efficient secret service department of our own: in fact, we may have to do any of the things which the packers have had to do during the Stock Yards strike. We do not anticipate, as stated, any very serious trouble, nor do we anticipate that many of the items mentioned above will occur or be necessary; but they are always possibilities and must be reckoned with by you in arriving at a decision in this matter; . . . .

Clarke's description of possible strife reveals a passion stronger than the anticipation of mere financial gain would seem to warrant. In fact, his enmity to labor is scarcely cloaked by his financial arguments. He seems to speak more truly as a crusader for his class:

we believe that the time is opportune to take a firm stand; that . . . we will have the sympathy and moral support of other manufacturers, . . . it is . . . a duty for this company, as a large employer of labor, to take some action which may be . . . an example in the community . . . . we believe that by taking a firm stand on this question and putting it through, we shall end up by having our men in better control; that they will respect us more, and that we will have less labor troubles . . . for several years to come than we would in adopting any compromise measure.

What the muckrakers of that day could have done with the Clarke report had it been available: the Harvester trust revealed as the epitome of the soulless corporation, its goal the pursuit of power and profit!

Those called upon to discuss this report were executives of various levels. First were the members of the owning families, who also held the top executive positions. The second echelon was the salaried manufacturing executives, who owned little or no stock. This group included the general manager of manufacturing, division heads, plant superintendents, and their assistants. Third was the banking firm of J. P. Morgan, potentially more powerful in case of disagreement than even the owning families, and represented by George W. Perkins. Perkins in

New York City was kept informed of the problems and consulted by President McCormick in a special interview in New York.

All Harvester officials, regardless of level, who participated in the labor conferences of August and September 1904 assumed that the company must cut labor costs. The prolonged debate was over how to accomplish this while minimizing the chances of a strike. The discussion was also concerned with policy toward the union. Whether or not Clarke's plan of increasing weekly hours from 54 to 60 for the same weekly pay was the wisest means of attaining the desired goals was seriously discussed. The chief concern was whether the company dared defy the general trend to shorter hours. B. A. Kennedy, assistant manager of the Deering Division, commented, "I cannot get out of my mind the fact that all manufacturers are going to a nine-hour day, and some of them to 8."[34] He worried "whether or no we would not have the public, and to a certain extent the press, to fight in this matter. . . . we might lose some of the good will of our men that possibly we have gotten back by the nine hour movement, ..."[35] More importantly, would the unions tolerate this major setback to one of their dearest goals? As Superintendent Borg of the Deering Works saw it, "the unions will stand a 5% reduction in pay, but when you affect their principle of nine hours, they will fight; if not this fall as soon as they feel strong enough to do so."[36]

In an attempt to evaluate these fears objectively, each superintendent was asked the comparative union strength at his plant then and at the same date in 1903 and 1902.

Borg said for the Deering Works: ". . . there are less union men now than there were two years ago, and . . . less . . . today than a year ago after the strike, ... I should say today about ten per cent . . . are members of unions . . . . If we should start hiring a full force of men and at the same time should increase hours and reduce wages, then the number of union men would greatly increase. . . ."[37]

"You speak of reducing the skilled high priced laborer. They will not stand much of a reduction. They will fight."[38]

Said Wood, superintendent of the McCormick Works: "I agree with Mr. Borg. . . . The machinists are our largest per cent of union men."[39]

Superintendent Robinson: "At the Plano the unions are not so strong as they were a year ago. . . . I think the percentage would be about twenty per cent of union men."[40]

Chairman of the Board and Vice President James Deering cautioned:

"It does not take many Union men to make a strike. We have discovered that at the Deering Works twice."[41]

After prolonged discussion had determined that the only danger of a strike lay with the skilled workers, the consensus was reduced to its arithmetical probabilities by General Manager Clarke: "I should say that the chances were probably 50 to 75% that we would have perhaps a little strike of machinists and pattern makers, but when you take a total strike of the Works, would say 95% that we would not have any."[42]

In spite of its promise of substantial financial gain at little risk, five of the thirteen executives who commented on it considered the Clarke recommendation too extreme.

One was Kennedy, the hard-boiled assistant manager of the Deering Division, whose brusque behavior toward shop steward Francke had precipitated the Deering strike. Not only was Kennedy the most forthright conferee in urging humanitarian treatment of the workers but, on the issue of the hiring rate, he dropped the detached tone of the conferees and gave the only spontaneous show of emotion, clashing with his superior, Clarke:

> The recommendations as put in by Mr. Clarke are, without doubt, the best thing to do, with the proviso that we have made up our mind to fight it out and establish ourselves as a ten hour factory. The benefits that would be derived by that are largely and naturally that we would get back again what we have lost and will also place ourselves in position in years to come maybe three and maybe not for five years, to adhere to a step that we may be forced to, namely, to come back to a nine hour day, or possibly we might be forced to an eight hour day. If we were to be obliged to adhere to a nine hour day now we may be asked to come to an eight hour day, not now but in three or four years perhaps, and we could hardly be expected to make a jump of two hours, but we might be expected to make a jump of one hour. If we take this step of going to the ten hour day I would say that if we gave a half day on Saturday I would not attempt to take it from the men, nor would I attempt to make any change . . . [that] would reduce the wages of any men in general, ... The day [common] labor I would not change. I do not think we can afford to reduce the day labor to less than 16 cents per hour. Living is higher today in Chicago than it has even been before, I think, and if you get a lot of the laboring class that are getting nine dollars a week to suffering or feeling that they are suffering, they are going to be ready to join any movement that comes along that is going to better their condition . . . .[43]

The minutes of the conference record the following exchange between Clarke and Kennedy:

Mr. Clarke: . . . there are concerns paying less than 16 cents an hour for their common labor. The principal ones that come to my mind are the Illinois Steel Company and our own steel mills, which are paying 15-½ cents.

Mr. Kennedy: I am afraid we ought to be ashamed of it.

Mr. Clarke: Not a bit of it.[44]

Several who objected to the Clarke plan offered less drastic proposals. The first, suggested by Flather, assistant general manager of manufacturing in the McCormick Division, was on the human side:

I do not know what the Pullman strike was for, but they have not had everything their own way since that time. It goes to show that at one works that has had a big strike they have not continued along without some trouble. Isn't it just as well not to anger them [the workers], . . . ? Suppose we should go to . . . a 9½ hour day and pay the men half the amount that you expect to make, and see if that does not avoid a strike. Pay this money to the men instead of the strike breakers.[45]

This plan was rejected because its higher labor cost did not seem to purchase a corresponding decrease in the likelihood of a strike.

The more seriously considered alternative was proposed by Frank Ericsson, International Harvester wage specialist, who had just completed a citywide wage survey.

I cannot see any logical reason why we should ask the men to work more hours at the same pay. Of course from the side of the Company there is a financial reason, but we have to consider both sides. If we want to control our business and our men, we have got to treat our men as well, or nearly as well, as the union does. If you do anything that is going to antagonize the men, they are going over on the side of the Union. If we treat our men right, they are with us. I cannot find any concern in the City of Chicago today that is making a fight to reduce wages. I cannot see where our men, except in very few cases, are receiving more wages than are paid elsewhere; in the majority of cases they are receiving less.[46]

His suggested compromise was to keep the nine-hour day:

In the first place, why did we adopt a shorter work day? Because at that time the general tendency was for a shorter work day without reduction in wages. Second, because the unions also forced us in the same direction. At present are conditions such as to warrant and justify us in increasing the hours of work without increasing the weekly wage? I would say—no. . . . I am in favor of a 54 hour week, 9 hours a day . . . . I think when it comes to adjusting wages, . . . We can save, . . . at least $225,000.[47]

Thus far Ericsson had mixed practical and humanitarian reasons for continuing the nine-hour day and for not cutting wages. But how was he to save the company money? His solution was simple. Fire 40 percent of the dayworkers, mostly skilled craftsmen, and replace them with cheaper help. He was quoted in the records of the conference.

Mr. Ericsson: . . . I would reduce our force just as low as we can get it. We have a certain number of day workers we must have. Would pay these men the same for 54 hours as we are paying for 60 and hire new men at our own terms. . . .

. . . . .

Mr. Flather: . . . you hire three-quarters of your day workers at a new [lower] price.

Mr. Ericsson: Yes, but not three-quarters. Say about 40%.[48]

Clarke, displaying the rigorous logic of the economic theorist, ingeniously used Ericsson's worker replacement proposal to support an increase in hours with no increase in weekly pay: "If the men are there anxious to take the job at $2.00 [per day] instead of $2.25, and so on, isn't that a pretty good indication that the supply of labor largely exceeds the demand, and for that reason there could be no trouble in putting through a 58-½ hour proposition? It is my judgment, rather than go out and see some new man come in and take the job on that basis, that they would sit pat on 58-½ hours."[49]

While foremen were not participants in the conference, the foremen of the three Chicago factories were polled as to their preference for the 54- or the 58½-hour week. The poll showed: for the 54-hour week with present pay, 41; for the 58½-hour week with pay reductions, 9. When reporting on the poll Superintendent Wood of the McCormick Works said, "Some of the men [foremen] were staggered a little bit when I asked them whether the day worker can stand 10% off."[50]

Ericsson's proposal for a 54-hour week was discarded when no subtle wage-cutting schemes could be devised. A flat reduction in wages was unacceptable. It was felt that piecework rates could be cut because, it was generally agreed, pieceworkers could work harder and make up the reduction.

Sentiment was moving toward the Clarke recommendations, but modified from the full 60-hour week by giving the men Saturday afternoon off, at least during the summer months. "It might help the situation, especially with the rank and file," James Deering suggested, "if they saw that there was a willingness on the part of this Company to make some fair arrangement for a Saturday half holiday in the summer."[51] Cyrus McCormick felt very strongly that there could be no plan which did not provide for the Saturday half-holiday.[52] The question debated was who would pay for this half-day, the men or the company. Clarke said, "We might formulate it in our announcement that the company would consider a Saturday half holiday during the Summer months"; to which James Deering added, "Then you can say if labor conditions are in our favor and we are strong—'Very well, have it on your own time.' If, on the other hand, we should feel as we did a year ago last April, we might give it."[53] Inasmuch as the men were enjoying a half-holiday at company expense every Saturday of the year under the 1903 contract, it is difficult to see how this new proposal would mollify the workers' attitude toward the longer work week.

In a study of labor relations in the steel industry during this period, historian John A. Garraty differentiated between the labor viewpoints of "bankers" and "steelmen" on the executive committee of the United States Steel Corporation. The bankers he characterized as posing as "friends, or rather patrons, of labor. . . . Industrial warfare was repugnant to the bankers; it was bad for public relations . . . . But they were never sympathetic to *organized* labor." The steelmen, on the other hand, "tended to be competing and uncompromising. To them workers were adversaries contesting against capital for the profits of manufacture."[54] The steelmen of the Harvester trust, the manufacturing executives, presented no such united front. On the whole they were much more sophisticated. Their posture was that of pure economic calculation, of complete emotional detachment from personal or class feeling. Only occasionally did emotion show through, as when Clarke demanded a "firm stand" so that "we shall end up by having our men in better control; . . ."[55] However, two of Clarke's assistants, Kennedy of the Deering Division and Flather of the McCormick Division, bore little resemblance to the steelmen as they urged the company to "Pay this money to the men instead of the strike breakers," and protested, "I do not think we can afford to reduce the day labor to less than 16 cents per hour."[56]

We turn now to the top echelon of Harvester executives, those in Garraty's category of bankers. In contrast to the situation at U. S. Steel, they were with one exception owner-executives: the McCormick brothers, Cyrus and Harold; the Deering sons, James and Charles, and son-in-law, Richard Howe. The only actual banker consulted was George W. Perkins, Morgan's influential representative on the Harvester voting trust, who was also a Harvester director and member of the executive

The McCormick Works, Chicago, 1847–1961. From 1847 until 1902 this was the sole plant of the McCormick Harvesting Machine Company; after 1902 it was one of many plants of the International Harvester Company.

Cyrus Hall McCormick, President of the McCormick Harvesting Machine Company (and its predecessors), 1847–1884.

Cyrus Hall McCormick II, President of McCormick Harvesting Machine Company, 1884–1902, and of International Harvester Company, 1902–1918.

Harold F. McCormick, Vice President of International Harvester Company, 1902–1918; President, 1918–1922; Chairman of the Executive Committee, 1922–1932, of the Finance Committee, 1932–1935, of the Board, 1935–1941.

Fowler McCormick, Vice President of International Harvester Company, 1934–1941; President, 1941–1946; Chairman of the Board, 1946–1951.

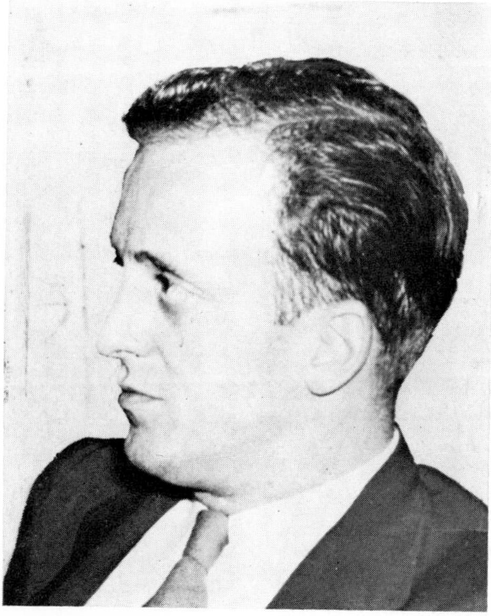

Gerald Fielde, McCormick Works employee representative who became a militant leader of the Farm Equipment Workers. (Courtesy of United Electrical Workers.)

An early blacklist, pinned to the flyleaf of the McCormick payroll ledger for 1872. The list contained, in all, the names of sixty-six molders.

VULCAN IRON WORKS
Nos. 80 to 92 North Clinton Street.
ATKINS & BURGESS,
—MANUFACTURERS OF—
Steam Engines, Steam Dredges, Steam Shovels, Steam Pile Drivers
MILL GEARING, AND GENERAL MACHINERY.

Chicago, Mch 12 1872

Mess C H McCormick & Bro

Gents

The Moulders named below discontinued work in our shop the 8 inst in consequence of our refusal to continue in our employ Strikers from the shop of N S Bouton & Co who were inadvertently hired by us last week.

Please keep names and act accordingly

Yrs Truly

Atkins & Burgess
pr Brooks

John Fichter
Arch Fichter
Pat McDonald
Jacob Sjohn
Fred Bossler
John Plaus
B Waggoner
John Minster

E Swenson
J. Longis
John Knight
John Bongue
P Keenan
Mike Connor
Mike Hypson
John Capert

Below: A petition of this sort, in the form of an ultimatum, was commonly used to notify employers of union wage demands. This one bore the signatures of ninety men, who walked out on schedule. Two weeks later the strike was extended to the entire plant; it was settled by the company's conceding to the demand.

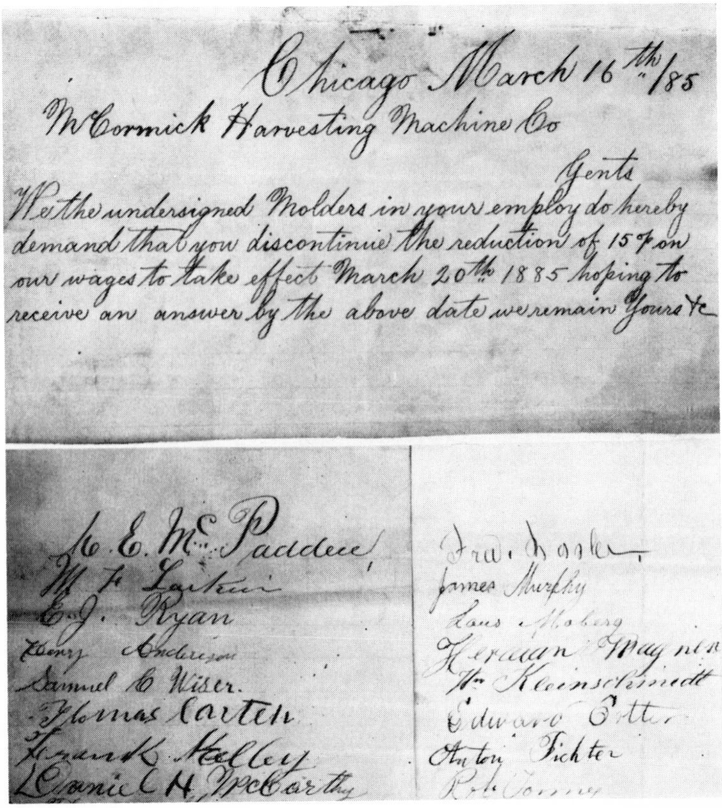

Chicago March 16th /85

McCormick Harvesting Machine Co

Gents

We the undersigned Molders in your employ do hereby demand that you discontinue the reduction of 15% on our wages to take effect March 20th 1885 hoping to receive an answer by the above date we remain Yours &c

M. E. McPaddee
W. F. Larkin
E. J. Ryan
Henry Anderson
Samuel C Wiser
Thomas Carter
Frank Kelley
Daniel H. McCarthy

Fred Booker
James Murphy
Claus Moberg
Herman Wagner
Wm Kleinschmidt
Edward Otter
Anton Fichter
Rob Conner

committee. Perkins similarly represented Morgan on the Board of Directors and executive committee of the U. S. Steel Corporation. Perkins pushed the same labor policy for both trusts. Consulted on Harvester's labor problem at a special conference in New York in August 1904, he said in true "banker" fashion that he wished to avoid a fight over cutting wages but believed this "an admirable opportunity to settle any issue we may have with the unions, as such, to forestall the opportunity of their trying to run our business."[57] The prime banker concern in both the Steel and Harvester situations, of course, was to avoid jeopardizing the newly created and already politically vulnerable trusts.

Among the owner-executives, the most important viewpoint was that of President Cyrus H. McCormick II. By 1904, though only forty-five, he had been the chief decision-maker of the huge McCormick Harvesting Machine Company for twenty years. Now, in the International Harvester trust, he had to administer by consensus—consensus of the owning families, of the Morgan banking representative, of the operating executives—and with regard for the workmen and public opinion. Despite the deep scars of the 1885–86 labor battles Cyrus faced the current labor problems without evident emotion. Acting in the mediator's role, he carefully drew out and listened to the diverse executive opinions. He did not express himself until after several days of debate. Then he directed his remarks toward clearing the air of minor details of wage cutting and focusing on the central issue, which he declared to be that of ridding the works of unionism. "Usually bad strikes are those fought for pecuniary purposes. The question is that of controlling your business and not recognizing unions, . . ."[58] He expanded this view in a letter to James Deering:

> Taking the broadest view of the whole matter and looking at the question, not for today only, but for a terms [sic] of years to come and our relations to the public, to our employes, to our finances, and to our general reputation in the community, I do not believe we should magnify the advantages of making our profits out of the reduction in the pay-roll of the workmen.
>
> Believing as I do, that the most important point for us to secure strategically is to get clear of our contracts with the unions, I would recommend as follows:
>
> . . . . .
>
> If at any time the labor officials come to see us we will treat them politely, according to the plan proposed by Mr. Clarke, but do not recognize them officially, or sign any contract.[59]

McCormick then proposed modifying Clarke's harsh 58½-hour plan to a 56-hour week, with 55 or 54 hours during the three summer months. He agreed to additional wage cuts of both dayworkers and pieceworkers totaling $200,000. At this point, August 31, President McCormick took off for Switzerland to attend the wedding of his brother Stanley, turning over the labor conference leadership to the third brother, Harold.

Harold McCormick consulted with Harvester wage specialist Frank Ericsson and was given the clear-cut information that Harvester wages were low for the Chicago area. His first problem as the new chairman of the labor conference was to resolve in his own mind the conflict which existed between the company's desire to cut wages and the low level of wages which already existed at Harvester. He wrote to Cyrus:

> I tried to review the question of hours and wages with Frank Ericsson, and my final conclusion on this subject was that we are not justified in reducing our wages directly or indirectly . . . except for the fact that our dividends and earnings of this Company are extremely low, and that it was more or less legitimate to curtail at the present time wherever we could; . . . .
>
> . . . general comparisons show that we seem to be below some large companies in wages paid and yet above some others. It is fair to say that we are below the union scale on the average. As against this, however, it is to be said that our men are not as high a skilled class of men as the trades, under which they nominally fall, actually represent.[60]

On September 7 Harold McCormick attended his first conference on the labor question. It was an amazing day, as his report to his brother shows:

> Mr. Deering [James] at once started in to discuss the general problem . . . saying that as a general proposition the 58-½ hour week was advocated.
>
> Both he and Mr. Howe talked pretty strongly on the 58-½ hour week and the advantages to be gained by establishing it now even though it would have to be surrendered later on, the advantage being that we might later have to go to a reduction which would put us about where we are now, but if we stayed where we are now, we might have to go to a reduction which would be lower."

At noon Harold attended the weekly luncheon where "the labor question was the principal feature discussed, ... it was the consensus of opinion that we should vote for a 58-½ hour day." After such unanimity for the 58½-hour week, Harold McCormick's surprise at the turn of events at the labor conference that same afternoon can be imagined. He reported to Cyrus:

> . . . At once the tone of these gentlemen [James and Charles Deering and Howe] changed, and I could at once see that something had happened. They all of them talked about the terrible consequences of strikes, the danger to life and property, the loss attendant upon both workers and employers and the question as to whether after all we would gain by a strike. . . . Mr. Howe then asked me what I thought would be the attitude of the papers in case a strike was made . . . and I told him that I thought arbitration would be demanded. This seemed to start them on the theme which was in their minds, and Mr. James Deering very strongly laid out the humiliation and disadvantages of arbitration. Mr. Howe then said . . . if we agreed to arbitration, we would undoubtedly lose at least one-half of what we thought of gaining; and this sum . . . might be brought about in time by continuing the 54 hour basis and pruning around where we could; . . . Mr. Clarke then said that he had not thought of arbitration, and that that was the worst thought that had been suggested.

Harold McCormick reported Howe's solution to these intolerable possibilities in guarded lines in which it is difficult to see any intention other than bribery of union officials:

> Mr. Howe then suggested pursuing the tactics towards the labor leaders which other Companies pursued, and he commenced to recite incidences where it was very general. He stated that he thought these tactics were pursued in the stock yards strike. He stated that two large labor employers had told him that they followed this practice, and Mr. Clarke broke in and said that he was sure that a high official of the Steel Workers' Association was treated in this same way by the U. S. Corporation. Mr. Howe then went on to say that if we did this, how easy it might be for us to get anything we wanted without trouble. He then looked at me once or twice furtively but I did not say a word and absolutely did not commit myself one way or the other, and I even did not comment upon it. I let the remark pass as if never mentioned.

These last sentences make one wonder if the bribery was not already quietly under way.

Harold McCormick inquired of other executives the possible reasons for this abrupt change of attitude. In his letter to Cyrus the picture of William Deering counseling his sons Charles and James appears: Harold "talked with Messrs. Mayer, Swift and Legge on this new development, and they all agreed that a personal element had apparently entered into the situation, and very likely Mr. [William] Deering had pointed out to them that the Deering Works might be in very bad shape in case of a strike, and they might have a repetition of last year's performance, viz: The McCormick Works running when the Deering Works could not." At the next morning's conference (September 8) Charles Deering verified this supposition; in Harold's words, "his father had stated his judgment to be that we would lose as much as we would gain by having any strike, and that he was against the program of going to 58-½ hours." At the final conference James Deering reported that ". . . Mr. William Deering stuck to a 54 hour week schedule, decreasing pay by finesse."[61]

On the whole these men who owned the company, whose names would bear the onus of a strike in the public mind, who understood the precarious legal and political position of the new trust, were more moderate in their wage-cutting proposals than the second-line executives had been. William Deering had given strong support for continuing the 54-hour week. Cyrus McCormick's plan had been for 56 hours during the winter and 55 or 54 hours in the summer. Harold McCormick had proposed a 55-hour week. For a time James Deering agreed with his father on the 54-hour week. Only Charles Deering held to the 58½-hour week, with some adjustment possible during the summer months—until the last day of the conference, when he voted for a 54-hour week with a 6.5 percent reduction in pay.

The owner-executives had no intention, however, of dealing with the unions on these matters. It was probably William Deering's fear of a strike which led his son-in-law Richard Howe to make the only suggestion favoring a labor contract that any International Harvester executive advanced during these many conferences. Harold reported: ". . . Mr. Howe put the question before the conference of the advantages or disadvantages of having an agreement with the unions and of dealing with the leaders, saying that many firms did it and that when once a contract was made you knew what to expect for the coming year. Mr. Clarke interrupted him and said that one did not always know because these agreements were broken."[62] Apparently no other member of the conference considered this proposal worth further comment.

The only other statement made in favor of above-the-table recognition of the unions was that of Ralph M. Easley, chairman of the executive council of the National Civic Federation.[63] In New York in August Harold McCormick had conferred with him about the Harvester labor situation. On September 11 Easley wrote McCormick these recommendations:

> To propose both a reduction of wages and increase in hours at the same time, is, of course, an invitation for war if there is enough resistance power on the other side to fight. (Generally speaking, the union leaders would rather do anything but increase hours.)
>
> . . . . .
>
> . . . it would be a mistake on your part not to talk this matter out with the committee which signed your contract, especially as it is signed by several very conservative men. To refuse point blank to confer with the union leaders, should they ask for a conference, would only be a declaration of war, ...
>
> In a conference with a reasonable committee, which I assume these men are, the exact situation could be put before them. It may be that you could leave the hours as they are and get their consent to cut wages as a business necessity. You know that most of the large unions have accepted reductions this year. . . . the Iron and Steel Workers accepted from 18 to 30% but they did this after a frank discussion. If the Fall River manufacturers had taken the committees of the men into their confidence, I feel sure that they could have prevented a strike but they simply put up placards announcing the cut. If employers would use the same tact and common sense in dealing with labor questions that they do in dealing with everyday business affairs, much trouble would be avoided.[64]

Evidently Easley's counsel was not considered seriously, since it does not appear in the reports of the labor conference discussions. While the exact amount of the wage cut and hours extension was debated at length, there was complete unanimity on the desirability of breaking off with the union.

A matter of expediency rather than principle was involved in a discussion of whether or not a plant shutdown was needed to make the wage cut more palatable.

Assistant General Manager Flather frankly expressed the reason for a shutdown: "You need to shut down . . . , to have your men in the attitude to stand that sort of thing. . . . I would have them lose as many paydays between now and September 15 as they can."[65] It was imperative that the shutdown should call no attention to September 15 as expiration date of the union contract, and should give no ammunition to the union leaders.

Before his departure Cyrus McCormick had advocated shutting down before the contract expiration:

Suppose you are running on the 15th and the labor committee comes to see you on the 20th, and on the 24th you shut down. Won't they tell all the men and won't the men construe that you shut down because the labor leaders came to see you? The chances are they would not come before the 10th, and when they come you are already shut down.

Mr. James Deering: When they come we can say we have no material and don't know when we will start up again.

. . . . .

Mr. Flather: If we are not running on September 15th, when we do start up we need not have any men go to work at the price they name, but each at a price to be agreed to mutually. If we are running and they shut us down, they have a strike. In the first case we would have a lock-out, which is a better situation.

Mr. Deering: Mr. Flather puts it too strongly when he says lockout. It would not even be that; we would simply be shut down.[66]

The motives behind the Harvester shutdown on September 10 fooled no one. The *New York Press* carried the following story datelined the next day:

NINE THOUSAND OUT OF WORK. International Harvester Company Shuts Down at End of Wage Agreement. Chicago, Sept. 11—Nine thousand men have been thrown out of employment by the closing down of the three big branches of the International Harvester Company, the McCormick and Deering divisions in Chicago and the plant in Plano. . . . The notices posted in each of the plants said the shutdown would continue indefinitely.

Officials of the company asserted to-night that the only significance in the move is that the dull season in the harvesting implement business has arrived and that extensive improvements are to be made while the big properties are not in operation.

Trades union leaders, however, assert that the move was made by the International Harvester Company because its agreement with the organized trades employed will end on September 15, and the union men believe the company does not wish to enter into another agreement.[67]

With the plants closed, the debate on the exact amount of the wage and hour change continued. But each day of worker helplessness during unemployment made the retrogressive views of E. A. S. Clarke appear more within reach of attainment.

At the September 13 labor conference James Deering "came again to the idea that a 57-½ hour week throughout the year was the best plan."[68] By September 14 Harold McCormick was able to inform Cyrus:

Our reports in regard to our men, indicate that the consensus of opinion is that the Company is going to start up soon; that it will start up on a 10 hour day and that a 10 hour day is preferred to a reduction in wages. Some reports indicate that both propositions would come about. Apparently the desire of the men is to be put back to work. Our reports indicate practically no dissatisfaction and it is the general consensus of opinion here that the men now realize that there has been a turn for the worse in conditions and times, and that their idea of meeting this will be to work longer hours.[69]

The day the union contract expired Harold telegraphed Cyrus in Geneva, Switzerland: "We all agree on working week averaging for year 57½ hours arranged by working 58½ hours nine months 55 hours three summer months making Saturday half holiday; sixty hours pay both cases; at proper time this program will be announced in full; . . . ."[70]

Just to make sure that there would be no trouble, the plants were kept closed another twelve days. When they were reopened on September 26, each plant posted notices of the following conditions, which represented an almost complete victory for the Clarke viewpoint:

The workday was lengthened from nine to ten hours with the same weekly pay. All overtime for pieceworkers was abolished. Double time after twelve o'clock midnight and on Sundays and holidays returned to 1¼-time pay. Overtime was further limited to skilled workers and their assistants.

Common labor was to be hired at 15 instead of 16 cents an hour. Those who demonstrated special ability and energy after trial could be advanced to 16 cents.

Skilled workmen such as machinists, millwrights, and patternmakers were to be fired whenever possible and replaced with others who would give the same service for less money.

Piece rates were to be cut so that workmen must work more hours to make the same weekly pay.[71]

In the face of unemployment, gross company discrimination such as the firing of union leaders and denying of stock to the unfaithful, and possibly even bribery of its leaders, the union collapsed without a whimper. On his return from Switzerland, Cyrus McCormick II had to face only the reproaches of his former welfare secretary, Gertrude Beeks, now working for Easley and the National Civic Federation:

While you are not likely to have any trouble now, I am greatly disappointed at the method pursued by the company inasmuch as it is simply a postponement of the "evil day." All that has been secured could have been arranged amicably through a conference, which the officials, apparently, denied the labor leaders. In this way the company would have made the labor men its

> debtors, but as it is, so far as the labor leaders are concerned, it can only appear that the company has taken advantage of them while they the unions are down, and it can only mean that the unions will "take the company by the throat" at the first opportunity. The method pursued will, of course, only cause the unions to go about the matter of organizing the plants at the first opportunity, and unfortunately, with a spirit that will not be productive of good.[72]

Eighteen years before, in 1885–86, as a neophyte president, Cyrus McCormick II had overthrown the unions. Then the violence and the publicity given the battle had damaged the family's good name. In this 1903–4 encounter with unionism, coercion and welfarism in the form of the stock gift were astutely applied in such proportions as to destroy the union without audible protest.

4

Welfarism, the Labor Program of a "Good Trust"

Sickness and Accident Benefits

To the McCormick Company, as one unit, the major adversary seemed to be unionism. From 1901 to 1904 the McCormick firm and its young successor, the International Harvester Company, found welfarism an efficacious weapon against this enemy. A trust such as International Harvester faced a second adversary: public opposition to monopoly. As Cyrus McCormick II had turned to welfarism to halt unionization of his factory, so George W. Perkins, most influential director of International Harvester, turned to welfarism to save the trust from the farmers' angry cries and the government's investigations.

If ever a corporation was "born in sin" from the standpoint of the Sherman Antitrust Act, it was the International Harvester corporation. At birth in 1902 it produced 85 percent of the nation's grain-harvesting machinery. Thereafter it continued a program of acquisition so vigorous that by 1907 there remained no semblance of competition. For International Harvester the competitive struggles of the marketplace were now replaced by the attacks of government agencies, irate farmers, and muckraking editors.

In December 1906 the United States Bureau of Corporations, pursuant to a Senate resolution, began a study of International Harvester. Company officials met with Bureau officials in January 1907 and agreed to give the Bureau any information requested about the trust in return for a pledge to keep it confidential. This federal investigation together with widespread resentment on the part of farmers against monopoly in farm machinery stirred up a hornet's nest of state legislative activity against the Harvester trust. Perkins, reporting to J. P. Morgan, described the situation of the company:

> We have been having one continuous battle all Spring with the various State Legislatures that have been attacking the Harvester Company right and left, and with the National Government that has threatened several times to bring the company before the Grand Jury in Chicago. . . .
>
> . . . no drastic laws against the Harvester Company were passed anywhere, although in February, March and April it was the storm center of 14 or 15 Legislative bodies, who wanted to tear it all to pieces.[1]

On August 22, 1907, President Roosevelt ordered Attorney General Bonaparte not to file suit against the company "for the present."[2] Another study of the Harvester books was begun in the summer of 1908 by Ben F. Wright, assistant commissioner of corporations.

By this time Norman Hapgood, editor of *Collier's Weekly*, had joined that attack with an article about a Harvester worker who had lost an arm in an accident at the McCormick plant. Entitled "Making Cripples and Dodging Taxes,"[3] the article accused International Harvester, on the one hand, of deceitfully trying to obtain the injured employee's signature to a release of liability in exchange for a mere $50 cash settlement and, on the other, of dodging Chicago property taxes by bribing a member of the Board of Review. While the two charges seemed to be unrelated, *Collier's* pointed out that the Harvester attorney who handled the compensation case was also a member of the tax appeal board. Without our passing judgment on the merits of either of *Collier's* accusations, a search of the donations file of the company reveals an even more questionable relationship than that of which *Collier's* was aware. For several years the McCormick Harvesting Machine Company had been making sizable contributions ($500 in 1898) to the election campaigns of the tax appeal board members.[4]

The article caused consternation among the Harvester Company's directors. Harold McCormick, in New York at the time, and Cyrus in Chicago conferred by telephone over this public relations catastrophe. After getting the "facts" from Harvester attorneys, Cyrus drafted a long letter to Norman Hapgood in defense of the company. The draft was sent to Harold in New York, who showed it to George Perkins for his advice. According to Harold, Perkins said that "under no circumstances could he . . . countenance handing that letter to Mr. Hapgood. He did not believe in letters. . . . He said that he would find out . . .

from some friends how Hapgood felt . . . ."[5] New Yorker Perkins knew better than to engage in an argument with a muckraking editor. He permanently vetoed Cyrus' letter to Hapgood.

Instead of letters to the enemy, Perkins planned and directed a bold program to change this hatred of monopoly to love for the "good" trust. His tactics are demonstrated by the Harvester Company's first published annual report, which appeared in 1908. Corporate annual reports of that era were often designed to conceal the corporation's operations. This one, on the contrary, was simply written, filled with facts, and intended to get across the notion that there was no water in the Harvester Company's stock. Hundreds of copies of this report were mailed to influential persons across the country, including one to President Roosevelt accompanied by a note from Perkins emphasizing its political and social implications.[6]

Perkins also instituted a comprehensive welfare program for International Harvester employees. A company relieved of the burdens of ruthless competition could favor its employees with profit-sharing plans, insurance programs, and pensions. As Perkins explained to the National Civic Federation in 1909: "If, as many of us have come to believe, co-operation in business is taking and should take the place of ruthless competition,—if this new order of things is better for capital and better for the consumer, then in order to succeed permanently it must demonstrate that it is better for the laborer; and if profit sharing, pensions, insurance, and the like mean anything, they must mean co-operation between capital and labor,—co-operation in the broadest, most helpful and enduring form."[7]

Perkins could explain the "good" trust where such an explanation would count the most, to trust-busting Teddy Roosevelt. George Perkins was a prominent fund-raiser for the Republican party, a caller at the White House. He found Roosevelt a sympathetic listener, particularly after the financial panic of 1907. On December 3, 1907, Roosevelt publicly advanced the good-trust approach. "It is unfortunate that our present laws should forbid all combinations instead of sharply discriminating between those combinations which do good and those combinations which do evil."[8]

One of Perkins' major programs to prove that International Harvester was a trust which did "good," not "evil," was a sickness and accident benefit plan. In May of 1907 President Cyrus McCormick II had ordered Mary L. Goss of the welfare department to dust off earlier welfare proposals in the company's files with a view to action. Miss Goss edited one such proposal; but it appeared headed for the file again when *Collier's* exposé broke on April 18, 1908. Within a week a committee of top-level management was hurriedly drawing up a new plan. By July 13, 1908, the committee submitted its recommendations to the officers of the company, calling its proposed benefit insurance plan the most liberal of all United States plans and even more liberal than the foreign corporation plans after which the United States plans were modeled. The basis of the committee's plan was simply a series of sickness and accident benefit payments for which the workers gave up 2 percent of their wages, the company contributing only the cost of administration.

A glance at the origin of benefit plans in the United States, as well as at the previous experience of the Harvester Company and of its predecessors, is necessary to understand the problems incident to establishment of welfare plans. One of the early activities of unions among American railway workers was securing union-managed sickness, accident, and death benefits. High accident rates on railroads often made railroad employees ineligible for commercial insurance coverage. After the railroad strikes of the 1870's and 1880's railroad management set up mutual benefit associations and pension systems in an effort to lessen employee dependence on the unions.

As unionism in turn invaded manufacturing, especially after the widespread strikes of 1886, manufacturing employers began to move in the same direction. In the companies which merged to form the International Harvester Company, several insurance and benefit plans were already in existence. Since 1894 the Plano Harvesting Company had deducted from all employee earnings 1 percent of the gross weekly wages for benefit purposes.[9] The Plano Company itself contributed about 10 percent of the fund's maintenance and operational costs. The Deering Harvesting Machine Company organized the Deering Workmen's Mutual Benefit Association in 1888. Membership was voluntary. Employees paid small monthly dues (30 cents) and after the first week of illness became eligible for $5 a week for eight weeks. Deductions of .75 percent were begun in 1899. Only $1,300 was dispersed during 1903, according to the report of this organization.[10] In addition, several smaller benefit associations operated. The workers and foremen of the

Deering paint department had their own fund. In the McCormick Harvesting Machine Company some of the German-speaking workmen had had their own fund since 1886, entirely independent of the company. By 1902 this benefit fund had 93 members, but only 45 still worked at the plant. The plant at this time had about 5,000 employees.

Interest in a sickness and accident association did not appear among McCormick management until 1901, when Stanley McCormick asked two of the company's lawyers to draw up a mutual benefit plan. Their suggested plan was completed in February 1902 and submitted to Stanley McCormick. The plan itself is not available, but Stanley's detailed comments on it are. They reveal that the attorneys' idea, typical of the corporate accident insurance plans of that day, was simply a money-saving device enabling the corporation, by token contribution to a fund, to escape legal liability and lawsuits, while the injured workman was cut off with totally inadequate resources.

Stanley McCormick's criticism of the plan is quoted at length because of the light it throws on his attitude toward employee welfare.

> In paragraph 15, membership to the association is made compulsory. I do not think this is advisable, unless the company should contribute the entire amount of money; since otherwise this arrangement will affect a man's wages independently of his own will; . . . . Mr. Allen [company lawyer] says in his letter that he would contemplate that the company's contribution should be quite small.
>
> . . . Viewed from the above standpoint, I think too much power is given into the hands of the company and not enough to the men. For example, the company has a majority of the Advisory Committee, and appoints the superintendent and medical director. My idea would be to consider this organization as an organization of the workmen which the company sanctions, and to which it contributes a certain amount, as a matter of broad policy. . . . it seems to me that the employes should elect the chairman and a majority of the Advisory Committee, and that the superintendent and medical director should be appointed by the committee.
>
> . . . . .
>
> . . . As to the Application for Membership, I do not think the company should ask for a release from legal liability. It is not likely that the benefits will amount to nearly the sum which could be obtained as damages in case the company was liable. Mr. Allen considers the contribution by the company as consideration for the releases. It does not seem to me, however, that the company should ask for consideration for its contribution, but should make it on the broad policy of better feeling among employes, etc. My fear is that the releases will cast suspicion about the scheme among the employes

and that would be fatal. I would suggest instead, providing that in case of damages secured, the amount of benefits should be deducted or else that the benefits should be void.

. . . . .

. . . Why should any limit be put upon the period of time during which a disabled employe shall receive benefits. I cannot see that his case would be any better after 18 weeks than before if he is still disabled. . . .

. . . I think that in the case of amputation the benefit should be surgical treatment with daily benefits *and also* the benefit for loss of member, instead of *either* one *or* the other. The former it seems to me is for the loss of time and expense incurred, and the latter for the loss of the member. It seems to me that the two items are distinct and should not be made mutually exclusive.

. . . It seems to me that the accident benefits are not made to cover a sufficient range of permanent disabilities. Why should not a man who loses one or both eyes be equally entitled to benefit as a man who loses one or two hands. I think benefits should be given as far as possible for all *permanent* disabilities. I notice also that no provision is made for loss of both hands or both feet.

. . . Should not the sick benefits be given for the first six days as well as later? or is this to avoid as much as possible pretended illness?[11]

Particularly unusual was Stanley's objection to using a small company contribution to the fund to evade legal liability.

Stanley's proposals were far too advanced for acceptance by his brothers. The demanding work connected with the founding of the International Harvester Company, in which he was deeply involved, probably caused him to drop further welfare fund planning.

In a 1904 company study of the legal damages paid out in workmen's compensation lawsuits it was estimated that the adoption of a mutual benefit association would save at least $10,000 a year in the McCormick Division alone. Despite Stanley McCormick's earlier demurrer, the 1904 recommendation of the company attorneys for a benefit association included an employee waiver of the right to sue the company for injuries.

The actual wording of the proposed Harvester release was as follows:

I also agree that, in consideration of the amounts paid and to be paid by —— the International Harvester Company, for the maintenance of the said Relief Department and of the guarantee by the said Company of the payment of said benefits, the acceptance by me of the benefits for injury shall operate as a release and satisfaction of all claims against the said Company for damages arising from or growing out of said injury, ...[12]

A company attorney justified this waiver thus:

The adoption of a mutual benefit association, wherein the Company contributes to its maintenance either in a monetary way or by assistance in its operation would produce a consideration sufficient to establish the validity of a release of the Company from liability for the injuries sustained if the injured accepted the benefit. The system in force at the Deering plant, I understand, is in a large measure wanting in this feature, that is, it is self-sustaining,—it costs the Deering Division nothing. The Plano Division has a mutual benefit system wherein it contributes about 10% of the cost of maintenance and operation.[13]

Thus the motive for the small contribution to employee benefit associations commonly made by corporations is here revealed as that of establishing a legal basis for escaping liability and not of assisting employees in distress.

In addition to saving money for the company by removing liability, the establishment of sickness and death benefit plans was advocated by at least one Harvester executive, C. E. Woods, as a general cure-all for personnel problems and as discouraging unionism:

this company would not only start a new line of welfare work but would reap great benefits from it. In the first place the issuing of such policies would greatly strengthen the loyalty of employes to the company, . . . the interests of his family would all bend in this direction, ... Further than this, the physical conditions required from medical examination in the granting of such policies would greatly increase the general physical condition of the help employed, with a corresponding physical and moral effect on the household. I believe at first sight that a weapon of this kind would be much stronger than any profit sharing proposition toward breaking up unionism.[14]

In December 1904, after three years of intensive study, S. M. Darling, secretary of the sociological committee, was only able to say that "while the matter of a benefit association for the employes in the factories of this Company has had a great deal of study and discussion, no plan has as yet been agreed upon."[15]

In 1905 the new Harvester welfare manager, C. W. Price, made an intensive study of sickness and accident benefit plans and came up with a concrete proposal. This 1905 benefit association plan was put to a vote of the workers in each plant. A rousing sales talk by Price preceded each vote. The large number of persons who refused to vote either for or against caused the company to drop the plan. As the superintendent of the Deering Works interpreted the Deering vote:

> You will notice that 50% of those departments that were canvassed voted in favor of it, 17% are opposed to it, and 33% noncommittal. I reason that a portion of the 33% had no idea to express on the subject either way: that is, they did not at that time know whether they should consider the proposition to their benefit or detriment. The remaining portion of this 33% are not in favor of the proposition, but did not have the strength of their convictions to come right out and say so, fearing that it might work to their harm to be found opposed to a proposition apparently favored by the Company. . . .
>
> It also must be taken into consideration that the foundries were not canvassed at all, and that, judging from the vote at the McCormick Works, a very strong portion of the foundrymen will vote against it.
>
> . . . . .
>
> To place the age limit at forty-five years is not good policy. It practically bars the employment of men above that age, and will be so understood, not only by the employees of the Company, but by outsiders as well, and will subject us to very severe criticism by the Press and public. I would rather have the By-Laws or rules of the Association state that men above a certain age will not be entitled to the death benefit, but by probably paying a somewhat increased rate, will receive the benefit of the accident and sick benefit.[16]

Even without a mutual benefit plan employees at the McCormick Works had not been entirely without recourse in case of injury. The facilities of the medical department were at their disposal, and it appears that in serious cases the company paid hospital expenses, costs of medicine, etc. A statement of the Relief Fund of the McCormick Works for 1904 shows that on the basis of a total payroll of $2,309,534.36 the relief department paid $3,016.83 in settlement for accidents. It incurred hospital expenses for employees of $3,711.30. The total expenditures of the Relief Fund amounted to $16,742.54, contributed entirely by the company.[17] Employees injured on the job received first aid and medical care. Two physicians and a nurse were on duty at the plant. In the event of serious injury workers were taken either to their homes or to a local hospital in the company ambulance. Employees and their families with medical problems were invited to take advantage of the free services of the facility. The total number of cases treated in 1904 was 23,903.[18]

As has been indicated, the 1908 benefit insurance plan contemplated a deduction of 2 percent from the wages of those who voluntarily joined the plan and passed the special examination; the company was to pay only administrative expenses. The committee on benefit insurance proposed surprisingly large benefits, including 52 weeks at half-pay for sickness, less the first 7 days (an item which even in 1960 remained a landmark in liberal employee benefit plans); 52 weeks at half-pay for accidents on or off duty; 1 year's wages for death; 2 years' wages for accidental death; 1 year's wages for the loss of a hand. Unique in this plan was a strong recommendation that the controversial waiver of the right to sue the company for accident be omitted. Thus employees could collect benefits from the plan for an in-plant accident and then sue the company for negligence. In support of this position, which was extremely rare, the committee gave the following arguments for consideration of the executive committee of the Board of Directors:[19] (1) Unless the waiver is omitted, "Great opposition will be met with on the part of the men, on the part of labor organizations, and also we fear that undue notice will be given this feature by the press, especially at this time"; (2) Professor Henderson of the University of Chicago urged omission of the release; (3) "The National Civic Federation, through Miss Gertrude Beeks, strongly urged that the release feature be omitted." The committee's fear of the press, "especially at this time," reveals the influence of the *Collier's* article, two months after its publication.

Though Miss Beeks had left International Harvester in 1903, she remained Cyrus McCormick's close friend and welfare adviser. Her argument to President McCormick was as follows:

. . . I had hoped that the International Harvester Company might take a step in advance of others . . . and by doing so meet the objections of labor men. . . .

1. The principal objection is where the employer binds the member of the relief department to release the employer from legal liability in case of accident if the employe who was injured accepts the *relief* money.

It is claimed by labor men that where this release clause is in effect, as it is on the Pennsylvania Railroad, that the company naturally sends the relief money immediately and it is accepted because it is not realized that the injury is serious or permanent. Sometimes it is accepted by the wife for there is nearly always immediate need in such a case. When it is found that the injury is permanent it is too late to bring suit against the company.

Furthermore, laborers believe that they should receive the financial aid for which they have paid dues to the relief department and still be entitled to damages if they are incapacitated for work. They do not accept the defense of the employer that they have been insured so long as their dues were paid, the same as in any accident company.[20]

The fact that the waiver was omitted in the plan as finally adopted was a triumph for Stanley McCormick's view, though the committee did not mention him at the time; he had left the company by the end of 1906 because of ill health.

Two reasons were given why immediate adoption of the plan was advisable: "The labor conditions make this fall [of 1908] an ideal time to install the working of this Association . . ."; "The effect of pending legislation has not been disregarded, and it is believed that by action at this time the Company gains the public opinion value of the voluntary act."[21]

Cyrus McCormick II wrote to George Perkins in support of the "Benefit Association and Pension Plan." The driving force behind his support was fear of antitrust legislation and a need to gain the loyalty of his labor force. "Is it not desirable that we should install this as soon after the first of September as possible? . . . it will help the Company greatly in the campaign [presidential campaign of 1908] and in its general standing before the public, and especially before all laboring men."[22]

In theory the committee recommendation on the benefit plan went to the company directors. Actually the man who would decide was the J. P. Morgan representative, Director Perkins, who besides casting the key vote on the voting trust was carrying the Harvester "good trust" case to the White House. When Perkins could not attend a late July meeting of the Harvester Board of Directors, the matter was deferred, Cyrus McCormick assuring him that "we are planning to await a conference with you before coming to a final conclusion."[23]

At this very time Perkins was presenting the Harvester case to President Theodore Roosevelt: "I was down to Oyster Bay twice lately,—" he wrote Morgan, "once in connection with some Steel and Harvester matters, which are going along satisfactorily . . . ."[24]

Perkins had only one criticism of the committee's very liberal benefit plan. It wasn't liberal enough: "the statement that we will pay the expenses of administering the fund which the men themselves wholly provide, does not sound good, . . . ," he wrote Cyrus.[25] This made it look as though the company came out ahead. Instead the company must make a really generous contribution. He proposed that, if 50 percent of the employees joined, the company contribute an amount equal to 50 percent of their contribution, and equal to 75 percent if 75 percent joined.

Perkins' deprecation of the committee's benevolence apparently was resented. Cyrus McCormick II reported back to the banker for the committee that if Perkins really wanted to spend that much money it would be better spent improving sanitary conditions in the core rooms and foundries and establishing badly needed dining rooms. He added what sounds like his own suggestion: "P.S. Another way to emphasize our benevolence, if it is thought wise to do so at the time, will be to add the amount you propose to the *Pension Fund*, ..."[26]

Though the Harvester committee rejected Perkins' liberalizing suggestions, the final result was a compromise. The company raised its contribution to a flat $50,000 provided 75 percent of the employees joined the plan. Though this percentage was not reached the first year, Perkins approved the company contribution of $50,000 anyway, plus an estimated $100,000 for administrative costs. To have done otherwise would have jeopardized the public relations investment. The plan became effective on September 1, 1908.

Meantime Perkins was keeping President Roosevelt up to date on the benevolent behavior of the "good trust." In October he wrote: "Thanks ever so much for your kind note in regard to our Harvester Pension and Benefit plan. I am sure you will be glad to know that already over 15,000 of the employees at the several works have joined the Association."[27]

With Roosevelt in the twilight of his term and hence of his ability to help the Harvester Company, Perkins was looking ahead to the next Administration. In 1900 and 1904 he had raised money for the Republican party. Now he redoubled his efforts, proposing a plan for systematically adding wealthy people in the new growing cities across the country to the party's solicitation lists. In the closing days of the 1908 campaign he raised a million dollars of desperately needed money—which made him the party's leading fund-raiser among businessmen.[28]

Perkins reported to J. P. Morgan that the Taft victory was significant because, despite Gompers' open efforts to deliver the labor vote to Bryan, it went to Taft. Perkins specifically interpreted the Taft victory as support for the antilabor injunctions issued by Judge Taft.[29] And, "Last but not least," continued Perkins, "on Thursday night after the election, at a dinner given to Mr. Taft in Cincinnati he came out in a very flat-footed, manly way and said that all legitimate business could now proceed without fear of being disturbed, and this has been taken by the whole country as a guarantee that we are going to have a more comfortable time."

But Taft's Administration gave the Harvester Company no comfort. Perkins pushed ahead with new welfare plans, to no avail. The year 1909 saw an expanded profit-sharing plan, and 1910 a completely company-financed workmen's compensation program. Despite all this "good trust" behavior, the United States attorney general filed an antitrust suit against the company in 1912. The company was actively harried through the lawsuit until a court decision in 1918. A final settlement did not come until 1927.

Pensions

The *Collier's* attack of 1908 had focused company and public attention upon business irresponsibility toward injured workmen. International Harvester responded not only with a liberal sickness and accident plan but with a far more expensive pension plan. Pensions at Harvester were in one sense descendants of the 1903–4 stock gift to McCormick Works employees. In 1904 employees of the Works who were over 60 years of age at the date of the merger (September 30, 1902) could choose either the stock gift or a pension. The amount of the pension was related to the worker's wage and length of service. In January 1907 there were 44 nonmanagement employees on the pension roll. The highest monthly pension was $43.33 and the lowest $2.00. The average monthly pension was $9.99.[30]

The motive for this early plan was to care systematically for employees too old to work. Prior to the pension plan the McCormick family was frequently approached by "old hands" who needed aid, and was supporting a number of such employees by monthly gifts.

It was only logical to extend this embryo pension plan to all International Harvester employees. To this end the welfare department had been studying various plans, with some suggestions from Gertrude Beeks. As with the insurance program, the leisurely study quickly became an operating plan as George Perkins built his tripod of welfarism—the insurance program, profit sharing, and the pension plan—to support the "good trust" image. The first companywide pension plan became effective coincidentally with the sickness and accident insurance plan, September 1, 1908. All employees (excepting executives) who were 70 years of age and over, with 20 or more years of service, were pensioned. All employees of 65 or more could "apply" for a pension. Monthly benefits were 1 percent of the average annual pay for the previous 10 years of service, multiplied by the years of service and divided by 12. Minimum benefits were $18.00 a month, the maximum $100. The employer paid the full cost; $250,000 was set aside for this in 1908. At the end of the year 32 employees were put on pension. Their average age was 71 years, their average length of service 31 years, and the average pension $19.00 a month.[31]

The Harvester pension plans of this era conferred no contractual rights upon employees. The trust agreement of the 1907 plan, for example, provided that "This certificate may be revoked at any time as to all or part of the pensioners named herein and the amount to be paid to any pensioner may be increased or reduced by the Trustees."[32] In the light of the cancellation of stock gifts to the strike leaders of 1903, there can be no doubt that both employees and management were aware of the possible consequences this language implied. Shortly after the companywide pension plan was established in 1908, *Farm Machinery,* a veteran agricultural implement trade paper, bluntly set forth the new plan's potentialities for labor peace.

PENSIONS FOR HELP WILL AVERT STRIKES. PLAN ADOPTED BY INTERNATIONAL HARVESTER CO. BY WHICH FAITHFUL, LONG-TERM EMPLOYEES ARE RETIRED—MAY BE USED BY OTHER BIG CONCERNS.

. . . An obvious merit is its tendency to establish better relations between employer and employe and thereby furnish a sort of protection to large industries against strikes. A man who can look forward to a permanent pension at the end of a term of years will not imperil the prospect thoughtlessly . . . .[33]

As late as 1919 the International Harvester's pension regulations provided:

A pension may be suspended or terminated by the Pension Board for gross misconduct or other cause. . . .

Neither the establishment of this plan . . . nor any other action . . . shall be held . . . as creating a contract or giving to any employee a right to be retained in the service or any right to a pension; and the company expressly reserves . . . its rights to discharge without liability any employee . . . whenever the interests of the company may in its judgment so require.[34]

President Harold McCormick in a 1919 letter to employees summed up the company's philosophy on pensions: "As you know, our Pension Plan is a purely voluntary expression of the company's desire to stand by the men who have stood by it."[35] This purely paternalistic pension arrangement was retained until, in January 1937, the pension system was integrated with social security.

That the pension plan was regarded by employees as a reward for not joining unions was indicated by comments of employee representatives on the Works Council of the McCormick Works in July and August 1936 when the Harvester pension plan was about to be replaced by social security. One such comment follows: "I don't feel there is any doubt in the minds of our management about [our] being real loyal employees of the Harvester Company and one of the things that has made it that is their pensions."[36]

From the beginning the Harvester pension plan was liberal in benefits. These were paid entirely by the employer. Improvements were made voluntarily from time to time. In 1913 the minimum monthly benefit was raised to $21.00, and in 1919 to $30.00. By 1919 the monthly benefit formula was raised to 1.5 percent of the highest consecutive ten-year average salary multiplied by the number of years of service. Full pensions were paid to men at age 65 after 20 years of service, at 60 after 25 years, or at 55 after 30 years. Women were eligible at 50. By 1919 545 employees had been pensioned. Out of a total of 30,000 employees, 364 were then on the pension roll. The average pension of the 115 employees who went on pension in 1919 was $32.25 a month.[37]

The pension appears to have been financially generous, and far ahead of those of most American firms of that era. Indeed the plan proved to be more generous than the company was willing to maintain; from 1919 on it was gradually curtailed. The first backward step occurred in the depression year 1922; on June 1 the benefit formula was cut back from 1.5 to 1.25 percent per month of the highest ten years' salary. The monthly minimum was cut from $30.00 to $27.00. Service and age limits were raised. No longer were men eligible for pensions at age 55 even with 30 years' service. The new requirement was age 60 with 30 years of service. Pensions at 65 for men of shorter service were optional with the company; twenty years' service was accepted on occasion. These new provisions hit foremen particularly hard since they were the ones formerly most often eligible for early pensions.

The next retreat came in 1925. A pension study revealed that fully 50 percent of the pensioners had not met the qualifications for age and for service when they began their pensions. These nonqualified workers had been recommended for pensions by superintendents and other officials, usually because they were physically handicapped and were not efficient workers. Pensioning them increased plant efficiency and was a humanitarian solution, but it was undermining the solvency of the pension plan. The major change in 1925 was that in the future all applicants must fully meet the qualifications. A second change applied only to workers with a break in service. Formerly a break in employment at the firm of two years did not destroy the pre-break employment period as a pension credit. Now this break period was cut to six months.

To make the pension plan actuarially solvent, even with these more stringent qualifications, great sums had to be poured into the pension reserves. From January 1924 through 1931 the pension fund reserve rose from $7,715,000 to $25,500,000.[38] But the demands grew even faster. The pension fund did continue to meet all requirements through 1936. The company was then on the point of raising age limits again and setting up a contributory plan.

When the Social Security Act of 1935 took effect in January 1937, the Harvester Company took this opportunity to cancel its traditional pension plan and put all employees on social security. The joint employer-employee contributions of the federal act plus the more stringent age requirements relieved the company of its rapidly increasing pension burden. All past credits earned by workers of more than five years' service under the old pension plan were honored, so that many workers received contributions from both plans.

Under the switch to social security, Harvester employees lost their rights to full pensions at age 60 and had to wait until 65. Much bitterness was felt by old employees who for many years had been looking forward to pensions at 60 and who feared that under the onerous working conditions they could not hang on until 65.

There is little question but that the economic reverses of the long depression of the 1930's caused the Harvester Company to curtail its pension plan. The plan had been actuarially unsound to begin with. To add social security in 1937 to the rapidly mounting pension demands would have been a double burden that the company could not reasonably afford. Social security furnished the company a welcome opportunity to escape from the expensive pension plan and at the same time put the company on an equal pension cost basis with the growing number of farm implement competitors.

The current pension plan, supplemental to social security, was negotiated with the union in 1950 as part of the widespread union bargaining pattern of that period. It has been substantially expanded in subsequent negotiations.

Profit Sharing

Before 1909 the International Harvester balance sheet had been discouraging enough to raise serious doubts as to the supposed advantages of monopoly. But early in 1909 it became clear that this great trust would pay off after all. The profits that year were embarrassingly large, 60 percent above 1908. This was cause for both joy and concern among Harvester officials; these profits for which they had organized the trust could also endanger it by destroying the "good trust" image. Director Perkins urged that these profits be concealed from the public by granting a common stock dividend; his argument, in President McCormick's words, was that "the rate of dividend was more important in the eyes of the general public than the . . . amount of the capital stock . . . ."[39] And just as Perkins had instituted the insurance program as a counterthrust to the *Collier's* exposé, he now introduced a new profit-sharing plan as a hedge against possible public criticism. Before the 1909 annual conference of the National Civic Federation he lauded the trust's generosity. After outlining the International Harvester programs of profit sharing, insurance, and pensions, he told the Federation:

> In the year 1908 the Harvester Company spent about $100,000 in its welfare work. This year it will probably spend a somewhat larger sum.
>
> The Company has been criticized by managers of other companies for making the plan above outlined too liberal and attractive. It has been said that the plans will be too expensive to the Harvester Company and that their cost will be very large. There is no doubt of the truth of this criticism insofar as the cost goes. No concern has ever put out plans that involved the application of so large a percentage of its profits to such plans. But the Harvester Company did not do this out of pure philanthropy. . . . It went into these enterprises in a purely business spirit, believing that the plans would so knit its vast organization together, would so stimulate individual initiative, would so strengthen and develop the esprit de corps of the organi-

zation as to make it possible for the Company to increase its business and its earnings,—and with the spirit of being willing to share this increased success with its organization. . . .[40]

The $100,000 welfare expenditure of which Perkins boasted was just under 1 percent of the corporation's $10,500,000 profits for 1908. Since the 1909 profits jumped to $16,000,000, the 1909 expenditures, including the new profit-sharing plan, were an even lower percentage.

The 1909 profit-sharing plan did not warrant all its fanfare. Its purpose was apparently to convince the government and public that the trust was sharing its profits with the employees. With only slight modifications the plan had been borrowed from one which Perkins had installed many years earlier in the New York Life Insurance Company. The Harvester plan was based on voluntary employee purchases of the company's stock, facilitated by means of payroll deductions. In addition to buying at slightly under the market price and receiving the regular dividend, the employee received a small supplementary dividend. These supplementary dividends were held back for a period of five years, at the end of which they were divided among the remaining plan members.

As a device for preventing turnover of executives, which is what New York Life had used it for, it may have had some merit. As a benefit enabling shop employees to share in the firm's earnings it was a total failure.

In the McCormick Works the first payroll deductions for the 1909 stock plan appear on the May 31, 1910, payrolls. In departments of unskilled workers no one subscribed. In a typical assembly department of semiskilled workers only two of 90 employees signed for stock-purchase deductions, and even this enthusiasm waned fast. A year later there were no deductions in this department. Among the departments of skilled workers the proportions of subscribers were little better. In the engine and boiler department three of 40 men began deductions, in steam fitting one of 25, among millwrights six of 92; in toolrooms Nos. 1 and 3 only four of 136 subscribed at the peak. The best response came in the highly skilled pattern shop, where 11 of 50 began stock purchases. By the end of the third year these men had dropped them.[41]

Profit-sharing plans were not new in European or American industry at this time. Studies of the origin of profit sharing published in 1889 and 1899 by Nicholas Paine Gilman show that profit sharing received its greatest impetus in France from the revolutions of 1830 and 1871, while in America the strikes of 1886 provided this motivation. For example, according to Gilman the famous profit-sharing plan of Procter and Gamble was adopted in 1887 following fourteen strikes the previous year. Procter and Gamble attributed its freedom from labor difficulties between that time and 1899 to this plan.[42] International Harvester's first profit-sharing plan, the stock gift, as we have seen, was also strike-born at the McCormick Works during the Deering plant strike. It was not company financed but was a gift from the McCormick family to McCormick Works employees only. The loyalty of most McCormick workers during this strike proved to Harvester officials the efficacy of the plan.

The first companywide profit-sharing plan at International Harvester had been quietly instituted at Christmas time, 1906. Bonuses were given to "men especially contributing to its success during the year."[43] The selection of men and the amounts for each were based on meritorious service to the company as determined by the Board of Directors. Under this plan annual individual bonuses ranging up from $25 to $50,000[44] were given every Christmas. The total amount available for bonuses each year was a percent of net profits over and above a "fair" return on capital stock and surplus. For 1906 the formula was 10 percent of the net profits in excess of 5 percent of the capital stock of the company. Through 1910 this bonus distribution, except for the occasional inclusion of a highly skilled workman, was never made below the foreman level.

In 1911, when it was clear that Perkins' profit-sharing plan was not reaching the blue-collar workers, President McCormick attempted to revise the annual bonus plan. Harvester works managers were specifically requested to recommend shop employees of special merit for the regular Christmas profit-sharing bonus. The Milwaukee works manager answered with a critical letter implying that such recommendation would be favoritism. He proposed instead setting aside profits to be given to all workmen strictly in proportion to wages received, on grounds that the better workmen had already been given the better jobs.[45] This suggestion received a negative response from the McCormicks, who continued giving the annual Christmas bonuses, receiving in return many letters of thanks from grateful employees and even from their wives.

The problems which had led the Harvester Company to institute profit sharing and other welfare measures persisted. The government suit which began in 1906 was not settled until 1927. Labor strife likewise became chronic, with strikes at Harvester plants in 1913, 1916, and 1919. Even strikes elsewhere in the country were portents of trouble. As the McCormicks had felt threatened by the 1877 and 1894 railroad strikes, so in 1914 they suffered vicariously through the violent dispute between the Rockefeller-owned Colorado Fuel and Iron Company and the United Mine Workers at the remote Colorado village of Ludlow. On business in New York City at the time, President McCormick wrote his son Cyrus III of the view below him opposite 26 Broadway (the Standard Oil offices), "where excited agitators were making violent speeches against Mr. Rockefeller and his son."[46]

The strong public and congressional reaction against the Rockefellers put increased pressure on business leaders to find some solution to the labor problem. The solution which appealed to President McCormick was profit sharing. A new plan, especially tailored for what McCormick called "the man lower down," was unveiled in 1915: "The complications of labor conditions . . . dictate the timely necessity of our doing something practical to win to us and hold our labor."[47]

The terms of the 1915 profit-sharing plan were indeed more generous than those of the 1909 plan. So proud of it was President McCormick that he wrote a glowing account to John D. Rockefeller, Jr:

> I am very glad to have your letter of the 11th, expressing your approval of our profit-sharing plan. It has had a great deal of careful study on our part and we think we have hit upon a system that is somewhat in advance of any other system which has been tried. The proof that it is taking with our people is that over twelve thousand applications have been made since Christmas for employes to come in under the savings and stock purchasing offer.
>
> You will notice that we touch the man of small wage favorably on four separate and distinct points:
>
> (1) We offer him an opportunity to save his money on which we give him 5%, while in a savings bank his money would earn only 3%.
>
> (2) While he is saving we add to his fund 1% of his annual earnings, with a further stipulation that this shall not be less than $10, even tho the 1% would figure out less;
>
> (3) We enable him to turn his savings either into cash or into stock, and if the latter, we give him an advantage of $3.00 per share under the market;
>
> (4) After he had acquired his stock, we give him 2% per annum more than the dividends of the company.

By the time the employee understands clearly these four advantages, it must be evident to him that we have no selfish purpose in view and that we are really trying to give him an advantageous deal which is better, proportionately, than any large stockholder can get.

It is evident that a plan of this kind would not be practical if applied to the upper men in the business, because it would run into money too fast; but, when applied to the man whose income is $1,000 or less, we estimate that it will cost the company less than $400,000 per annum, and we are very glad to make such an appropriation for the benefit it will be to the man of low wage whom heretofore we have been unable to reach with any profit-sharing system.

I shall take great pleasure in sending a few copies of this circular to Dr. Eliot, as you suggest.[48]

In contrast to the very limited acceptance of the 1909 plan by the blue-collar workers, an amazing total of 63 percent of the entire work force began deductions under the 1915 plan.

Yet in the midst of their presumably favorable reception of the profit-sharing plan the employees went out on the bitter month-long strike of May 1916. President McCormick, who had been giving sage advice on employee relations to strike-beleaguered industrialists like Rockefeller, was himself embarrassed as angry Harvester employees picketed his plants.

A Chicago labor paper used the Harvester experience to attack profit sharing:

ANOTHER "PROFIT SHARING" FAILURE

Events at the plant of the International Harvester Company the past week go to show the failure of the so-called profit sharing plan to bring justice to the workers. Two days before last Christmas the daily press announced a wonderful philanthropy on the part of this company. . . .

. . . The employes were to at once become stockholders and share in the great profits of this institution. They would be transformed from common workers into capitalists and visions of the millennium were reflected from the publicity this wonderful plan received.

A brief four months has shattered the dream and the employes of the Harvester Company find themselves worse off than before, for living costs have been soaring and wages are inadequate. A strike has resulted and the profit sharing plan has failed.

. . . the plans are intended to make the employes "loyal" to the company, for while they are deluded into the belief that they are stockholders, the theory is that they will refrain from organizing and keep silent on a wage issue.[49]

The Harvester Company, as a leader in both welfare activities and opposition to unions, had been a frequent target of earlier union attacks on profit sharing. Samuel Gompers had singled out Harvester for criticism in 1908, stating that it had cut wages after installing a profit-sharing plan. Perkins tried to correct Gompers' impression by talking with him through the National Civic Federation, in which they were both active. Gompers did not change his mind; and, when Perkins presented his views on profit sharing before the Federation, Gompers was extremely blunt in his criticism.[50] There was some basis for Gompers' accusation. The McCormick stock gift had been promised to the McCormick employees during the Deering strike of 1903 but not actually given until well into 1904. Wages were cut in September 1904, upon expiration of the union contract. It may be that some employees received their stock gift about the time of the wage cut.

Cyrus McCormick never lost his faith in profit-sharing plans, though their continuance created difficult problems: during World War I additional compensation based on stock ownership was considered by the Treasury Department as subject to the excess profits tax; expanding the amount of stock in employees' hands diluted the McCormick family's share of ownership (40–45 percent in 1920); the fluctuation of profits, arising from such uncontrollable factors as antitrust suits and wartime losses of properties in foreign countries, made the formulation of profit-sharing plans very difficult.[51]

In 1920 the 1915 profit-sharing plan expired. That was a year of unsettled labor conditions and high company profits, hardly a time to abandon profit sharing. Consequently the plan was not only at once renewed but substantially sweetened with a new supplementary plan called "extra compensation." This extra compensation gave stock to all workers, even those who would not subscribe for it voluntarily.

The essence of the new plan was simply to give cash and stock outright to employees who met all the qualifications. Forty percent of the 1920 profits over and above 7 percent on the net worth of the company was set aside for distribution to the workers. Two-thirds of this distribution went to employees below the supervisory level; 20 percent of earnings in excess of 7 percent on invested capital was distributed to the managers or executives. The *Annual Report* for 1920 listed extra compensation of $2,760,263.66 to be given out on May 1, 1921.[52] The downturn of business apparently caused a change in plans, for the report for 1921 lists only $694,600 worth of stock as having been distributed.[53] Even assuming that this was matched with an equal amount of cash (of which no mention is found in the 1921 report), the extra compensation actually granted for 1920 would have fallen about $1,450,000 short of the determination in the 1920 annual report. The depression of 1920–22 cut the earnings of the company so sharply that, measured by the 1920 formula, there were never after 1920 any excess profits for distribution. Depression layoffs and wage cuts (30 percent) wrecked the 1920 profit-sharing plan. As early as June 1921 less than 5 percent of the McCormick Works production workers were subscribing for stock, in contrast to the earlier 63 percent under the 1915 plan.[54]

After his retirement from active management in 1920 Cyrus McCormick continued to study profit sharing, calling upon scholars at several universities for assistance. Professor David McCabe, Princeton economist, was his chief consultant. But at the depth of the depression in 1921 McCormick suspended his study, as he informed Professor McCabe, "until the sky is somewhat cleared from our present economic difficulties."[55]

Since that depression had nullified the extra compensation plan and ruined the regular 1915-style profit sharing, the company began a new voluntary stock purchase plan. During the later prosperity of the 'twenties the company promoted employee stock purchases vigorously, but sold the employees only the 7 percent preferred stock. Beginning in 1924 management went to extreme lengths to high-pressure employees into subscribing for stock. Even works council representatives were urged to peddle stock to their constituents. A gigantic competition was set up to promote the sale of stock. In a procedure reminiscent of safety contests, plant was pitted against plant and department against department. After two months of this, 50 percent of the Harvester Company's Wisconsin Steel employees, both blue- and white-collar, had subscribed to the enormous average of $800 of stock each. By July 1925, 19,840 subscribers companywide were signed up for $14,000,000 worth. But management still was not satisfied. Employee representatives of the works councils were given lists of nonsubscribing employees as sales prospects. The company was critical of employee purchasers who subsequently sold their stock. Company officials explained to employee representatives that it was foolish to sell stock to finance winter coal bills, sickness, or the purchase of an auto; all of these should come out of current income.[56]

Somehow Harvester's high-pressure stock sales campaign struck the attention of William Green, president of the American Federation of Labor, who wrote the company for details.[57] The Harvester plan appears indeed to have been a good investment for the workers. As in the 1915 plan, the company paid 5 percent on all money deducted from the paychecks until enough was collected to buy a share of stock. In the beginning preferred stock paying 7 percent was sold at par. An additional 2 percent dividend was paid to employee stockholders from 1925 to 1930. One percent of annual earnings was awarded also. Thus an employee purchaser received a near-guaranteed return of about 10 percent. Employees could invest in a home mortgage instead of Harvester stock if they wished, or have the company purchase non-Harvester securities.

It is hard to see why the company was willing, not to say anxious, to acquire capital by this expensive procedure. The incentive may have been the hope that the generous dividends would replace wage demands and spur the workers' interest in more efficient operations and profits. Though any increase in stock somewhat diluted family control, sale to employees, with the wide dispersion that involved, was less likely to have this effect than public sale.

To attract more employee capital, and perhaps to satisfy employee demands for some of the real fruits of prosperity, the company in 1929 formulated a common stock purchase plan for employees. Fortunately, as it turned out, this was not ready until the summer of 1930, well after the first stock market bloodletting. But the seriousness of the recession was improperly assessed by company executives. Common stock in 1930 was offered to employees at $75.00 a share, down from the 1929 peak of $140. A year later the stock which the plan was to purchase had fallen far below $75.00. A new bargain price of $50.00 was heralded in mid-1931.

In the early years of the depression the stock sales were surprisingly large. Those workers who were still employed did not receive a wage cut until the fall of 1931. At the McCormick Works in the millwright department, where employment fell from 105 men at the time of the stock crash to 45 at the end of November 1931, the number purchasing stock remained constant at 35. In the pattern shop the number of stock purchases fell only from 42 to 40; in the engine and boiler room the number buying stock rose 50 percent despite a 40 percent drop in employment.[58] Insecure workers may have imagined that in some way continued stock purchase would aid them in avoiding layoffs. However, when the second wage cut appeared in the spring of 1932, and the value of the stock which they had agreed to purchase at the new bargain price of $50.00 a share fell to $16.00, cancellations forced the company to drop the plan. At the same time, low operations cut off the need for expansion capital. Employees were notified to withdraw all money which the company was holding for them under the stock purchase plan. The week of July 30, 1932, saw the last stock deduction. A few employees wished to leave their savings on deposit with the company in the belief that the company was safer than the banks; but the company, unwilling to pay 5 percent interest, canceled the entire scheme, offering only to buy stock on the open market for those who insisted. Thus did forces beyond its control destroy one of International Harvester's fondest hopes for labor-management harmony. The collapse of the securities market made a revival of employee stock purchase plans out of the question for many years.

When in 1936 the CIO came knocking at Harvester's gates, extra compensation was suddenly revived in a completely new form. To the surprise of everyone, on October 31, 1936, the company gave an extra week's pay to all nonmanagement employees with between one and two years' service, and two weeks' pay to those with more. Those working less than a year received extra pay on a pro rata basis. Persons who deposited this money in the bank for a year were entitled to receive one extra dollar for each four saved.[59] This plan was supposed to resemble that of 1920 and split profits above a certain level with employees. Actually it did nothing of the sort. It was hastily devised and bore little relation to the 1920 plan, after which it was named; it smacked of an effort to buy employees' loyalty in the face of the mounting pressure from the trade unions. The loyalty of older workers was particularly precarious because at this same time the company canceled its famous pension plan, which had been in operation since 1908, in favor of the new federal social security plan. As of January 1, 1937, employees were no longer eligible for pensions at 60; they had to wait until the social security minimum age of 65.

In September 1937 a second surprise distribution was made under this new extra compensation plan. This year $4,400,000 was distributed, or almost double the 1936 distribution. Workers with one year's experience received one week's extra pay, those with two years' experience two weeks' pay, and those with three or more years' experience three weeks' pay. In 1938 no money was distributed thus. In 1939 the company merely announced that a formula for a plan would be made public by April 1940. In 1940, in the midst of a renewed CIO organizing drive, the formula was announced: (*a*) 25 percent of profits above $3.00 per common share would be distributed to employees of three years' or more experience in proportion to their wages, and (*b*) such employees who deposited money for savings would have one-half of their savings, not exceeding 2.5 percent of their wages, matched by the company.

This plan functioned for only one year. As a result of the CIO election victory at major Harvester plants in July 1941, the company was finally brought to the bargaining table. Here it readily became clear that the union did not consider the extra compensation scheme a substitute for an hourly pay increase. In fact, the union looked upon it as an antiunion gratuity. In the light of this lack of appreciation the company ruefully abandoned the plan in 1942 while making a general wage increase.[60]

5

Harvester, a Political Pariah

The Wagner Investigation

In 1912 and 1913 the force of public opinion which had stimulated the Harvester welfare program of 1908–10 made itself felt as an important determinant of wages and working conditions. Unionism, which had been the moving force for wage changes in 1903–4 and in the nineteenth century, was nonexistent in the Harvester plants from 1905 to 1912. During this period there were no general wage increases at Harvester despite a 10 percent rise in living costs. The last general wage increase had occurred in January 1904 according to the terms of the union agreement of May 1903. Upon expiration of the union contract in September 1904 wages were cut across the board. A second general cut took place in January 1908. There were selected individual rate increases, chiefly for skilled craftsmen, during this time.

The "public opinion" that chiefly influenced the Harvester Company was perhaps that of important government officials and candidates for office who could affect legislation and the policies of government regulatory agencies. Thus in 1912 Harvester Director George W. Perkins, who was then managing Teddy Roosevelt's bid for a third term, suddenly found that unpopular Harvester labor policies were seriously jeopardizing Roosevelt's candidacy. The famous Triangle Shirt Waist Company fire of March 25, 1911, in New York City, which caused the deaths of 146 women, had jolted the state legislature into setting up a Factory Investigating Commission headed by Democratic State Senator Robert F. Wagner. In August 1912 the commission visited the Harvester Company's Twine Mill at Auburn, New York, where 400 women were employed. The *New York Tribune* of August 22 announced the committee's findings with the headlines: "HARVESTER CO. 'SWEATS' WOMEN, PROBE SHOWS. WORKS THEM 10 HOURS IN TWINE MILL, WITH NIGHT SHIFTS, AND VIOLATES LAW. SENATOR WAGNER'S STORY TELLS OF UNSANITARY CONDITIONS AND SMALL PAY IN SHOP RUN BY TRUST G. W. PERKINS AIDS IN MANAGING."[1]

According to the committee:

> . . . In the course of the inspection several of the women were seen pulling piles of hemp, weighing 150 pounds each, across the floor. These piles, in many instances, were higher than the women themselves.
>
> In the spinning room the clatter of machinery was so frightful that a voice could hardly be heard below a shriek. The appearance of the women workers was very disheartening; they were wan looking and pale, and their clothes, faces and hands were covered with oil and hemp dust.
>
> No attempt whatever was made to remove the dust by any system of exhaust, but it was breathed continually by the workers, some of whom testified that they had frequently suffered from sore throats, colds, etc. The dirt and dust were so thick upon the clothes of the working girls that at noon, when they went to luncheon, and at 6 p.m., when they left the factory, they had to sweep one another off with brooms.[2]

Even the hours of work were substantially above the 58½-hour week in Chicago.

> A number of the women questioned said they began work at about 6:30 every morning, lunched from 12 to 12:30 and then worked up to 6 o'clock at night. On Saturdays they worked until 5 o'clock, making a total of sixty-four and a half hours a week, according to their testimony. This is, of course, in direct violation of the labor law. The luncheon period provided by the labor law was also entirely disregarded.

The piecework pay system often yielded the women as little as $5 a week.

The Wagner commission report appears to have been accurate. The Harvester Company's well-publicized welfare work begun by Gertrude Beeks at the McCormick and Deering works in 1902 and 1903 had been extended but sparingly to the Auburn mill.

When newsmen cornered Perkins and demanded an explanation of these conditions at Auburn, he could only refer lamely to the Progressive Party platform favoring improved working conditions for women, and report the many thousands of dollars that Harvester was spending on employee welfare.[3] Clarence Funk, general manager of the company, countered the committee's criticisms more specifically:

> It would be only fair, however, for our critics to go further in their study. If

they should they would learn that at each plant there is a matron, whose sole duty it is to watch the condition of the girls at work and take them to the rest room if they show signs of fatigue. They would also learn that we have not had one report from Auburn of collapse or suffering from overwork.

They would also learn that the night work is not compulsory, but that to obtain employes the company has paid higher wages than were given in the day, and that the people benefited by the extra employment were in the main immigrant girls who by inability to speak English were unable to earn anything like as much money elsewhere.[4]

The use of the Wagner report to attack Roosevelt was more political than reasonable. Though Perkins appears to have been the only International Harvester director who supported Roosevelt, Perkins and Roosevelt were given the blame for Harvester's bad labor conditions. Papers did not mention that Harvester President Cyrus McCormick was a long-time friend and supporter of Woodrow Wilson or that other directors were supporting Taft. It is true, however, that none of the other directors was so politically active as Perkins, who was both chief fund-raiser for Roosevelt and very active in the campaign of the Progressive Party.

President McCormick wanted to dismiss the criticism as simply a political attack: "No sooner had I returned . . . than I had to . . . investigate a scandalous attack made upon us by the Democratic elements of the New York Legislature, who wanted a crack at Perkins and consequently used us as a convenient weapon. The attack they made was with regard to the conditions of the work of the women in the twine mill at Auburn and, although there were some things which needed improving, the sensational report as a whole was unjustified and was nothing but a political move."[5]

Not only the Democrats but the Taft Republicans were merciless in their use of the labor situation at the Auburn Works to attack Roosevelt. Over and over again emphasis was placed on the long hours of work by "young girls, young mothers and women about to become mothers . . . ."[6] Taft Republicans openly declared that Roosevelt had delayed antitrust prosecution of International Harvester from 1907 to 1909 because of the political contributions of George W. Perkins. These charges were particularly unfortunate for the company at this time—September 1912—when the antitrust suit was in full swing in the courtroom in St. Paul.[7]

Harassed Cyrus McCormick tried to extricate the company from its uncomfortable political position and sought to separate it from Perkins' support of Roosevelt. Privately he wrote of the cooperation the firm had given the Taft Administration during the preceding four years. He sent his personal contribution to the campaign fund of Woodrow Wilson. But such a pariah was the Harvester trust by now that no one would take its money. Wilson's campaign manager returned the check.

This public exposure by the Wagner commission forced International Harvester to comply with the New York State law by reducing the work week for women to 55 hours. To deny this shortening of hours to all Harvester workers, men and women, across the country would be to invite further political attacks. On October 1, 1912, the 55-hour week was installed in all International Harvester plants—bringing the work week back to within one hour of the 54-hour week which had existed under the union contract of 1903–4. To compensate for the reduced hours, a wage increase across the board of a 2½ cents an hour was granted. Thus 1912 saw the first general wage increase since the abolition of the union in 1904.

The newspaper publicity about bad working conditions for women at Auburn also engendered new pleas for abolishing night work for women. Mrs. Louise de Koven Bowen, who described herself as "the owner of two thousand shares of International preferred stock and seven hundred shares of common," wrote to President McCormick "to protest against the employment of several hundred women who work at night."[8] In replying, McCormick stated his personal opposition to night work for women while explaining the company's desperate need to continue this practice: "The policy of the Company has always been against night work, especially for women, and we have allowed the twine mills to be operated at night only because we have felt our responsibility to the farmers was so great that we must produce an adequate supply of twine for the binding of grain, which could not otherwise be secured; and we have not, and cannot, within a reasonable time, obtain sufficient spindles to manufacture this twine in the day time."[9] He did assure her, however, that the company had "instituted a very careful examination of the whole question . . . ."

Mrs. Bowen then joined forces with some powerful allies: Nettie Fowler McCormick, Cyrus' mother and the company's largest single stockholder; Cyrus' sister, Anita McCormick Blaine; and Jane Addams.

This impressive delegation called on Cyrus McCormick to protest the continuing night work for women. In writing to his son Cyrus, President McCormick described the meeting and went on to state a new and, he believed, progressive company policy on plant improvement:

> Before receiving her [Mrs. Bowen's] letter we had already begun to consider substitution of men for women in the spinning of twine at night, so these ladies, . . . were pleased to hear our reports and appeared to be satisfied that we are doing all we can to have the conditions of women's work satisfactory. . . . The I.H.C. desires to be the foremost in welfare work. . . . Many companies are beginning to realize that it is just as legitimate to use the stockholders' money for the improvement of the conditions of work at the mills (within reasonable limits) as it is to appropriate for physical properties . . . .[10]

Thus under political pressures and women stockholders' demands Cyrus McCormick ordered the replacement of women on night shifts by men in both the Auburn and Chicago twine mills and the appropriation of $50,000 for installing apparatus to remove the dust from the twine mills.[11]

The O'Hara Investigation

Establishment of the 55-hour week and abolition of night work for women did not rescue International Harvester from the current concern for the welfare of working women. No sooner had the New York legislative investigation died down than a committee of the Illinois legislature headed by O'Hara began an investigation of prostitution. The theory of the investigating committee was that women were forced into prostitution to supplement the scant wages paid by niggardly employers. Chicago department store executives as well as prostitutes made lively copy as they testified about wages and working conditions in the metropolis.

Vice President Harold McCormick learned that he or Cyrus would be called to testify before the legislature's "white slavery" committee. To head this off he recommended immediately announcing an $8 minimum wage for women. Harold's letter of March 15, 1913, to Cyrus urging immediate action clearly establishes the primary role the legislative investigation played in this wage raise. ". . . I believe you or I will be subpoenaed to testify in regard to the International, and I believe that if we should adopt the proposition as suggested by Mr. Ranney [Harvester manager of manufacturing], to publish it [the $8 minimum for women] in the papers, that we would not only avoid investigation, but we would by this act boost along what really on the merits of the case seems fair and just, ..."[12]

The $8 minimum announced on March 20 was described by the company as a humanitarian move voluntarily instituted. President McCormick's explanation was as follows: "The International Harvester Company has been, for many years, studying the question of how to bring better conditions to all its employees, and especially the women. Since last summer we have been very carefully studying the condition of our women employees, ... Our last step, just recently taken, has been to adopt eight dollars as a minimum wage. This we did upon expert advice that eight dollars is as little as a young woman needs for her own support if she is not living at home, ..."[13] Fifteen hundred girls were affected. The *Chicago Tribune* labeled the new Harvester minimum wage for women "the first concrete result of the white slavery senatorial investigation . . . ."[14]

The Strike at Auburn

On the day that the $8-a-week minimum wage for women went into effect the Harvester Company's Auburn Twine Mill went on strike. It began rather quietly as a sympathetic strike in support of employees at the neighboring Columbia Rope Mill, but the Harvester workers soon had demands of their own. President McCormick concurred in the recommendation of his subordinates that, rather than pay the increased wages, the company should dismantle the plant—which had had an unprofitable record anyway—and move it to Germany. No public announcement of this dismantling was made. About April 11, Cyrus McCormick, on his way to Panama to visit the company's sisal plantations, discussed the plant-closing plan with Director George W. Perkins. Perkins strongly objected. McCormick phoned the Auburn plant and before leaving for Panama reported to Perkins that the matter was in process of amicable settlement. Actually the strike was not settled, nor had McCormick rescinded the dismantling decision. On April 15 newspapers carried an announcement by Harvester Assistant General Manager Alex Legge that the plant was being dismantled for shipment to Germany. The announcement that American workers' jobs were being handed over to foreigners roused strong newspaper and political repercussions.

In an effort to save the jobs of his constituents, New York Governor William Sulzer sent the State Board of Arbitration to Auburn and appealed to his political friend, Harvester Director Perkins, for help. The New York newspapers took up the cudgels in behalf of American workers. Nettie Fowler McCormick, then 78 years old, learned of the dismantling from the newspapers and immediately went into action. Appearing at the Chicago offices of the firm, she interrogated Assistant General Manager Alex Legge and extracted from him a promise to stop the removal of machinery and to delay a final decision until Cyrus returned from Panama. What was remarkable was not the reversal in policy she achieved, as the largest stockholder and mother of the company president, but the cogency of her arguments.

> If it is best to move it, as a business measure, let it be done; but not now in the lime-light of angry publicity, and also of passion, inviting further outrage from unreasoning employes. . . . The Government law-suit causes us to be now still in the public eye, some defending us, some saying, "well, new troubles for the International Harvester Company." . . . wisdom bids us walk more circumspectly than if we had not been several times on the gridiron.
>
> . . . we should not reject the proffered advances of the first officer of the great State of New York.[15]

She put Assistant General Manager Legge on the spot by reciting the lessons of the Haymarket affair, "the awful episode in 1886, which resulted in the hanging of the anarchists—all arising from the unwisdom, of Averill, superintendent."

A day later, from New York, politically alert Director Perkins was bombarding Chicago executives with telegrams demanding revocation of the decision to dismantle the plant. "You wired me yesterday that eight directors had met in Chicago and considered the matter. I did not receive any notice . . . . How can a meeting of directors be legal unless properly called?"[16]

When President McCormick returned from Panama on April 28 he had a long talk on the Auburn situation with Perkins. Thereupon he called together all the New York directors he could locate. Besides Perkins, they were Judge Gary and Messrs. Saunders, Lamont, Reay, and Deering. It was inevitable that these men with their broad banking and industrial experience and their public relations orientation should reverse the dismantling order. Three carloads of machinery which had already arrived in New York City were ordered returned to Auburn and reinstalled. Employees who wished to work were offered their jobs. If they did not wish to return to work the plant was to remain idle for the time being.[17]

Perkins received much of the credit for this reversal from his friend Governor Sulzer. The governor, with his eye squarely on the political scene, even requested, through Perkins, that a Harvester press announcement of the return of the Auburn employees to work should make "mention of the fact that Albany had used its good offices, etc."[18] Perkins phoned the suggestion to Cyrus McCormick in Chicago, also suggesting a telegram of thanks to Governor Sulzer. McCormick obliged.[19]

While the striking union was a factor in the outcome at Auburn, it was manifestly too weak to tangle successfully with the Harvester trust in the collective bargaining arena. However, the political considerations engendered by the strike were prime influences upon Harvester policies at this time. Governor Sulzer's motivation in opposing removal of the Auburn Twine Mill to Germany was political as well as humanitarian. One motive for Perkins' vigorous and effective intervention was probably the strike's obviously harmful effect on any future political influence he might wish to wield. He was even more concerned for the political vulnerability of the Harvester trust and the antitrust suit pending in the federal courts. Mrs. McCormick's timely intervention was probably primarily humanitarian, but she too was conscious of the trust's vulnerability and, with her vivid memory of the Haymarket tragedy of 1886, anxious to avoid a repetition of the inept labor policies which had led to it.

6

Management Divided: Perkins vs. McCormick

After the end of the union contract in 1904 International Harvester spread successive layers of welfarism, profit sharing, pensions, and sickness and accident benefits liberally over its traditional antiunion policies. By 1916 the company officers could look back on twelve years of labor peace marred only by the strike at the Auburn Twine Mill in 1913. Had the combination of repression and welfarism achieved permanent immunity from unionism? A labor explosion in 1916 proved welfarism no more than a veil spread over the basic, unmet needs of the Harvester workers.

Allied war orders brought rising living costs and mounting discontent to American workers, while booming war industries provided increasing job opportunities. Before long workers lost their former close dependence upon any one employer. In the midst of this ferment, in the spring of 1916, the Harvester Company was experiencing a period of sluggish business because it was avoiding war orders. Quite unrealistically, in the light of the general labor market, the company cut piece rates for twine workers and put certain departments where work was slack on a reduced work week. These actions touched off spontaneous strikes in three of the four Chicago works: McCormick, Deering, and Tractor.

There was little leadership among the workers. These mass walkouts were not planned by unions. The union leaders were outsiders who appeared and took hold after the initial walkouts had occurred.

The walkouts began on April 26 with the McCormick twine workers, who had suffered a piece-rate cut. The next day metalworkers, who had been cut from ten to nine hours a day because of shortage of work, followed the twine workers out on strike. The company rapidly made concessions, but the strikes spread from department to department and from plant to plant.

As President McCormick described the origin of the strike to Perkins:

> Suddenly, out of a clear sky, on Wednesday, April 26th, trouble was reported at the McCormick Works, being a dissatisfaction in one small department which had been put on a 9-hour basis because of the lack of work. This plan of reducing slightly the hours of work instead of laying off men has been one which we have successfully used for the last two years, and it has been much preferred by the men. This action, taken in the regular course of business, by the superintendent, seems to have been the tinder which started the whole labor conflagration.
>
> Promptly we acquiesced in the requests of this small group, and immediately requests came from other quarters, minor in their character, which were also promptly granted. Nevertheless, the men came back and said that they were going out anyway. There was no general grievance nor any general demand. The men did not seem to know why they went out; they simply went out. There was no feeling of bitterness, and for two or three days it was difficult for the superintendents to find out why they were going. They did not all quit in a body, but went out department by department, each day a few more men failing to turn up.[1]

G. A. Ranney, now Harvester secretary, said: "The strike in both twine mill and foundries came as an absolute surprise to us, because the employees brought no urgent grievance to our attention, nor revealed their intention to quit work . . . . Sets of demands asking more money and shorter hours were placed in our hands and without waiting for an answer the men and women walked out."[2] R. G. Brooks, superintendent of the McCormick Works, commented: "It looks like spring fever to me. The foundry men certainly had no better reason to take such action than the seasonal lassitude could furnish."[3]

If management was actually as much in the dark about the real grievances as it pretended to be, the cause lay in the long-time policy of the company not to recognize unions and to fire employee leaders whenever they exposed themselves. The inevitable result was the complete breakdown in communications described by corporate officials.

The real demands of the strikers were clearly revealed to the newspaper reporters if not to company officials. Though they differed in detail among departments they were in general: (1) restoration of former twine piece rate plus an increase, (2) equal pay in the twine mill for men and women, (3) a 9-hour day (foundry 10 hours), (4) a 10 percent increase for pieceworkers, (5) abolition of piecework, (6) abolition of the Employee's Mutual Benefit Association, (7) recognition of the newly formed union, (8) establishment of collective bargaining through delegates of employees.[4]

The company, as in earlier labor disputes, rapidly made sweeping concessions on wages and hours but was implacable in its refusal to grant any form of recognition of the union. Two days after the strike began the company conceded (1) 10 hours' pay for 9 hours' work, equivalent to an increase of 11.1 percent at the old hourly rate, (2) piece rates increased 11.1 percent, (3) time and one-half for overtime, both day rate and piecework, (4) a minimum wage rate of 25 cents per hour for men (formerly 20 cents).

But the workers did not return. Full-page ads urging workers to come back to work were run by the company in all Chicago papers, including the foreign language ones. The perverseness of the workers exasperated company officials. President McCormick explained by letter to the directors on May 2, 1916:

> We hoped that the consideration of the matter during Saturday and Sunday would bring back on Monday morning most of the operating force.
>
> On Monday, May first, all of the men at the Tractor Works came back. None of them expressed a grievance, and yet after luncheon only half of the men came back, and this morning none are at work.
>
> At the McCormick Works about 3500 came to work in the morning and 1500 stayed out. After luncheon these figures were changed, so that at quitting time only 1200 remained in and all the rest—about 4,000—were out. Today (Tuesday) all the men at the McCormick Works have gone out.
>
> At the Deering Works conditions are much better. Not more than half the men have gone out, and today they are working while the McCormick and Tractor Works are practically closed.[5]

On May 5 Cyrus wrote to his mother: "The conditions are rather better today. The trouble is that while we were waiting for conditions to improve so that men who are friendly can go to work, the labor agitators may work on others."[6] To company attorney Cyrus Bentley he reported: "The molders at the Deering Works came to work on Monday morning, but were appealed to by outsiders not to go to work, and on Tuesday morning they all failed to show up."[7]

By May 23, after three weeks of strike, President McCormick was able to report substantial gains in employment, except that the twine mills and foundries were lagging: "It is our judgment that the Deering Twine Mill employees have been more thoroughly unionized than any other part of the works."[8]

By May 29 all departments, including twine mill employees at the struck Chicago plants, were at work except the molders. In a letter to the directors McCormick reaffirmed the company's uncompromising open shop policy: "We have about 250 molders at each of the Chicago works out of a normal 1694 at the McCormick and 874 at Deering. The indications are that since these troubles began the labor unions have taken most of our foundrymen into their union, so we shall probably have to build up a new organization, which we can do, . . . but it will take some time and will cause us more or less expense."[9]

The 1916 renewal of the feud with the Molders' Union must have reminded Cyrus of the bitter strikes of 1885 and 1886. Then it was "the Irish" among them who were the troublemakers. Now it was "the Poles." To the directors and to his mother he reported on June 5: "The labor leaders still are exerting a strong influence on our foundrymen to keep them from returning to work. One of the advantages of building a new foundry organization will be that we will not have such a large percentage of Poles. It does not have a good effect to have so large percentage of one class of men. While they are no doubt wellmeaning and are good workers, they are very excitable and easily led astray."[10]

A unique feature of the 1916 labor dispute was the light it focused on the divergent labor policies of President McCormick and Director Perkins. When during the Twine Mill strike at Auburn in 1913 the company began dismantling the plant, Perkins was bitterly critical of the company management, and particularly of the lack of breadth and understanding of Harvester second-line executives. Cyrus McCormick escaped direct criticism because he was in Panama. Since Perkins and Nettie McCormick intervened for the same end—to reverse the Auburn decision—there was no direct clash with the McCormicks on this occasion.

The widely publicized Harvester strike of 1916, coming so soon after the similarly publicized labor troubles of 1912 and 1913, outraged Perkins. Because the bitter attack he made on Cyrus McCormick II included more than the company's labor policy, the past relationships of the two men are relevant.

Perkins, as we have seen, was no ordinary director. From 1901 to 1911 he was a Morgan partner and through 1902–11 he represented the Morgan firm on the Harvester Board of Directors, with powers to hire and fire executives—given him by the trust agreement—which made him a virtual dictator. In this situation it was almost inevitable that the McCormicks should come to regard him as an intruder. When by 1906 the trusts profits had failed to revive adequately from the 1904 recession, Perkins moved in, hand-picked his own general manager, C. S. Funk, and reorganized the company. The McCormicks, who even at the time of the merger were determined to emerge from the ten-year agreement with control of the company, deeply resented Perkins' assumption of power. By borrowing from Harold's father-in-law John D. Rockefeller, they had succeeded in buying up enough International Harvester stock so that upon expiration of the agreement they would gain control of the corporation. When the ten-year period ended, Perkins no longer had the deciding vote on the board; the McCormicks promptly asserted their control by firing his man Funk. In addition, Perkins' political activity on behalf of Theodore Roosevelt in 1912 had hurt the Harvester Company, thus offending the McCormicks. At this time Cyrus McCormick seriously considered removing him from the Board of Directors.[11]

Perkins' blunt and detailed criticism of Harvester's labor relations policies from his vantage as a director of the firm stands out as unique in a long period devoid of such internal examination. But its acerbity perhaps stems partially from the otherwise strained feelings between Perkins and Cyrus McCormick II.

At the first report in the New York papers of the Harvester strike, Perkins telegraphed Cyrus McCormick in Chicago, ". . . I strongly recommend immediate ten per cent [wage] increase matter should be settled and announced tonight."[12] As further reports from Chicago indicated that the situation was worsening, Perkins wrote McCormick on May 4 an uncommonly frank and discerning exposition of proper corporate labor policy:

> I think the trouble with the labor situation in the Harvester Company is that it was not handled with a strong, direct and broad enough policy some time ago. The heads of the departments have undoubtedly temporized with it, fussed around, and pusseyfooted on the question of a real general raise and settlement of the question, and the result is what one always gets in such a

> method of handling the case. I suppose you noticed what the Steel Corporation has done in the way of wages and also that we [U. S. Steel] have had very little trouble, even at Pittsburgh where the disturbances have been so serious.[13]
>
> I was very anxious about the situation in the Harvester plants when I was in Chicago and that was why I telegraphed as I did. I believe firmly in the heads of the Corporation taking information and advice from the under officers and heads of departments, but I do not believe in letting the heads of departments assume the responsibility for a policy and use their discretion as to whether literally it shall be carried out. As I have said so many times in the past years, this is one of the serious failings in the Harvester organization. If we had followed it in the Steel Corporation we would have been in more labor struggles than you could shake a stick at, for on more than one occasion the presidents of subsidiary companies have been dead against wage increase, but they have been overruled by the Finance Committee and allowed no discretion practically as to the carrying out of the policy laid down by Judge Gary and his associates. I think the way wages have not been raised, the way the heads of departments have sort of tried to make believe they had raised them without raising them, you will find is more largely responsible for your labor troubles than anything else.
>
> I think it very unfortunate. It will cost the Company a great deal in its prestige and, besides, a lot of money, all of which from my point of view ought to have been avoided.[14]

Perkins spoke with authority here of the labor policies of United States Steel. Throughout 1901–11 he was the elder Morgan's eye on the Steel Company's Board of Directors. His regular reports to Morgan on U. S. Steel activities included special analyses of the "labor situation." In that period Perkins was certainly one of the architects of U. S. Steel labor policy.

Of special interest is Perkins' charge that department heads at Harvester had been sabotaging wage increase directives from top management. Perkins probably knew whereof he spoke. When department heads and superintendents were judged—as they commonly were—by their ability to keep down costs, they had a real incentive to resist wage increases. With the wide latitude which production officials had over wage policies, what Perkins charged is very plausible.

A study of Harvester wage policy over the years gives some support to Perkins' analysis. In the long history of the company from 1848 through 1916 there was never a general wage increase until after a catastrophic event such as a strike or, as in October 1912, a legislative investigation. U. S. Steel met the 1916 labor crisis with a three-cent increase over 1915, as against one and a half cents at Harvester. More important, the U. S. Steel increases were put through in time to forestall strikes. In the long run, however, as Table 2 shows, the wage advantage for 1902–16 had generally been with Harvester.

TABLE 2

Average Hourly Earnings, 1900–1916

Year	*International Harvester, McCormick Works**	*U. S. Steel†*
1900	—	—
1901	—	—
1902	19.4¢	20.1¢
1903	20.9	20.7
1904	22.0	19.2
1905	21.8	19.8
1906	22.2	20.4
1907	21.8	21.4
1908	22.0	21.4
1909	21.6	21.6
1910	22.8	22.4
1911	23.8	23.4
1912	22.9	23.8
1913	26.4	25.2
1914	26.3	25.7
1915	27.6	26.0
1916	29.1	29.0

* Source: 1902–12, District Court of U.S. for District of Minnesota, U.S.A., International Harvester, 2: 168. 1914–16, G. J. Kelday, memo for Cyrus McCormick, Jr., Sept. 15, 1930. CHMcC II papers, unindexed materials.

† Source: U. S. Steel Corporation, 47th *Annual Report*, 1948, p. 28.

Cyrus McCormick's answer to Perkins' May 4 criticism is contained in two communications. Despite the polite language the replies bristle defensively and at one point move to the attack with a deft dig at Perkins on the Pennsylvania militia being called at the U. S. Steel plant at Braddock:

Believe our labor situation has had and is having careful and intelligent attention. If we had given ten percent increase before demand for shorter hours came that would not have prevented demand for nine hour basis and we would have had a general increase of twenty percent. Our men so far as they have been reached with exception of molders are satisfied with nine hour basis which amounts to an increase of eleven percent already given.

We are in conference with committees of our men continually and good feeling prevails. Large numbers of our employes ready to go to work as soon as general labor conditions better. . . . Our organization here including directors and managers are a unit as to method of handling present situation in which I fully concur. Believe if you were on ground you would feel same way. Will write further Monday when we expect some further favorable action.[15]

I note your statement that the Steel Corporation have had very little trouble. This I am glad to know, but it is reported here that at Braddock the situation was so serious that the militia had to be called out to protect the Steel Corporation's Works.[16]

Throughout the six-week strike Perkins was kept informed of its progress. The newspaper appeals to the men to return to work were all sent to him. With particular pride General Manager Ranney called attention to the company's ultimatum that workers return by Monday or lose their jobs. Perkins in New York continued his long distance kibitzing of Harvester strike management. His reply on the return-to-work ultimatum was sharp and prophetic: "I have yours of the 13th and think the advertisement enclosed [the ultimatum] was an unfortunate utterance. I should doubt if it would produce anything except an unfavorable impression on the men."[17]

Cyrus McCormick admitted that the effect of the ultimatum "was not as completely favorable as we had hoped," but defended his management of the strike:

The peaceable and businesslike methods which we have used in dealing with our men; the early announcement that there would be no strike-breakers brought in to force an issue; the patience that we have shown in waiting for the men to come to their senses; the reasonableness we have exercised in discussing with the men grievances and requests which were trumped up after the strike began and which were most of them in reality absurd—all of this has called forth, not only from business men in Chicago and the public, but also from the labor leaders themselves, and especially the president of the Federation here, most favorable comment.[18]

The last sentence of one of Cyrus McCormick's letters "All of our operating men are satisfied that we can work out the present problem to our entire satisfaction . . . ," spurred Perkins to write a final sarcastic attack on McCormick's executive management:

I have yours of the 29th. The trouble with this whole labor business, which is a source of very great disappointment and disturbance to me, is covered in the last three lines of your letter, which clearly indicate what I have so often said, viz., that the Harvester Company is managed by a group of operating men and not by the officers. The operating men form the policy and the officers adopt it, which is absolutely contrary to any sound, able management that I have ever known of. There is no doubt or question that the advice and recommendations of superintendents and all other under officers should be earnestly desired and freely sought after, but this having been done, the final decision should rest with the officers of the Company, and the directors as to what the policy of the Company should be and this policy should be determined not only by the reports of the under officers but by other information bearing on the great problem which the under officers cannot possibly have.

I doubt if you realize the serious position in which the Harvester Company has been placed throughout the country by this unfortunate labor disturbance and the manner in which it was handled, or rather in which it was not handled.[19]

In 1913 Perkins had been able to rally the directors to his side and to reverse the company policy of removing the Auburn twine machinery to Germany. In his attack on Cyrus McCormick in 1916 he rallied no support. Thomas W. Lamont expressed the majority viewpoint of the directors in a letter to Cyrus McCormick: "Contrary to Mr. Perkins's opinion, I don't see very well how you could have handled the whole situation any better than you have."[20]

Despite Perkins' willingness to make concessions to labor in the Harvester strikes of 1913 and 1916, he was in no sense prounion. In 1904 he had advised Cyrus McCormick that it appeared to be a good time to settle with [destroy] the unions. His attitude toward labor stemmed from his role as trust creator. A trust lived always in the shadow of government sufferance. The Harvester Corporation, after the initiation of the antitrust suit of 1911, was living by grace of the United States courts. Perkins was aware, as the operating officials were not, that the Harvester trust could not afford to jeopardize favorable public and judicial opinion through ruthless behavior of any sort. He looked upon good wages and fringe benefits as a small price to pay for the freedom to monopolize an industry. As a man of political experience and ambition, he knew that his candidates needed the labor vote as well as that of other segments of the population. The ineptness of Harvester management in 1912 and 1913 in handling labor matters had hurt Perkins and his candidate Theodore Roosevelt politically as well as endangering the trust's precarious legal position.

Perkins promoted profit-sharing programs for both U. S. Steel and International Harvester. However, his early proposals were gimmicks which he had learned in the insurance business for the purpose of rewarding executives who stayed many years with the company. He always insisted that the industrial reforms which he pushed—profit sharing and sickness compensation—arose from business motives rather than philanthropic ones. He cannot be correctly labeled a "reformer" but he did have a much broader appreciation of the public responsibilities of business than did most of his colleagues.

Both Perkins and Cyrus McCormick were members and financial supporters of the National Civic Federation, Perkins being more deeply involved than McCormick. This organization attempted to promote recognition of unions by employers; it offered its services for mediation and arbitration of strikes; and it served as a forum for discussion of the wide variety of employer welfare proposals. It is interesting that both Perkins and McCormick, despite their personal and financial commitments to the Federation, flatly rejected its basic principles in dealing with labor in their own corporations.

Labor relations was a series of crises for the rest of 1916–19. There was no special welfare or labor relations department. Welfare and labor relations work was being handled by the line officials, already overburdened with difficult war production problems.[21] Nothing new in welfare or labor relations could even be attempted. Vice President Harold McCormick spent much of the war in Switzerland attempting to salvage what he could of the company's foreign operations. Assistant General Manager Alex Legge was loaned to the government to aid in food procurement. Cyrus McCormick personally shouldered the added burdens for the duration of the war. At the request of President Wilson he participated in an important presidential mission to Russia.

Despite the press of war production problems, labor relations could not be kicked under the rug. Given impetus by a tightening labor market and the friendly Wilson Administration, union membership zoomed upward. A national membership of 2,500,000 in 1915 had doubled by 1920. Strikes came with increasing frequency and hit an all-time national record in 1919 for the percentage of workers participating. To firms like International Harvester with an avowed antiunion policy, the increasing tempo of trade union activities called for extreme vigilance. The 1916 strike and Perkins' criticism caused the company throughout the rest of the war to pursue the policy of heading off labor trouble by granting wage increases before strikes materialized. Writing to his brother Harold on the handling of labor problems in the spring of 1917, Cyrus declared, "We are carefully considering every point daily with our Manufacturing men."[22]

The rising cost of living, the tight labor market, and the threat of unionism brought wage increases twice a year during the war period. So critical was the threat of unionism that Cyrus McCormick privately broke with his long-time friend and classmate Woodrow Wilson over the President's support of the Adamson Eight-Hour Law for railroad workers and his general encouragement of trade unionism. Cyrus' quiet vote for Hughes in 1916 is an indication of how deeply he felt on the issue of trade unionism. Not only had the McCormick family traditionally been Democrats, but Cyrus as a Princeton alumnus had kept in close touch with Wilson during the latter's presidency at Princeton. In the national presidential campaign of 1912, as we have seen, McCormick had offered financial support—even though the offer was turned down. The break with Wilson in 1916 had nothing to do with foreign policy: writing to his brother Harold, Cyrus said of Wilson, ". . . he has alienated almost the entire business community because of the way he openly espoused the cause of labor and yielded to the threats of labor leaders."[23]

Despite its vigilance International Harvester became entangled in the upsurge of trade unionism accompanying the end of the war. In July of 1919 the McCormick Works, which had twice voted down the company's proposed system of employee representation, went out on strike. Three months later the company's Wisconsin Steel Works in South Chicago went out on strike in conjunction with the national steel strike of that period. McCormick Works pickets shut down other Chicago plants of the company; but in both the implement strikes and the steel strike Harvester steadfastly refused to make concessions to the unions. Though plants were closed for about a month in the case of both strikes, management would not meet with union committees. As in earlier strikes, employee rolls were purged of workers who had taken an active role in union leadership. Attributing the strike vaguely to "radicals," the company's public statement at the time of the July implement strike declared: "No demands were made by the employees or have since been presented. The average hourly wages at this plant have increased 114% since June, 1914. In the absence of information to the contrary, the Company is inclined to attribute today's action to the prevalent spirit of industrial unrest rather than to any specific cause."[24]

The 1919 implement strike was led by an AF of L federal labor union with its main strength in the McCormick Works. The Chicago Federation of Labor gave substantial support to the strike. Its publication, *The New Majority,* stated the goals of the strike as "recognition of the union, a shorter workday, a new wage scale and the complete elimination of all piecework."[25]

The plants were reopened in the middle of August. As in 1916 the molders showed the most militance, and it was several months before employment in the foundries reached its prestrike level. The total union defeats in the 1916 and 1919 strikes ended active unionism at Harvester plants for many years and gave the company an aura of invincibility. It was to be twenty-two years before Harvester employees again challenged the absolute company power.

7

Employee Representation

Origin

From the viewpoint of American management the labor relations climate at the end of World War I was menacing. The Russian Revolution and uprisings in Hungary and Germany put American industrialists on edge. They generalized the anti-German feeling of the war into a broad anti-foreignism augmented by the anti-Red hysteria. These fears caused them to turn against their own employees, who, spurred by inflation, high demand for labor, and a relatively sympathetic government policy toward collective bargaining, were aggressively demanding union recognition and improved wages. In 1919 20.8 percent of the nation's workers were involved in strikes, a figure which is still the national record 50 percent above 1946, the next highest year.[1]

Chicago was one of the centers of this labor unrest. On July 19, 1919, the *Chicago Evening Post* ran the following front-page account of strikes then in progress: ". . . 10,000 . . . at the big packing plants . . . 115,000 building trades workers are idle . . . 5,000 workers of the Corn Products Company . . . 5,000 employees of the Standard Steel Car Company . . . 65,000 factory workers of the Crane Company . . . 5,000 workers at the International Harvester Company . . . 249 fire department engineers have resigned . . . ." Later the same year the Chicago area steel mills went on strike in connection with the national steel strike of 350,000 workers.

In 1914 and 1915 the McCormicks had loaned industrial relations know-how and personnel, in the form of Clarence Hicks, to the Rockefellers, hard pressed by the tragic dispute at Ludlow. But the war brought a resumption of labor troubles at International Harvester, and it was now Rockefeller who in 1918 came to the aid of the McCormicks by releasing Arthur H. Young of the Colorado Fuel and Iron Company to head a newly established industrial relations department at International Harvester.

Young shrewdly anticipated the strike holocaust of the postwar period. As early as October 1918 he called in his mentor at Colorado Fuel, the internationally famous labor relations consultant McKenzie King, whose novel and ingenious "company union" plan had succeeded in rescuing the Rockefellers from the United Mine Workers. Together they drew up for International Harvester a slightly modified version of the Colorado Fuel plan. As the postwar strike activity began to crackle like fire around International Harvester, this plan was the backfire that Young set to protect the company from advancing unions.

This company union, formally entitled the Harvester Industrial Council and referred to as the "Works Council" in each local plant, was announced without warning to Harvester employees on March 10. Voting on its adoption took place in all plants only two days later. Employees in seventeen of the company's twenty plants approved the new plan. Three Chicago plants rejected it. Petitions for new elections were circulated in these three plants, and on the repeat elections the works councils were approved in two of the three. The huge McCormick Works, where an AF of L federal labor union had a following, continued to reject the Industrial Council Plan until 1921. Adoption of the works councils initiated twenty-two years of employee representation at International Harvester.

The haste with which these adoption elections were conducted, and their being managed by supervisory employees on company property, make it doubtful that the outcome was a valid indication of employee feeling. Still more significant was the rejection of the plan by workers at three of the twenty plants. Although it carried by a vote of 1,152–712 at Wisconsin Steel, many key departments there rejected it: e.g. Nos. 2 and 4 merchant mills and the blast furnaces. The big pro–works council vote throughout most of the plants was actually built from overwhelming majorities in departments which were salaried and management-oriented: office, storeroom, restaurant, labor and safety; civil engineers, draftsmen, watchmen.

Of historic interest are three company statements of purposes in establishing the Industrial Council Plan. One is the public statement addressed to the employees:

> The directors and officers of the Company have for some time been working out a plan to establish closer relations between the employes and the management. To this end they now offer the following Harvester Industrial Council plan for the consideration of the employes, hoping it may meet with their approval.
>
> The Plan provides for a "Works Council" in which representatives elected by the employees shall have equal voice and vote with the management in the consideration of matters of mutual interest.
>
> It guarantees to every employe the right to present any suggestion, request, or complaint and to have it promptly considered and fairly decided. Provision is also made for impartial arbitration.
>
> Should this plan be adopted by vote of the employes, the officers pledge their best efforts to carry it out in letter and spirit.
>
> It is my hope and belief that the plan, if adopted, will materially strengthen our relations in the work we have in common, and will make for the greater contentment and well-being of us all.[2]

Here President McCormick makes clear that the entire initiative came from management. The ostensible purpose was "to establish closer relations between the employes and the managment," and to guarantee prompt grievance settlements, including impartial arbitration.

The second statement of purpose elaborates on the first; it is a refutation of an accusation at the 1919 AF of L convention that the numerous company unions being adopted were intended to prevent real collective bargaining with an AF of L union. Vice President Cyrus McCormick III specifically denied this charge for the Harvester Company in October 1919:

> So far as trade unionism is concerned our friends of the American Federation of Labor have mistaken the trend of employee representation. In the very important convention held at Atlantic City in June of this year, there were adopted elaborate resolutions condemning employee representation, on the ground that elections were unfair; that democratic organization was not permitted; that the committeemen were intimidated, and that an employee in pleading his case could not have the aid of an expert walking delegate to help him marshal his facts. No one who, as I have done, has sat through meeting after meeting of a Works Council, could believe that any one of these charges is justifiable. The basic object of organized labor is to improve the condition of workmen through collective bargaining. Without doubt this was necessary in the past, and is possibly [s]till necessary in many cases, but now with employee representation, working sincerely and successfully,

organized labor should welcome it as an ally which is seeking the same fine result and achieving it with more immediate and intimate satisfaction than is possible for an organization not controlled by the men of any factory themselves. Employee representation has not been set up in opposition to organized labor. It is not an endeavor to create company unions or to do anything to deprive the men of the results which long years of industrial history have secured for them.[3]

McCormick went on to eulogize the Industrial Council Plan as a step toward sharing management with labor and a movement comparable in politics to the growth of democratic government: ". . . the most significant feature in labor conditions of the day is the expressed desire of labor to share in the management of business. There is a close parallel existing between the movement in favor of employee representation and the growth of democratic government. . . . until recent years our industrial system was . . . a benevolent despotism." He gave one further reason for some employers [but presumably not the Harvester Company] being interested in employee representation: "Syndicalism has made such rapid strides in Eastern Europe that some men, not recognizing the fundamental solidarity of the American people are afraid that this country is about to deliver itself to Bolshevism; . . . ."

A third, and conflicting, statement of purpose in setting up the Industrial Council Plan is a letter from Arthur H. Young to President Cyrus McCormick II written in November 1918, three and a half months before the plan was unveiled. Here, while the plan was being formulated, Mr. Young explains in detail its antiunion potentialities.

Recently in a discussion of the subject of Industrial Relations, the question of the advisability of the announcement *at this time* of such a Plan as we have contemplated was brought up, the suggestion being made that it might possibly be to our advantage to wait for a period (of say six months) when, if present indications materialize, the labor supply will be much more plentiful, and reception of such a Plan consequently regarded less in the light of a concession to an implied demand.

It was suggested that possibly any radical action by our company at this time might be capitalized by organized labor as indicative of a general stampede on the part of employers.

I feel very strongly that, if we contemplate going ultimately to the adoption of the Plan we have discussed, it would be unwise to delay much farther in the announcement of our action. It may be true that, six months from now, labor will be more plentiful, but on the other hand it may also be true that conditions will be less unsettled in that period, and that a condition of unemployment will possibly bring with it greater anarchical and "bolshevik" activities than has before attended similar periods. I feel certain that the activities of the labor organizers will be much more radical in character, now that the war is over, than they have been heretofore. Furthermore, there is a greater need for the adoption of clearer statements of fair and democratic principles by leading industries, because such pronouncements will serve as beacons on the very turbulent sea of industrial relations existing just now. If we withhold action and make no move to combat the efforts of labor agitators and anarchistic workers, it is certain that some of our empolyes will be influenced by their propaganda. And I think that the general condition of society is such that there is a distinct danger, because of the world-wide unrest of what we popularly term the "working classes."

I still feel that our Industrial Relations Plan, as now developed, would have a distinctly stabilizing effect in our own organization, and in addition would contribute materially to the national welfare.[4]

In this argument for the employee representation plan, the major objective appears to have been to "combat the efforts of labor agitators and anarchistic workers." "Democratic principles" are offered as a reason for its adoption but they are subordinate to fear of the "working classes" and the wish to forestall action by "organized labor."

Organized labor indeed had a foothold in the Harvester Company. Two of the main Chicago plants had substantial AF of L membership: at the McCormick Works an AF of L federal local was already in existence, with considerable employee support; at the Wisconsin Steel Works in Chicago's South Side the AF of L's nationwide steel organizing drive of 1919 was gaining recruits. Both of these plants were among the four Chicago Harvester plants to suffer prolonged strikes within the year.

The Harvester Industrial Council Plan

A summary of the Harvester Industrial Council Plan, as given in *Decisions and Orders of the NLRB,* is quoted below:

The Plan provided for a "Works Council" composed of representatives of the employees and representatives of the management. The employee representatives are elected by the employees, the plant being divided into voting divisions, each entitled to one representative. Nomination of candidates and election of representatives are by secret ballot. All employees, except foreman, assistant foreman and salaried employees, are eligible to vote. Employee representatives must be citizens of the United States, at least 21 years of age, and must have been employed at the plant for at least one year immediately prior to nomination. The management representatives, not to exceed in number the employee representatives, are appointed by the management. Provision is made for filling vacancies in the Works Council and for the recall of employee representatives. The Works Council holds regular monthly meetings. The Manager of the respondent's Industrial Relations Department, or his designee, acts as Chairman of the Works Council; the Secretary is appointed by the plant Superintendent. Chairman and Secretary have no vote. When a vote is necessary the management representatives vote as a unit and the employee representatives as a unit, the majority determining the vote of the unit. The vote shall be secret unless otherwise ordered by the Council. If the Council reaches an agreement on any matter, its recommendation is referred to the plant Superintendent for his approval or disapproval. The Superintendent, if he deems the matter of such importance as to require the attention of the general officers, shall refer it to the respondent's President. The latter may either approve the recommendation or utilize the same procedure as in the case of a tie vote. In case of a tie vote not resolved by further discussion, the matter may be referred to the President, who may either propose a settlement or refer the matter to a General Council. If a proposed settlement is not satisfactory to the employee representatives, the President may likewise refer the matter to a General Council. If the President does not so refer the matter, or if the vote of the General Council is a tie, the President and a majority of the employee representatives may mutually agree to submit the matter to arbitration. The General Council is composed of employee representatives chosen by the employee representatives in the various plants designated by the President as being interested in the matter, and of appointed management representatives.

The Works Council may investigate, consider and make recommendations on all questions relating to working conditions, protection of health, safety, wages, hours of labor, recreation, education and similar matters of mutual interest to employer and employees. It may appoint sub-committees, with employee representatives and management representatives having equal voting power, whenever such committees are deemed necessary. Provision is made for the manner in which an employee may have a matter brought before the Works Council. The respondent is to provide a meeting place for the Council. Employee representatives shall receive their regular pay from the respondent while on Works Council business. The Plan may be amended by a majority vote of employee representatives and a majority vote of the management representatives. The adoption or rejection of an amendment shall not be the subject of arbitration. The Plan may be terminated, after six months' notice, by a majority vote of the employees or by the Board of Directors of the respondent.[5]

The Harvester plan differed from that of the Colorado Fuel and Iron Company principally in exerting closer management supervision, and in permitting arbitration only with company permission. Local meetings of employee representatives were held in the presence of management representatives. In the Colorado Fuel plan employee representatives normally met by themselves, except for quarterly meetings of representatives of all plants with top management; employees were also permitted to resort to arbitration in case of disagreement with management.

In one important respect the Harvester plan was the more democratic. In the Harvester works councils unit voting of the employee group and the employer group prevailed. In the Colorado Fuel plan if one employee representative voted with a solid management, his would be the controlling vote.

Other significant elements of the Harvester plan were as follows:

1. *Powers of the council.* Theoretically the council could only recommend action to the superintendent; but since under the unit rule no action could be passed without management's affirmative vote, the recommendation of the council was tantamount to enactment.

2. *Scope of the council.* The scope of the council was as wide or narrow as management wished. On occasion the councils were asked to make far deeper invasions into management prerogatives than was customary for unions of that day; and yet often they were limited to after-the-fact announcement of management's decision. In practice the council had no exclusive power.

3. *Veto power of management.* Management held the veto power over employee proposals. If management and labor representatives of a works council, each voting as a unit, failed to agree, the only appeal was to the company president. Arbitration was possible only by mutual agreement. There were no cases of any matter referred to arbitration, nor, in the councils studied,[6] of employee representatives ever requesting it.

4. *The isolation of employees.* The plan seems to have been carefully designed to keep rank-and-file employees from ever getting together. It made no provision for any employee meetings. Employee representatives, elected by plant departments, had no written right to call a meeting of their constituents. Even nomination of employee representatives occurred without a meeting.

No provision was made for separate meetings of employee representatives, except that during council meetings they might withdraw temporarily to meet in private. In practice some of the council employee representatives did meet regularly. Those at Wisconsin Steel Works met privately at least once each month on company time and pay. The Tractor Works employee representatives met regularly but with the plant superintendent present.

The plan effectively isolated Harvester employees by plant. Joint meetings of representatives from all Harvester plants could be called only by the president of the company. In all the years of the plan he exercised this right only once, in December 1919, on the occasion of the adoption of several minor amendments to the plan.

5. *Composition of the council.* Originally the employee side of the works council included both salaried white-collar and blue-collar employees. The votes of the white-collar employees had been needed in getting the plans adopted in 1919. By 1923 management philosophy had evolved to the point where Harvester executives decided that such salaried employees should be treated as management and separated from the hourly paid workers. When Vice President H. F. Perkins learned of the proposed transfer of professional and clerical forces to the management side of the works council he was alarmed lest the change "would unduly strengthen the employee group."[7] Upon being assured that this would not be the case, he approved the change. At two plants where perhaps the councils were already considered too strong, an exception was made and the salaried departments were left in the employee unit.

Thus, far from being self-governing democratic bodies where equals dealt with equals, the works councils were intentionally kept weak and dependent. One decision by top management, such as the removal of white-collar departments from the employee side of the councils, could bring about a unified management policy in every works council. Employees under the Harvester plan, separated in twenty-five plants without communication with each other, never could exhibit the common unified front that management always displayed. Management's manipulation of the councils went to such lengths that in getting works council approval of the transfer of the white-collar departments it was able to have the employee groups in the various works councils inaugurate the proposal, which, the works managers were told, "is management's desire."[8]

Harvester Strikes of 1919 and the Entrenchment of the Works Councils

While the works councils were a protection from unions, to the surprise of the company they were no protection from demands for wage increases. The new works councils deluged the company with these. Vice President Cyrus McCormick III described this period:

> In the beginning it was quite natural that the first demands were all for large increases in wages. The plan passed successfully a very severe test when it had to be explained to the men, through their representatives, that the financial condition of the Company and of the business were not such as to justify a flat increase of wages. Later, when the cost of living rose again, as it did last summer [1919], the question was again brought up, and this time the management representatives accepted the point of view of the employee representatives just as sincerely and fairly as in the beginning the latter had accepted the view of the former. The International Harvester Company, since the inception of its plan of employee representation, has never held back any information from the men. Business policies have been discussed and figures shown which it was our former custom to keep secret.[9]

Just how these early requests for wage increases were handled by the works councils may be seen from the minutes of the Wisconsin Steel council.[10] At its second meeting (April 1919) the first item of business was a request for a wage increase presented by employee representative Shupnick. The sparse minutes report that after some discussion and a private caucus of employee representatives "a motion was made and seconded that Mr. Shupnick be allowed to withdraw his proposition, for the time being, in order that the matter could be given further consideration by Mr. Shupnick's constituents. Motion carried unanimously. Mr. Shupnick then withdrew the proposition."[11] This is the last reference to this wage increase request. The minutes of the next meeting merely mention Mr. Shupnick's resignation as employee representative but give no hint as to the cause. Mr. Shupnick's mysterious fate, however, did not discourage other wage increase proposals. At the next meeting, May 1919, two employee representatives submitted a new proposal for an eight-hour day for dayworkers, who were then working a ten-hour day. The proposal called for nine hours' pay plus a 16.5 percent wage increase. The purpose of the proposal was to give dayworkers the eight-hour day that had been given to shift workers in 1918. The matter was ably presented by employee representative Kelso and thoroughly discussed. Industrial Relations Director Young forcefully summed up the management case:

In balloting, if this goes to a deadlock, and we are unable to get a decision in this council, it must be referred to the President as a wage demand from all employes. The officers will realize it as a labor demand over and above union rates; over and above similar rates in similar industries, we are asked to do something pretty nearly out of reach.

I look forward to the actual 8-hour day as much as you do, and would put my shoulder behind a fair and square movement affecting the whole industry. I come here as a spokesman from the General Office. I do not take the position here in preference to the Superintendent. I am not neutral. I feel this is an improper request, and at that, I have not made a single unfair statement.[12]

The secret ballot on the wage increase showed

	For	*Against*
Management representatives	0	15
Employee representatives	9	6

However, while the matter was pending, awaiting presidential action to resolve the deadlock, a special council meeting was called to reconsider. A so-called rank-and-file committee of employees appeared before the council to demand withdrawal of the wage increase proposal. Somehow this unofficial committee had been permitted by management to conduct a special vote among employees of certain departments on whether or not the proposal should be withdrawn. The officially elected employee representatives seeking a wage increase were thus not only strongly opposed by top management, but harassed by an unofficial worker committee that joined with management to block a wage increase at this time. A motion to reconsider the wage increase passed with the following close vote:

	For	*Against*
Management representatives	14	0
Employee representatives	8	7

On the unit rule reconsideration carried 2–0. After more vigorous discussion and a private employee caucus, the orginal motion favoring a wage increase was again voted on. The results were:

	For	*Against*
Management representatives	0	13
Employee representatives	8	7

By the unit rule the result was a 1–1 tie, thus kicking the matter up to the president of the company for decision.

Harold McCormick, president since 1918, resolved the tie vote promptly. Appearing at a special Wisconsin Steel council meeting only one week later, he reversed the position of Industrial Relations Director Young and the Works management representatives, and granted the employees' request almost *in toto.* This meant an eight-hour day and a substantial wage increase for 25 percent of Wisconsin Steel's work force.

There is no evidence to indicate why Harold McCormick reversed his industrial relations department. This was no doubt one of the first wage requests to reach him under the Industrial Council Plan, and the company had a good deal to gain by winning the employees' confidence in the plan. At the Steel Works the outside unions participating in the AF of L steel-organizing drive were serious rivals for employee loyalty. In presenting his arguments in favor of the wage increase, employee representative Kelso had declared, "I have the honor of working with a department that has a union organization."[13] Or, President McCormick, who was proud of the company's leadership in employee welfare, may have seen this request for an extension of the eight-hour day as a logical continuation of this leadership.

Other works council requests for general wage increases in the agricultural implement industry were withdrawn by council representatives or refused by the company; but by mid-July of 1919 the pressure of the rising cost of living and of competing outside unionism led management to grant agricultural implement workers a 10 percent adjustment. The next day the AF of L federal labor union at the McCormick Works went on strike. Pickets from the McCormick Works closed down the other Chicago Harvester plants except for the Wisconsin Steel Works, idling 11,500 workers.[14]

At the conclusion of the July–August agricultural implement strikes Harvester management gave its works councils a power which was destined to enthrone them for a generation. First at the Tractor Works and then at other plants, striking employees who wanted to return to work were interviewed and interrogated by a Works Council committee. This committee held the power of life or death over the workers' employment. At the Tractor Works, management made this unprecedented grant of power to the employee representatives of the council alone.[15] Never before nor since has the company permitted tenure of employment to be determined by an employee group.

At the Wisconsin Steel Works, whose employees joined the nationwide steel strike in the fall of 1919, this power of determining who would be permitted to return to work was exercised jointly by the employee and management representatives of the Works Council. At no time did the employee representatives ask for this power; it was thrust upon them by plant superintendent G. E. Rose.

This power was first established at the Wisconsin Steel Works in the course of discharging from the Works Council employee representative Jensen, who was also a member of the Union of Structural Iron Workers. As a union member, Jensen did not report for work on the opening day of the strike; but since the plant was shut down by noon, he was willing to enter to attend the Works Council meeting held on the second day of the strike. Superintendent Rose confronted the council with the question of striker Jensen's presence:

> Last Wednesday we had a meeting of the Council and decided to go ahead and operate the plant. . . . as I take it, that meant that the council expected every man to be here Monday morning, . . . and therefore anyone who was expected here, but absented himself, was violating the Council's instructions and therefore must be recommended by the Council for re-instatement before he can again be considered an employee of this plant.
>
> I believe we have present here this morning in the Council meeting, one representative who was not present for duty Monday morning. Before we can proceed at this meeting, the Council must take action in his case.[16]

Rose's remarks contained several incongruities. First, the Works Council had not decided to operate the plant in the event of a strike. The week before the strike Superintendent Rose announced that a new blast furnace was ready to be blown in. He asked the council whether it thought, in the light of a possible strike, that this should be done. Since the council had never been consulted on such a problem before, no employee representative dared to voice opposition. The Works Council did vote to blow in the furnace. There was nothing in the motion about operating the plant in case of a strike. Dismissal of employees who failed to report for work on the day of the strike was entirely Superintendent Rose's idea. Secondly, under the constitution of the works councils, the only way council member Jensen could be removed from office was by a two-thirds vote of his constituents.

Management escaped these dilemmas with a single proposal: Jensen and all employees who had failed to report for work on the morning of the strike had automatically resigned from employment, unless the council recommended their rehiring.[17] Severing Jensen's employment at Harvester would automatically remove him from the Works Council. In the discussion the employees were reluctant to assume this power but were pushed on by Rose. A high degree of intimidation is indicated by the fact that the voice vote to dismiss representative Jensen and the other striking employees was unanimous although among the employee representatives voting on this proposal were three other union members who were themselves subsequently dismissed. Thus the power to hire and fire strikers was given to the Wisconsin Steel Works Council.

In order to put before the employees an image of a powerful Works Council, the company throughout the strike maintained that it was the council which ordered management to operate or to close the plant. In the council sessions, held daily during the steel strike, Superintendent Rose had to explain their vast power again and again to the astounded employee representatives:

> . . . as I see it . . . the Council ordered this plant to run at its meeting Wednesday, Sept. 17; the management on instruction from the Council endeavored to run the Plant straight through until the Council took other action which it took last Monday, Sept. 22nd, instructing to close down the plant even though there were 75% of the men supposed to be here on the job. . . . The Council decided to close down on account of threatened violence . . . all that is necessary for the Council to order resumption is [for management] to be informed by the members of the Council that the employees of this plant no longer fear to come or go from work. . . .[18]
>
> This Council can put the operation of the plant on the "bum" entirely if it wants to. That's the responsibility this Council has and I have only one vote as a member of this Council, just simply a member . . . As Superintendent of the plant I feel it my duty . . . to run the plant as far as the question of employment is concerned, in accordance with the instruction of the Council. . . . The constitution explicitly states that this Council is concerned in the shaping of the policy of management with regard to employment.[19]

This picture of a powerful Works Council was true only in the sense that it had some power derived from management. Despite Rose's claim, the council minutes reveal no vote ordering the company to operate during the steel strike, although the matter was discussed informally by the council a few days before the strike. So far as closing the plant is concerned, during the first morning of the strike, Monday, September 22, 1919, the Works Council did vote to close the plant, but not until it was already plain that too few men were on hand to operate even had the company wished.

During the strike the company used the Works Council to build up sentiment for a back-to-work movement. Employee representatives were urged to visit workers' homes and urge a return to work. Daily Works Council meetings were spent interrogating employee representatives as to just how soon employee sentiment might support a back-to-work movement. In this endeavor it would appear that management was badly deceived. Three of fifteen employee representatives were apparently secret union members. Daily they reported that the workers were afraid to return to work. Their deceit perhaps delayed by a week or two the Works Council vote to resume operations. The company, having maintained the fiction that an employee vote had closed down the plant at the beginning of the strike, could hardly open without a favorable council vote. When Superintendent Rose really wanted to reopen the plant he went all out with a patriotic motif to bludgeon the council into voting for it:

> I'd like to say, gentlemen, that before we do retire it seems to me this strike condition has taken quite a different angle within the last week. When it was first called, it was perhaps called by American unions, with Americans in control. I believe we can all see that this matter is getting around into the hands of people that are pretty Bolshevik in their ideas, and that it is attracting the attention of the American government, that is the Federal government. I just submit this to you as members of this council to think about. I think we are getting into a situation where a man with good red American blood in his veins will not want to be identified with them. You may have different thoughts on it; I think it is a good thing to consider at any rate. Of course, we as a council here, I take it every man here to be a good red-blooded American, and I believe this organization has energy and force, and of course, we can't sit idly by until this whole thing is calmed throughout the whole country and here in this district. If we do, we are not doing our duty as a council organization in American industry, just consider as to what will be our situation, or how we will be viewed as an industrial organization by a great majority of people of the country if we simply sit idly by in a situation like this. Put that up to yourselves; I do not care what organization you belong to outside of this council organization. Just put it up to yourselves, and decide for yourselves.[20]

The voice vote following this speech was unanimous to proceed to set a date for the plant reopening. To open the plant an announcement signed not by the company but by the Works Council was sent to all employees at their homes. When many workers still refused to come back the Works Council sent out the following letter:

TO EMPLOYES OF THE WISCONSIN STEEL WORKS:

We, the Works Council, acting as we believe for the best interest of the employes, recommended that the plant be closed down September 22d. Again, acting upon the expressions received in replies to our letter of October 1st, we recommended the resumption of operations Monday morning, October 13th.

Up to the present time the Works Council has recommended the operations of the plant be carried on with old employes. A number of new men have been inquiring for jobs and the Council has felt that it was only fair and just to hold your jobs for you.

However, some of you have given us no indication that you intend or desire to return to work. Therefore, in justice to those who have returned, and in recognition of their expressed desires for effective operation, we feel it proper to notify you that unless you return to work by noon of (date——) we shall feel free to instruct the Employment Department to fill your job.

After that date former employes will be considered as on the same basis as new applicants and, therefore, to secure a job in this plant must be rehired through the Employment Department.

We wish to say to you however, that it is the earnest desire of all Works Council members that our plant continue its operation with the same employes who have successfully operated it in the past.

WORKS COUNCIL
of
WISCONSIN STEEL WORKS

By C. M. BRADING,
Secretary, Works Council.[21]

The council had already been delegated the job of passing on the re-employment rights of all workers who failed to report for work on the opening day of the strike. This letter setting a deadline for return to work handed the council the additional task of passing on re-employment for all who remained off the job past the deadline.

A special Works Council committee on employment then spent several weeks reviewing loyalty records of employees. In view of the desperate need for workers, strikers were generally forgiven if they appeared personally before this committee and gave a pledge of allegiance to the council. Exceptions were a list of "intimidators" supplied by the company. Even one of the "intimidators," an old employee with a good record, was reinstated after a written apology. He had declared that the "whole electrical department were scabs." Before the committee he recanted completely, declaring, "I was a damn fool, and the Electrical Department was right."[22] Some strikers were completely reinstated. Others were taken on as new employees, losing pension and welfare coverage.

By the end of November 1919 the fratricidal duties of the Works Council's employment committee were finished. Minutes of the proceedings, including names of strikers asking for clemency, were printed and passed out to all employees. But a proposal to discharge the committee was blocked by a management representative who declared, "Instead of discharging this committee, I'd like to make a motion that the committee be continued. I do believe there are a good many times when it will be a good idea to talk to certain individuals."[23] Superintendent Rose then moved that "the Committee on Employment be made a permanent committee and have authority to deal with all violators of Council orders in regard to employment . . . ."[24] The council minutes passed out to each employee put all workers on notice that the Works Council permanently held the power of life or death over job tenure.

The Works Councils during Inflation

The year 1920 was a banner one for Harvester works councils. The complete defeat of the AF of L strikes in the Chicago agricultural implement plants and in the Wisconsin Steel Works, together with the company grant to the councils of power over re-employment of strikers, established the councils as formidable organizations.

In the early years the councils appear to have represented primarily the aristocracy of workers. The council constitution restricted employee representatives to American citizens, yet at Wisconsin Steel 50 percent of the workers were foreign born, most of them not naturalized.[25] At the Tractor and McCormick plants the proportion of noncitizens was even higher. During the anti-foreign hysteria of the period, the privileged American-born employee representatives were more likely to find common cause with management. This was especially true at Wisconsin Steel after the 1919 strike had purged union members from the council. Throughout 1920, a year of inflation, there was not one request at Wisconsin Steel for a wage increase, though on management's initiative a 10 percent raise was handed out on February 1 to match a similar increase in the entire steel industry. Instead the council busied itself with such activities as running contests for vegetable gardens and home yard beautification, elaborate prizes going to the winners; with cutting living costs by getting the company to buy and resell to employees jams, potatoes, and 25,000 men's suits made in England; running an interdepartmental baseball league; recruiting citizenship classes among Harvester's many foreign-born workers; and helping management explain, particularly to the foreign-born, the 1920 version of Harvester's profit-sharing plan, known as the "extra compensation" plan. Council members accompanied this last endeavor with pleas for increased productive effort, for greater efforts to eliminate waste of materials, and for less loitering: ". . . if everyone of us wasted 15 minutes a day it would be 3,000,000 hours wasted and if the average pay per employee was 50 cents per hour that would equal $1,500,000 . . . ."[26]

While these activities may seem less significant than pushing for wage increases, some of them, particularly the sale of commodities in order to evade the rising cost of living, appear to have been much appreciated by employees. Some of these ventures came to grief despite the assistance of the Harvester Company purchasing department. Many of the British-bought suits were not matched in coats and pants; there were far too many odd sizes. Several carloads of potatoes were green and inedible. And between the time of ordering and delivery, prices fell, so that employees could buy more cheaply at the stores. By far the most successful item merchandized to employees was coke from the company's own ovens.

The YMCA, one of the McCormick family's major charities, had a full-time office in the Wisconsin Steel Works, from which it recruited foreign-born workers into citizenship and English classes. The Works Council joined management in cajoling the foreign-born into enrolling and attending these classes.

The Works Council, sensing its weakness in achieving wage increases and protecting basic employee rights, seems to have compensated by doing an outstanding job on those grievances which it could handle. Such a grievance was the overcrowded condition of the streetcars. Periodically the council's committee on education and transportation would spend several days and nights in the dead of winter, on company pay, recording the exact arrival and departure time of each streetcar that passed the Works. It also recorded the seating capacity of each car, the number of passengers aboard as it took off, and the number of passengers left stranded. These facts were then used to overwhelm the transit company's arguments during the frequent requests for improved transportation.

Voting for Wage Cuts

During the prosperous years of 1919 and 1920 when it could award wage increases, the Harvester Company no doubt achieved a certain passive acceptance for its work councils. The depression of 1921–22 presented unexpected problems. How would employee representatives and employees respond to wage cuts?

Harvester plants, except the Wisconsin Steel Works, received 20 percent cuts on April 1, 1921. The Steel Works cut came a month and a half later, timed to coincide with the wage cuts in big steel. Under the constitution of the works councils, proposals for wage changes had to be put up to a vote of the council. In the Works Council of Wisconsin Steel, management began softening up the employee representatives as early as January 1921. At each meeting management would call attention to the low rate of plant operations, would cite examples of wage cuts at other plants, and imply that the only way to get the men more hours of work was to become "competitive"—which implied cutting prices and wages. In April the council was told how cooperatively other Harvester councils had approved wage cuts. Out of councils at twenty plants only two had been ungracious enough not to support the wage reduction unanimously.[27] On May 9, 1921, plant superintendent Rose explained to a special council meeting the details of the proposed cut. Industrial Relations Director A. H. Young was on hand to emphasize the falling cost of living, the tumbling income of the Harvester Company's farm customers, and the high hourly wages of the Wisconsin Steel workers. After considerable speechmaking by management and a few innocuous questions by two employee representatives, a management representative moved the 20 percent cut. The employee representatives then withdrew for a 20-minute caucus. They returned and amended the motion to make the cut 15 percent. After more haranguing by management a secret ballot was taken. The employee representatives voted 13–3 for the 15 percent amendment; management voted 15–0 against. No sooner was the vote announced than an employee representative jumped up to move "that the employee representatives accept the 20 percent cut unanimously."[28] A voice vote was then taken on the original management motion to cut wages 20 percent. It carried unanimously. The reason for this quick capitulation was that Young had met with the employee representatives during their caucus and explained the inevitable outcome should the matter be sent to the company president.[29] The 15 percent amendment had been merely a prearranged face-saving gesture to aid in relations with their constituents.

This willingness of the employee representatives to vote for a wage cut was one of the major factors that sold the council plan to top management. The moment the Wisconsin Steel employee representatives voted to cut wages, Industrial Relations Director Young, oblivious to the circumstances surrounding the vote, expressed to the council Harvester management's satisfaction with the works council plan:

> I take it there are a number of things might be said by me as to the complete satisfaction of those connected with industrial councils. There are a lot of fellows who say, "You can go along with your employe representation scheme and take the men into your confidence when everything is going good, but wait till you have to shut down the plant. Where are you going to get off at?"
>
> . . . our answer has always been that we believe both sides are playing fairly and squarely. We will get, if we come through with a fair proposition, the confidence and support of the men, and have a better understanding between the employes and management than by simply putting up notices on the bulletin boards, "Effective May 16th, there will be a reduction of 20 per cent in wages," . . . .
>
> We have had the Council in operation for more than two years, and I have spent a great deal of my time watching what we are doing and what the other fellows are doing, and I believe that if industrial peace and justice is to come that it must proceed along this line. In this way we will establish here in America industrial peace and justice.[30]

The 20 percent wage cut of May 1921 was hardly in effect before management began a new brainwashing program leading up to a second cut. This time the employee representatives held the power to block the cut: Article XIX of the constitution of the works councils prohibited wage readjustments oftener than six months. As Young interpreted it, this prohibition could be waived by a vote of employee representatives.

The president and vice president of Wisconsin Steel paid a special visit to the council on August 2. They described the vast volume of business which the company could attract with another wage cut to make the new business profitable. Building trades unions in the community were castigated for their refusal to accept wage cuts, thus holding up the cost of living and rents of Harvester workers. It was hinted that without a second wage cut the company might have to shut down completely. Employee representatives listened to speech after speech by company officials. There was no one to speak for the employees.

The employee representatives then recessed for a special meeting of their group and passed a resolution agreeing to waive the six-months rule if the new wage cut was limited to 10 percent. Management praised the employees for their attitude but explained that the wage cut must be 27 percent for the dayworkers and 32 percent for shift workers. This was in addition to the 20 percent wage cut of May.

This drastic proposal did arouse two or three representatives to argue and protest. Some seemed resigned to anything management might propose. Most of the employee representatives were tongue-tied in the presence of management. On a secret ballot the employees representatives rejected the proposal 11–3. Management representatives voted 14–0 in favor. Superintendent Rose then asked why the employees voted against the cut. One representative blurted out, "The men come to me and say, 'Mr. Joe, better starve without working then to starve and work too.' "[31] Rose replied, ". . . looks to me as though they [top management] would be forced to close down the plant. . . . if the plant is shut down, you can feel pretty sure that it was your action that caused it."[32] At this point an employee representative moved for a second vote. Fearing for their jobs, the employee representatives reversed their vote, now favoring the 27 and 32 percent wage cuts 10–4. Management was again unanimous. The one-sided performance ended with Rose making new vows to try to get more orders. Young seems to have sensed that the situation in which the employees had been persuaded to vote themselves a second big wage cut was humiliating for them. He showed the good taste this time to spare everyone his speech on the merits of the works councils.

Despite the wage cuts, production continued to decline. During the succeeding months the cordial atmosphere in council discussions became strained, as this exchange of October 4 between the chairman of the employee representatives, L. H. Cook, and Superintendent Rose indicates:

Mr. Cook: . . . a month or six weeks ago we granted the Company all the concessions asked for. We would like to know why the Sales Department hasn't brought in more orders on the mills than we have had.

Superintendent Rose: . . . if these wages had not been cut like other Steel Companies, do you think we could have operated here as much as we did . . . ? The chances are this plant would have been shut down tight, and everybody laid off.

Mr. Cook: They probably would have been better off. Maybe some could have gotten out and got better jobs.[33]

Election of works council representatives occurred every six months, in December and June, with terms running for a year. In the election of December 1921, the first held after the two wage cuts, considerable dissatisfaction was evident at Wisconsin Steel. Not only was the turnover high as enraged workers tossed out the incumbents who had voted for wage cuts, but in two departments frustrated workers made a mockery of the election: in the Bessemer Mill department the workers elected an employee who could not read or write or speak English; in the works council district constituted of the office, laboratory, and engineering departments, the winning candidate was apparently a janitor, who immediately resigned, stating that he was not capable of representing this district. The Bessemer winner also resigned, but he could not write a resignation and was ashamed to put his "X" on a resignation. The council meeting discussed the elections and resignations with considerable resentment, and with a clear recognition that the elections were a grave slap at the entire council system.

Other districts put aggressive men in office, such as E. W. Schneider, who introduced a new mood into the Works Council. Schneider's aggressive spirit brought on a real test of management's willingness to abide by the protective clause of the council constitution, guaranteeing that employee representatives would not be discriminated against by management. He pushed hard for wage restorations. He was willing to challenge management on any issue. On one occasion he objected to approval of the minutes of the previous meeting because some remarks by the superintendent to the effect that the men ought to work harder had been deleted: ". . . such a statement," he commented, ". . . is pretty good reading for the rank and file around the Works . . . for those fellows who have a straw boss standing over them the whole day long."[34]

Schneider's independent behavior particularly antagonized the foremen of the departments which he represented. When his term as council representative was up, they campaigned openly against him, instructing the men to vote for his opponent. Schneider fought back and was re-elected. At the next meeting of the Works Council he proposed an amendment to the constitution forbidding such management interference in employee elections. It did not pass, but the occasion brought forth clearcut top management repudiation of the foremen's interference. Not only did the offending foremen write a letter of apology to the council, but Superintendent Rose henceforth at the time of each employee election sent a special warning to all management personnel to keep hands off the election.

Wage Restorations, 1922–23

The defeat of wage-cutting representatives in the council elections and the independent spirit of men like Schneider stiffened the backbone of the employee representatives on the council. They began a series of demands for wage increases, moving on May 2, 1922, for a 20 percent raise.

The secret ballot taken after considerable discussion showed employee representatives voting 16–0 for the increase and management 12–0 against it. Under the constitution this meant a 1–1 tie, to be resolved by the company president upon request of either party. The employees voted to refer the matter to the president. Ten days later Harold McCormick, president, and Alexander Legge, vice president, appeared at a special Wisconsin Steel Works Council session. McCormick stated that the company's answer was "No" to the wage request but that if the request were deferred from May 26 to July 5 the company could give it further and perhaps more favorable consideration. The council, somewhat overawed by the presence of such eminent men, as well as convinced by the logic of their reasoning, voted for deferral.

A week later all Harvester employees received the discouraging news that the company unilaterally was cutting their pension benefits. No longer could 20-year men retire before age 65. Pensions which had been based on 1.5 percent of average compensation for the last ten consecutive years were dropped to 1.25 percent. Minimum pensions were cut from $30 a month to $27. This pension cut was merely a matter of information; it was not discussed nor was the council consulted.

This cut is an example of the frequent bypassing of the council on important matters of worker welfare. The employee representatives could have little assurance of the scope of council powers: at times enormous problems, such as the re-employment of strikers, were dropped in their laps; at other times they were ignored.

The company came to a decision on the wage increase request sooner than July 5. At a special council meeting on June 15, 1922, the new Harvester president, Alex Legge, stated that the company would increase wages 10 percent for Wisconsin Steel employees. This raised common labor from 34 to 37½ cents an hour. Workers in Harvester's agricultural implement plants received no general raise until February 12, 1923.

Instead of being pleased, the employee representatives, to the consternation of the industrial relations department, voted to reject the offer on the ground that 10 percent was a pittance which would scarcely help. After much discussion they decided to delay acceptance or rejection while they consulted with their constituents. The new meeting was held June 26. President Legge showed up for the third time in seven weeks. The employee representatives voted to accept the 10 percent increase, after being assured by Legge that if the steel industry made any adjustments of more than 10 percent the Harvester Company would immediately match them, waiving the six-months rule. On September 1 the Harvester Company brought the increase up to 20 percent to match the steel industry raise of that date. This brought the rate for day labor at Wisconsin Steel to 40½ cents an hour.

This partial wage restoration of September 1, 1922, did not satisfy employees for long. On January 26, 1923, the employee representatives meeting unofficially as a committee of the council and without the presence of management agreed to present to the council a request for a new wage increase of 20 percent "to relieve the shortage of labor and . . . bring a more efficient class of workmen to our plants . . . ."[35]

Neither Superintendent Rose in a conference nor the full council meeting on February 6 could dissuade the employees from proceeding with their wage request. The secret ballot that day showed employee representatives for the raise 14–0 and management representatives 14–0 against it. The employees voted to send the matter to President Legge. In this case Legge met not with the Works Council but with the employee representatives in a specially called session. He persuaded them to abandon their request. No minutes of this meeting were printed.

Later minutes (April 16, 1923) of the council make clear that President Legge had informed the employee representatives that the steel industry was preparing a general wage increase for the very near future, and that when it occurred Harvester would match it for Wisconsin Steel employees. These minutes refer to newspaper announcements of an 11 percent raise in the steel industry. Industrial Relations Director A. H. Young and Superintendent Rose explained the matching Wisconsin Steel raise. Common labor rates went from 40½ to 45 cents an hour and other rates increased 11 percent. The council in a voice vote unanimously approved the proposed raise. This raise put common labor rates seven cents above the rates in the Harvester implement plants in Chicago, which had been raised on February 12 to 38–41 cents for light common labor and 42–45 cents for heavy common labor.

Not only were the employee representatives now pushing aggressively for wage increases, but they began circumventing the constitution to make the council more responsive to workers' needs. The only constitutional reference to employee council members meeting together is the following: "Both the Employee Representatives and Management Representatives shall have the right to withdraw temporarily from any meeting of the Works Council for private discussion of any matter under consideration."[36] This section contemplated merely brief recesses during council meetings. At Wisconsin Steel, however, as early as April 1921 employee representatives began meeting regularly, in private and at company expense, a week before each council meeting. Abbreviated minutes of these meetings were regularly printed as part of the council minutes and distributed to all employees. By 1922 these meetings had developed a cohesiveness among employee council members. No longer did they split their votes on council motions. They constituted in effect a subcommittee of the council, unique in that this committee met without the presence of management representatives. Although this body was not an official council committee it became an important source of new council business. It proposed wage increases, vacations with pay, and occasionally even reprimands for various management personnel. In fact, the employee representatives in 1923 began so to resemble a union that management attempted to squelch their group activity.

When in August 1923 the employee representatives through their private meeting passed a resolution requesting a paid vacation for all employees with a year's service, management applied the brakes. The representatives from the industrial relations department declared the resolution out of order since it was passed by an unofficial body and had not come up through the proper procedure—from individual employee to foreman to department superintendent to plant superintendent to the secretary of the Works Council, the steps prescribed by the council constitution for handling grievances. The ridiculousness of this procedure was shown up by astonished employee representatives who asked, "Don't we understand that the foremen couldn't grant us a vacation?" "If we have to see the foremen on a proposition it will take a pretty long time to settle a matter. There are a lot of foremen in the plant," and "Could a Department Superintendent give a vacation on his own hook?" Management could find no sensible answers to these questions, yet it stuck doggedly to its defense of the routine procedure. George Hodge, one of the representatives of the industrial relations department, tried to bring Wisconsin Steel procedures in line with those of other plants where the employee representatives had not gotten out of hand:

> In this connection I would state that each Council has its own little way of doing business. I think the Wisconsin Steel Works is peculiar, in that they have the minutes of the Employees Representatives' Meetings and submit them to the Council. . . . I know that in the other Councils they have not the odd procedures that you have; . . . any matters that the Employee Representatives want action on they take up with the plant superintendent, and if he says, "no," if they want to bring it up and carry it further, they go to the Secretary of the Council with the request that it be made an order of business at the next meeting.[37]

This particular request for vacations never did get formally presented. The informal discussion of it so discouraged the employee representatives that they did not carry their proposal through the many constitutional steps. These required steps also discouraged the presentation of most workers' grievances. Consequently, unlike unions today, the Works Council handled practically no grievances.

Prosperity: The Bankruptcy of the Works Councils

This curbing of the employee representatives seems to mark the beginning of the end of their militancy. The last general wage increase of the 1920's at Harvester's Wisconsin Steel Works was that of April 16, 1923. For two more years, 1924 and 1925, the employees' representatives brought in requests for additional wage increases. In both years they were refused. Never was the overwhelming advantage of management in respect to access to information more clearly demonstrated. The Harvester industrial relations department deluged the Works Council with cost-of-living and comparative wage statistics proving that Harvester workers were about the most fortunate in the country and should be thankful to avoid a cut. Moreover the company claimed it was suffering from competition of German steelmakers whose employees worked for a fourth of American wages.

The employee representatives complained that the company had more than once promised to raise wages when it reached a higher operating rate and that now was the time for it to repay the employees for their wage cuts and part-time work during the depression of 1921–22. But statistics overwhelmed the unsupported feelings of the employee representatives, who, after listening to the sad plight of the company, withdrew their motion for a wage increase. Two months after pleading poverty before its own workers the Harvester Corporation increased its common stock dividend 20 percent on the basis of the very favorable 1925 profit showing.[38]

The only vital matter of employee welfare to come up at the Works Council of Wisconsin Steel from 1926 to 1929 was the paid vacation plan. The employees had not renewed their request for a vacation plan since its rejection in 1923. This plan, however, was proposed by management before the August 1928 Works Council meeting and was instituted by the company in 1929.

During the last years of the 'twenties, 1926–29, the Works Council turned its emphasis from wages and employee welfare to joint employee-management matters. For example, its representatives took responsibility for increasing sales of company stock to employees. More and more time at council meetings was spent on safety problems. In fact almost every accident appears to have been discussed before the council. Employee representatives at Wisconsin Steel seemed glad to turn from the one-sided task of fighting management over wage levels to joining management in its concern over the standing of the plant in relation to other Harvester plants on such matters as Red Cross contributions, number of noncitizens in the work force, and purchases of Harvester stock. The detailed minutes of council meetings, which had through 1925 been filled with discussion of wage levels, proposals for shorter hours, requests for vacations, or names of reinstated strikers, now became an unbroken sequence of employee bowling scores, health tips by the company surgeon, Boy Scout contributions, and reprints of speeches by Cyrus H. McCormick III.

The employee representatives' meetings, which in the early 1920's had ignited the fireworks of wage demands and vacation plans, now atrophied. Years of frustration had reduced their discussions to trivia. Typical was the meeting of November 12, 1929. The first item on the agenda was the purchase of potatoes, onions, and Christmas candy; a representative proposed that a No. 1 Idaho Russet potato be considered. The second item of business was absenteeism from Works Council meetings. The Works Council secretary complained that in three tries he could not muster a quorum for the meeting of the committee on safety, health, and sanitation. The employee group put in the minutes of another meeting its concern over employee indifference: "The Group deeply regrets the chronic habit of some of the members in not attending the monthly meetings of the Employee Representatives, ..."[39] There was a discussion of inadequate showers and toilets. Lastly, the month's accidents were discussed; and the meeting adjourned after having been in session from 2:00 to 4:30 P.M.

While employee interest in the council was on the wane, top management after ten years of experience gave the works councils its unqualified approval. The following excerpts are taken from a speech that Vice President Cyrus McCormick III delivered in 1929 in Australia on "How USA Prevents Strikes."[40]

> There is not in America that sharp demarcation between employer and employed that is found in other countries. The young American wants to get ahead and he knows from examples all around him that the highest positions are open to energy, integrity and intelligence. . . . Everyone of our factory superintendents was once an ordinary wage-earner. I started on our payroll at eight shillings a day—to be precise, two dollars—which was at that time, I believe, the minimum wage.
>
> . . . . .
>
> From 1916 to say 1924, was a period in which American employers gave workmen an opportunity of deliberating upon and practically deciding their own destiny, through the Works Councils. . . .
>
> . . . . .
>
> The workman recognizes that his interests and those of his employer are not separate but demonstrably one and the same.
>
> Fear that the elimination of labor will mean loss of employment has been proved to be groundless. . . . That knowledge is engrained in the minds of American workmen, and that is the reason they are so interested in methods of efficiency.
>
> The Works Councils have to listen to few complaints, and what are made

are very quickly attended to. The councils are largely engaged on constructive work.

. . . . .

. . . about the working of these industrial councils. The plan provides for a Works Council at each plant . . . through which council the employees have an equal voice and vote with management . . . .

. . . there is frank "fifty-fifty" discussion and participation in the settlement of any question of mutual interest.

. . . In case of a deadlock the matter goes direct to the president of the company for settlement. No provision is made for arbitration. In practice there has been no appeal to the president since 1922,[41] as all matters have been settled at the works to the satisfaction of all concerned.

Atrophy of the Works Councils, 1929–33

Prior to 1929 the greatest failure of the councils had been their inability to capture some of the prosperity of the 1920's. Now they were to undergo a new series of trials in the economic collapse of the nation's deepest depression, 1929–33.

The subject of wages, which had vanished from the Wisconsin Steel council agenda after 1925, was reintroduced in 1931 when the company proposed a 5 percent cut for salaried employees in April and a 10 percent cut for all workers in October. After long and agonizing discussions reminiscent of those of 1921, the employees unanimously voted to accept the cuts. It is, of course, remarkable that in this depression the United States Steel Company, whose wage pattern Harvester followed for its steel plant, waited so long—two full years after the stock market crash—to cut wages of hourly employees. Once steel wages had been cut, Harvester steel employees knew that theirs would follow, as night follows day. The great bulk of Harvester employees were in the agricultural implement and truck plants. Their cuts occurred at the same time but were 15 instead of 10 percent.

In April 1932 Harvester implement workers were given a second cut, this time 10 percent, while the steelworkers were cut 15 percent a few months later in accordance with the pattern of the steel industry.

Severe economic recessions are enough to destroy the resistance to wage cuts of even powerful unions. But the second wage cut at Wisconsin Steel aroused bitter protest since it highlighted not only the Works Council's helplessness on this occasion but its gross failure to get wage increases during the years of prosperity. Ironically, on the agenda of the Wisconsin Steel council meeting just before the wage cut proposal of 1932 was a discussion of the annual Harvester financial report for 1931. With the mill operating at about 10 percent of capacity and only 25 to 30 percent of the men working at all, employee representatives stoically listened to a central office accountant describe the 1931 dividend payments of $16,759,000—fully equal to the peak payments of 1929 and 1930. These were paid out of company savings, since profits had fallen to almost zero. A month later representatives were asked to vote themselves a second wage cut of 15 percent. Employee representative E. C. Lechner gave the most serious indictment of the council: "During all the years of prosperity we didn't come to management for additional wages. We were satisfied to leave it to a fair minded management that they would see that we got a just proportion of the profits. . . . The thought I gather from conversations with my constituents is the fact that since 1923 there has been no general raise in wages and the stockholders have been deriving all the benefits."[42] Representative Lundstrom added: "In 1928 this company paid out $10,555,000 and in 1931 they increased dividends to $16,758,000 [sic]. In other words an increase of 60%. Well that looks as though that would kind of reflect on us, wouldn't it?"[43] These arguments must have carried conviction; they were followed by a slight modification in company plans. The proposed 15 percent cut was reduced to 10 percent for the three summer months of 1932, when the slackest period of steel operations was anticipated. The full 15 percent cut was then instituted in September.

The Works Council's fortunes were at an all-time low. The most important items on the agenda that summer of 1932 were an unsuccessful attempt to have the company sell Mason jars to employees and a campaign to stop pilferage of the garden plots.

In responding to company wage-cutting proposals throughout the depression, 1929–33, Harvester works councils repeated their remarkable performance of 1921 by dutifully voting to approve a series of three wage cuts for salaried employees and two wage cuts for hourly employees. Even the arguments for the 1931 wage cuts were identical with those of a decade earlier; competitors have cut wages, so in order to get more business and provide more employment Harvester must reduce prices; if the employees do not vote for a wage cut, the plant will be closed completely. With employment already drastically reduced, this threat never failed.

As management went through this tortuous process of gaining employee support for every wage cut, doubts arose about the value of the works councils. At wage-cutting time the company became entangled in the net of works councils' rules. For example, the cuts were company-wide in the truck and implement plants. Yet according to the Harvester representation plan each of the twenty-five councils individually considered and voted on these cuts. In the early days this dilemma troubled the works managers (a Harvester executive group located in the Chicago office), who debated whether or not to take wage decisions made unilaterally by management before the works councils for a vote, and, if so, how to do it so it would not look like a sham. Yet management did not trust the employees enough to bring together the representatives from all plants for purposes of wage discussions. The problem was resolved by scheduling special meetings for wage proposals at each works council so close together that the next council to meet might not learn that the same proposition had already been presented and accepted by all preceding councils. Was what the company gained from it worth the cost and trouble of maintaining this complicated works council procedure? The costs included the lost-time wage bill for all the council meetings, the salaries of highly paid executives who represented management on the councils, the expenses of the central industrial relations department of three to five men who were on a constant travel schedule attending council meetings, the secretarial and printing costs for each meeting, and the time that top executives had to spend attending crucial council meetings. Many corporations refused to be so tortured, and allowed their works councils to atrophy as soon as the success of the national antiunion drive of the early 'twenties had dispelled the danger of unionism. Several Harvester plant superintendents had proposed abolishing works councils in 1923, but management had refused to make any substantial changes in a device which had so recently saved the company from the unions. Other firms abolished their councils in the early days of the 1929–33 depression rather than again go through the expensive and unpleasant sham of getting employees to approve wage cuts.

In 1931 a Harvester superintendent at a meeting of works managers proposed discontinuing works council meetings during the period of low plant operations.[44] With the company losing money, new programs were out of the question and council meetings were little more than joint gloom-spreading sessions. The deep unemployment had brought resignation, not militancy, to the work force. Trade unionism, on which the company kept an apprehensive eye during the period of prosperity, vanished with the onset of unemployment.

But again, as in 1923, Cyrus McCormick III took a long view of the works councils. He recalled their usefulness in 1919 "in times of labor disturbances." He praised their helpfulness in the depression of 1921 and the prosperity which followed. In the current recession he expected the employee representatives to assist the foreman and superintendent in explaining to the workers the unpleasant necessity for wage cuts and severe layoffs, thus maintaining "Harvester enthusiasm" and "mutual contact." "The Representative has been elected by the workmen to represent their interests in the discussions of mutual business problems. He is a man from among the men, and his duty as a Councilman is the fair interpretation of the desires and needs of his constituents. Such a man is an absolutely necessary link between management and men."[45] The works councils were costly, but they were insurance Cyrus McCormick III would not be without.

The Councils Fight Outside Unionism, 1933–41

In 1933 Harvester management's long and expensive support of works councils through the 'twenties and early years of the depression began to be vindicated. Section 7A of the National Industrial Recovery Act, which put the Federal Government on record in favor of collective bargaining as national policy, together with the rise of trade unionism from 1933 on, made some form of collective bargaining a practical necessity. Companies without employee representation plans were forced to establish them immediately or fall prey to outside unionism. Those companies which hastily set up plans in 1933 risked having them outlawed as company dominated. Here Harvester had a great advantage: no one could claim that its works councils, in operation since 1919, had been formed to circumvent Section 7A.

The Harvester Company suddenly found itself deluged with inquiries about its works councils by other companies, which were scrambling frantically to comply with the law without dealing with or recognizing outside unions. It looked as though the Harvester works councils, with a little shoring up, might be brought into compliance with Section 7A. Industrial Relations Director George Kelday recommended certain minor changes in procedures: (1) Councils from now on were to meet regularly. Some had been skipping meetings when there was no urgent business. (2) In order to generate some rank-and-file worker support for the councils, detailed minutes were to be kept, with the comments of employee representatives reported completely. In the past some minutes had reported only management comments. (3) All minutes were to be printed in sufficient quantity to give each employee a copy. This was to replace the former practice at some plants of merely posting one copy on the bulletin board. (4) The clause in the constituition requiring all elected representatives to be citizens twenty-one years of age was to be waived to comply with the NIRA code and the Wagner Act.[46]

In addition to this artificial resuscitation of the works councils by management, a real breath of life came from the workers. Excited by Roosevelt's election, Congress' talk of new labor legislation, and the revival of unionism, the workers goaded their quiescent council representatives into action. A new aggressive spirit infused the works councils; requests for wage increases and other benefits such as improved vacations and call-in pay came thick and fast from 1933 to 1941.

At Wisconsin Steel the employee representatives pushed for wage increases, though with limited success, in July 1933, even before the NIRA steel code was adopted. They strongly urged return to the wage which had preceded the 15 percent cut of 1932. The company, after much argument, offered a lesser increase, the 15 percent raise proposed by the steel code. To the employees' rejoinder that workers had had no voice in the formulation of this steel code, Kelday replied that the workers had been represented at the NIRA code hearings in Washington by the company vice president. Though they threatened to reject the 15 percent offer, the employee representatives reluctantly accepted it on July 20.

In 1935 the Wisconsin Steel Works Council requested a 20 percent raise. Council members may have been short on research but they were long on emotion, as the following bitter expressions indicate: "How would you feel if you were making $18.80 for five days a week . . . ? And in the [company] restaurant, some of the girls earn $13.20 for five days. Do you think these people can live? They are not living, they are barely existing." "The attitude of big business in the United States in the past has been 'Never let go of a dollar until you see two more dollars coming in.' "[47]

The real pressure on the company to grant wage increases was not the bitter statements of representatives but the calculated though veiled threats by council representatives to replace the Works Council with an outside union. Since the company was diligently striving to block outside unionism during these years, this was a potent threat. It was expressed as follows in March 1935, when the employee representatives were attempting to have a 5 percent wage offer made retroactive: ". . . this request . . . is one of the most vital wage adjustments we have ever asked for, because of the simple reason that every man in the plant is looking forward to getting something in the way of a wage adjustment. If it isn't forthcoming this Works Council isn't worth half what it is cracked up to be. The less attractive this compromise is that we have written up during our recess the less prestige this Works Council is going to have when we take back to our constituents what you have given us here today. When we tell the men what we were able to obtain for them, I don't think that this council will be very well thought of by them."[48] The clinching arguments by which the employee representatives won their retroactive pay in this case were made in a private conference with the president of Harvester's Wisconsin Steel subsidiary. The Works Council minutes omit the discussions at this meeting, but no doubt the blunt realities of outside union pressure could be plainly expressed here without being printed in the minutes for distribution to all employees.

In fact, the closer outside unionism approached, the more frequent were the wage increases. In 1936 Industrial Relations Director Kelday reported to the Harvester executives at the works managers' meeting that labor organizers were becoming more numerous, that unions had substantial money for organizing, and that the steel situation was extremely critical. He cautioned the executives to settle labor problems with tact and speed and to mutual satisfaction lest controversies which seemed insignificant grow to serious proportions.[49] That year, Harvester made two wage increases, liberalized vacations, and gave a cash bonus of two weeks' pay—improperly labeled "extra compensation," in an effort to make it resemble the actual "extra compensation" profit-sharing plan of 1920. However, these employee gains were offset by abandonment of the Harvester pension plan as of January 1937, when social security took effect.[50]

This agitation for higher wages by the employee representatives was hardly the company's idea of what the councils might do to stop outside unions. The company looked to the council members to sell the workers by words rather than by deeds on the efficacy of the works councils as opposed to outside unions. Thus in 1933 Harvester works managers assigned plant superintendents to give talks to the "council members and foremen" for the purpose of counteracting outside influences. It was felt, however, that such talks should be given "in an informal way . . . . the discussion should not be a part of the Works Council meetings as they would then have to be recorded in the minutes which is not desired."[51] Thus the fact that management's wishes, not spontaneous worker initiative, were behind the antiunion activity would be hidden from rank-and-file workers. When the AF of L was attempting to organize the Harvester Fort Wayne plant it was reported at a works managers' meeting that the plant superintendent "is doing very good work in a quiet way with his foremen and council members in counteracting union influences."[52]

The Harvester Company also enlisted works council representatives to convince the Federal Government of the validity of the Harvester employee representation plan. In 1934 four employee representatives from the Wisconsin Steel and McCormick councils went to Washington at company expense to testify before the Senate Committee on Education and Labor against that section of the Wagner bill which would abolish company unions such as the Harvester works councils. They gave a vigorous defense of the Industrial Council Plan, reciting the many gains the workers had wrested from the company. In charge of the Washington expedition were Industrial Relations Director Kelday and Harvester Vice President Elliott. Elliott's testimony confirms that freedom from strikes endeared the Industrial Council Plan to the company: ". . . I do not intend to go into the details of the plan. I will simply state that it has produced satisfactory relations, harmonious relations, without strikes, for 15 years, . . . how can this committee know but what many of the plans of like form recently put into force may also have a 15-year record of industrial peace, which is what we want?"[53]

When in 1935 the Wagner Act was passed, Harvester management was apprehensive about the future of the works councils. These fears were transmitted to the employee representatives, who filled page after page of the July 9, 1935, Wisconsin Steel council minutes with flowery testimony to the superiority of the works council system over unionism. One loquacious older employee representative declared:

And so this Council Plan has sprung from a strong desire to preserve as far as possible under modern giant incorporated industries the old-fashioned friendly contact between employer and employe that existed in the early stages of the company's development—to preserve, if you will, the "McCormick Spirit."

. . . . .

I am aware that amongst the men at Wisconsin Steel Works there are some who do not like the council. I have heard them speak contemptuously of it. They would do away with this peaceful, democratic, American, manly organization for promoting social and economic justice. Men have been slandered and vilified by them to fellow workers and have been pilloried in that scurrilous sheet that used to be handed out at the gate in bold type, all because of enthusiastic espousal of our Employee Representative Plan.

. . . . .

I have had some experience with organized labor but I wish to say that I can get more and I have been able to get more from management for the men, than any business agent ever got for his men.[54]

The chairman of the employee representatives went out of his way to deny that the works councils had been organized to defeat outside unionism.[55]

Management's fear of the Wagner Act and other New Deal labor legislation was well founded. This national labor legislation jeopardized and finally killed the works councils. The NIRA encouraged outside union activity, thus putting company unions on the defensive. The Automobile Labor Board in April 1935 held elections in the Harvester truck plants in Springfield and Fort Wayne. The works councils won majorities in these elections, but on the basis of proportional representation utilized by the Labor Board, the AF of L got four seats on the Fort Wayne council and two at Springfield. Following passage of the Wagner Act, the National Labor Relations Board, on the basis of a union complaint, charged that the Harvester Fort Wayne Works Council was a company-dominated organization and ordered it disbanded on November 12, 1936.[56]

In this decision and order to terminate the Harvester Industrial Council Plan the NLRB stated the following conclusions, among others:

The role of the employees as a group in the workings of the Plan is . . . negligible.

. . . . .

. . . On one side are management representatives possessing complete information, statistical and factual, relating to the business and able to command the resources of a huge and efficient organization. On the other are employee representatives with no information other than that which their working experience has given them. . . . The only possible weapon of the employee representatives—the assistance of outside experts—is effectively denied to them, since the management controls the purse strings.

. . . . .

. . . As a result, its employees possess only the shadow, not the substance, of collective bargaining.

. . . . .

. . . by careful manipulation and scrupulous adherence to the outward forms of collective bargaining, the respondent has so interwoven the Plan into the numerous beneficial activities designed to improve the welfare and morale of the employees and thus increase their efficiency—vacation plan, Credit Union, Athletic Association, pension plan, safety measures, etc.—that the Plan receives credit for many of these benefits in the eyes of the employees.

. . . . .

With equal skill and subtlety the respondent controls the procedure of the Plan. Its Industrial Relations Department sits at the controls, keeping constant watch. The normal operations of the Plan may be steered in any direction by means of the many checks carefully established—preliminary meetings, management officials as Chairman and Secretary, appeals to higher executives, etc. . . .

The Plan is thus entirely the creature of the management.[57]

At the Fort Wayne hearing an employee representative testified that the most important thing he had received for his constituents between 1933 and 1936 was ice water coolers. Another named as his most important demand asking "management to change the paint grates in the paint booths every week."[58]

The adverse NLRB decision in the Fort Wayne case in November 1936 did not immediately end the works councils, since the company had foreseen and countered this eventuality. Even before the Wagner Act was passed, Harvester management, in concert with other employers who were members of the Special Conference Committee, had agreed to continue its employee representation plan and contest the act in the courts.[59] Hence the company appealed the decision to the U. S. Circuit Court and announced to its employees that the NLRB decision, ". . . is of no effect."[60]

The effect of the Supreme Court's Jones-Laughlin decision of March 1937 was to force the Harvester Company formally to disband all its works councils. Thereupon, simultaneously in the key plants threatened by outside unions, the employees, presumably unaided by the company, set up new plant unions unaffiliated with any outside union. The leaders of these new "independent" unions were the leading employee representatives of the old works councils.

These "independent" unions continued to function, holding off outside unionism for four more years—except at the Chicago Tractor Works, where the company recognized the Steelworkers' Organizing Committee, which became the Organizing Committee of the Farm Equipment Workers (CIO). While CIO unions rolled up impressive victories over General Motors, General Electric, U. S. Steel and many other companies during this period, they could not enroll enough members to risk an election at the main International Harvester plants.

Though the Industrial Council Plan could not hold the Federal Government at bay, it had served well to protect the company from outside unionism, in large measure through the vigorous support given to the works councils by some of the employee representatives. Management proved to be very appreciative of such capable employees. It was inevitable that, without any prearranged *quid pro quo,* management material would be discovered among the employee representatives. Once the promoting of employee representatives to management positions was begun, representatives were put under a tremendous temptation; there were innumerable opportunities to do favors for management by taking a "constructive" position on controversial propositions.

The chairman of the Wisconsin Steel employee representatives who had gone to Washington in 1934 to defend the works councils before the Senate's Education and Labor Committee was promoted to foreman upon his return. His successor on the Works Council took leadership in setting up an independent union when the councils were disbanded; the company recognized his ability by promoting him to a position in the industrial relations department of the plant at Springfield, Ohio. At Milwaukee too the Works Council leaders formed an "independent" union in 1937, and then in 1941 led the employees into an AF of L federal labor union in a successful election fight to block the CIO's Farm Equipment Workers from gaining recognition. Several of these men were promoted to management positions. The same thing happened at the West Pullman Works. The domination of works councils and "independent" unions by promotion of leading employee representatives appears to have been an established Harvester technique.[61]

Harvester executives were not unmindful that such a promotion policy could be good management practice as well. On March 29, 1937, at the works managers' meeting, Industrial Relations Director Kelday reported on the recent meeting of the Special Conference Committee. He reported that in the recent General Motors sitdown strikes union leadership rested almost entirely "on union men of short service. These men are quite outstanding, having fairly good education but with socialistic ideas. General Motors feels that they did wrong by not watching such individuals who are aggressive and have initiative and give them special training and inducements to keep them satisfied."[62]

Evaluation of the Industrial Council Plan

In terms of its major objective for International Harvester, that of blocking outside unionism, the Industrial Council Plan was especially successful. Undoubtedly for all except the periods 1919–20 and 1933–41, Harvester could have blocked unionism without works councils. However, this would have meant open repression, as in the past. By 1919 this was no longer acceptable to a cautious company as much in the public eye as the Harvester trust. Furthermore, open repression made a mockery of the vaunted Harvester welfare programs. What top Harvester management needed was a righteous way of blocking unions. The works councils filled this bill. They enabled the McCormicks to talk about "extension of industrial democracy," "frank fifty-fifty discussions between management and labor," "an equal voice for workers and management," and "a spirit of cooperation" without surrendering any of the absolute power that the management had historically wielded.

The works councils accomplished less for the employees in wages and welfare benefits than outside unionism would have because the councils never were able to exert any serious pressure on management. They had no way to call a strike. Their only bargaining power was a derived power, the threat that workers might desert the council for an outside union. In 1919 and from 1933 to 1937, when outside unionism was an active threat, the works councils made their only wage gains. In the years of prosperity, 1924 to 1929, when economic conditions were favorable, they achieved nothing, while profits and dividends rose substantially; the quiescence of outside unionism during the period had robbed the councils of their only leverage.

The entire atmosphere of the works councils reeked of paternalism.

On those rare occasions when a McCormick visited a council and discussed employee problems, appreciation was shown by a rising vote.[63] The contrast of the generally obsequious behavior of works council members with the bluntness and aggressiveness of outside unionism is vividly illustrated in the behavior of one man who at different times held leadership in both types of organizations: Gerald Fielde, the mild-mannered, humble spokesman of the knife department on the Works Council at McCormick Works. The minutes do not record a word uttered by him from his election to the Works Council in December 1935, until July 24, 1936. At that July 24 meeting management announced unilateral abandonment of the long-established pension which permitted retirement beginning at age 60. It also announced a gift, small by comparison with the withdrawal of the pensions, of one week's pay, labeled "extra compensation" for workers with one to two years of service and two weeks' pay for all employees of longer tenure. Instead of expressing outrage at the poor exchange, Gerald Fielde jointly authored the following resolution, humbly thanking management for the gift of a week's pay: "Whereas employees of the McCormick Works realize the fairness and confidence which Management has always shown in matters concerning the well being of its employees therefore be it Resolved that they pledge themselves to complete cooperation in the improvement in quality and efficiency, in accident prevention, and to aid in every way possible in making the extra compensation and savings plan at the McCormick Works a complete and lasting success."[64] Four months later Fielde was still so grateful for the company's vacation-gift benevolence that he declared to a Works Council committee that "the fact the employees had now been given an opportunity to share in the company's profits would be an incentive to them to do all they could to reduce scrap and spoiled work in every way possible."[65] After the Farm Equipment Workers union was formed, Fielde became a leader in it and a *bête noire* of the Harvester Company. Company wage offers became "that paltry nickel," the McCormicks "that greedy family."[66] The thousands of employees known in company publications as the Harvester "family," who had not been on strike since the formation of the works councils in 1919, walked out time and again and shut down the plants for months at a stretch until that ex-McCormick Works Council member, Gerald Fielde, gave them the word to return to work.

The great welfare programs which had made the Harvester Company famous were all started before the works council period of 1919–37. The only new program in this era was the paid vacation, begun in 1929, but even this had not been requested by the works councils in the five preceding years, nor was it by 1929 a pioneering venture. In fact, the benefits of the vacation plan by no means compensated for the curtailment of the pension plan in 1922 and 1925. The reason for the lack of welfare improvements during the works council period is that the councils themselves were a substitute for welfarism. They proved far superior to and cheaper than welfarism in preventing the development of outside unions.

While the works councils from an employee viewpoint suffer by comparison with outside unions, they were a step forward compared to the totally autocratic labor relations which preceded them. In the works councils, superintendents sat down with worker representatives to discuss wages and grievances, as they had not done since 1903. The interminable man hours consumed in council committee meetings and in the full council meetings brainwashed employee representatives with management's viewpoint but also to some extent acquainted management with workers' problems. Under the works council system even the company president had to appear in person before elected worker representatives and explain why he refused wage requests. In his entire tenure as president of the company, from 1884 through 1918, Cyrus McCormick II had only once, in 1886, had to explain to a worker or union representative face to face his decisions on wages and working conditions. His younger brother Harold, who was president from 1918 to 1922, had to undergo this ordeal many times. Appearing before the docile works councils, which could not lead a strike no matter what the president's decision might be, was not as educational as facing a real union; but for Harvester officials it was a distinct change in the direction of greater understanding of employee opinion.

Administration of the works councils required full-time industrial relations specialists. Even though the industrial relations department manipulated councils to get them to vote as management wished, it provided a buffer between the frequently autocratic superintendents and the workers. In addition, the industrial relations officials were a link between workers and top executives. Communication was imperfect, but at least in the works council minutes management read at times some amazingly frank comments by worker representatives. In earlier years foreman and superintendent had presented an impenetrable wall between worker and top executive. Normally no protest short of a full-blown strike reached the president in the years before the works councils.

During the period of the councils there were no strikes, no surprise employee outbursts. The elected employee representatives may not have been the most able leaders among the workers, but with management's help they were effective enough to block the rise of any other leadership.

Employee representation was a big-industry bulwark against unionism. It gave the firm an appearance of compliance with public policy, which was gradually moving toward support of collective bargaining. Furthermore, to succeed, such a plan as Harvester's needed relatively well-satisfied employees. Successful plans were usually found in firms with extensive welfare programs.

While the employee representation movement nationally siphoned off some worker leaders and suppressed others, it did almost nothing to alleviate workers' grievances. Workers therefore had a calloused apathy, generally tinged with the bitterness of frustration, toward the representation plans. The failure to win wage increases during the prosperous 'twenties or to get protection from the deep wage cuts of the 1921–22 and 1929–33 depressions caused these frustrations to mount. With the passage of the Wagner Act, ably led union drives toppled most company unions. Harvester employee representation and the successive unaffiliated unions that followed it lasted longer than most other such plans, yet were outlived by the unaffiliated unions of the oil industry and those of the DuPont Company. Company unionism at Harvester could not withstand the onslaught of determined outside union drives because employment in agricultural implements was too seasonal and irregular. The large number of piecework jobs probably contributed to the workers' discontent.

The Special Conference Committee

Harvester's employee representation plan was not an isolated phenomenon but part of a concerted program carried on by American big industry through a secret committee known as the Special Conference Committee. The first public knowledge of even the existence of such a committee came in the 1937 hearings of the civil liberties committee.[67]

The McCormick and International Harvester companies had always kept clear of entangling employer associations which might restrict their freedom in labor relations. The late 1880's and 1890's were periods of areawide and even national negotiations in the metal trades. However, the McCormick Harvesting Machine Company refused to join such organizations as the National Metal Trades Association or the National Founders Association which at the time of their origin recognized unions. These were defensive associations of relatively small firms banding together to resist the great power of the molders, machinists, and patternmakers. The member firms aspired not to become nonunion but to contain the power of the unions by presenting a common front. Large corporations such as McCormick had learned that they could handle unions by themselves and did not need help from other manufacturers.

This does not mean that Harvester labor relations and wage policy were not influenced upon occasion by the policies of other employers. This influence, however, was the result of an ad hoc exchange of information and only rarely the result of any binding agreement with other manufacturers. As early as 1863 the proprietors of iron foundries west of the Appalachians, including the McCormick Harvesting Machine Company, jointly agreed on a policy goal for limiting wage increases. In 1867 the employers of Chicago openly banded together to resist the demand for an eight-hour day. In 1872 the McCormick Company was cooperating with other employers in blacklisting striking molders. Most of these joint efforts, however, were of the informal variety in which none of the employers was pledged in advance to any particular form of action.

Later International Harvester did join the usual employer associations; but the openly antiunion employer associations, such as the National Association of Manufacturers, did not meet the real needs of the nation's largest corporations. The behemoths wanted to discuss labor relations out of the glare of publicity and quietly take such antiunion action as they felt met their own needs. They did not wish to appear to lead any movement against organized labor. As trusts they feared arousing public and congressional opposition.

When unionism became sufficiently menacing at the close of World War I, ten of America's large corporations secretly formed the Special Conference Committee, an exclusive labor relations organization. The members were Bethlehem Steel, E. I. DuPont de Nemours, General

Electric, General Motors, Goodyear Tire and Rubber, International Harvester, Irving Trust, Standard Oil of New Jersey, United States Rubber, and Westinghouse Electric. In 1925 American Telephone and Telegraph was added and in 1934 United States Steel. Eight of the original ten firms had company unions at the founding of the committee. After NIRA, DuPont, U. S. Steel, and American Telephone and Telegraph established company unions, leaving only the Irving Trust without one.

All that is known about the origin of this secret organization is the statement of Clarence J. Hicks that A. C. Bedford, chairman of the Jersey Standard Board of Directors, and Owen D. Young of General Electric decided in April 1919 that it would be useful to set up such an organization.[68] At the time, Hicks was the top personnel executive of Standard Oil Company of New Jersey. According to the La Follette civil liberties committee (subcommittee of the Senate Committee on Education and Labor), which began investigating it in 1937, the Conference Committee had no listed telephone, no letterhead on its stationery, and no bank account or dues. The Standard Oil Company of New Jersey picked up the tab for all expenses, which were later divided among the member companies.[69] From 1923 on the Special Conference Committee employed a full-time executive secretary, E. S. Cowdrick.

For two decades the personnel executives of these companies met regularly and secretly in informal session to discuss problems of labor relations, personnel, employment, wage movements and, additionally, during the 1930's, state and national legislative movements to regulate labor-management relations. During the period of reduced union activity, in the depression of 1921–22 and the prosperity which followed, Conference Committee discussion of unionism gave way to discussion of labor market shortages and surpluses and broad personnel problems. By reading the AF of L *Federationist,* Secretary Cowdrick managed to present some report of union activity across the country at most of the Conference meetings even during this quiet period. The fact that once or twice a year the principal executive officers of the firms joined the Conference Committee meetings demonstrates the importance they attributed to the committee's work.

The exchange of information among the Conference members probably had a significant influence on the labor policies of each company. For instance, the wage patterns of these companies bear a marked similarity. In December 1922 A. H. Young, Harvester industrial relations director, brought back information to the effect that the members of the Conference Committee were considering wage increases, probably in the spring of 1923, if business conditions continued to improve. Harvester put a general increase into effect in February 1923. Goodyear had already raised wages 7.5 percent. In 1926 Harvester Industrial Relations Director George Kelday brought back word to Harvester works managers that Goodyear had recently cut certain piecework prices 12 percent without reducing the employees' earning power or causing any unfavorable reaction on the part of the employees. The same year the Goodyear Company reported that it had turned down a request for an 8 percent increase in pay which had been made through the employee representatives. Conference members seemed to have looked to each other's wage policies with special concern during the severe recession of the 1930's. General Motors reported to the meeting of March 20, 1931, that it was opposed to any downward adjustment in wages. DuPont planned no reduction in wages. American Telephone and Telegraph reported no change in wages and salary rates although some earnings were reduced because of short work weeks. General Electric, whose production was running 25 percent below the same period of the previous year, declared it hoped to avoid any reduction in wages or salaries. On the other hand, Goodyear announced that it was prepared to go ahead with a general wage leveling in order to adjust to the continuing decline in business. Bethlehem Steel had saved on wage costs by reducing the work week of salaried employees.[70]

These companies also held other labor policies in common, at least in part because of their sharing of ideas and experiences through the committee. International Harvester's relief fund for unemployed workers was instituted shortly after General Electric described its insurance fund for unemployed workers to the March 1931 Conference Committee meeting. In 1932 Cowdrick spent some time in Madison, Wisconsin, observing the legislature's passage of the first unemployment compensation bill. He was accompanied by representatives of the four Conference Committee companies which had plants in Wisconsin. Kelday represented International Harvester on this trip. Probably the most significant area of common concern and influence in the Conference Committee prior to 1933 was the employee representation plans operated by eight of the companies.

With the upsurge of unionism beginning in 1933 the antiunion work of the Conference Committee went into high gear in Congress as well as in the plants. Committee members George Kelday of Harvester and Arthur H. Young, then vice president of industrial relations for U. S. Steel, instigated and coordinated testimony in opposition to the Wagner Act. When the Wagner Act became law, Conference members along with some other companies refused to obey it.

The Goodyear Company described in detail to Conference members its use of specially selected "flying squadron" employees to smash union meetings and to beat up and give "rides" to union organizers. So interested were Conference members in the Goodyear tactics that Secretary Cowdrick went to Akron in 1936 to study and report on the situation firsthand. He made certain criticisms of Goodyear's methods, principally the tactless cutting of piece rates and the way the company-union employee representatives milked the company for off-job pay.[71] Each company was, of course, free to pursue its own labor policy and did so. Harvester, for example, did not practice in the mid-'thirties the gross discrimination against prounion employees or union organizers that the La Follette committee uncovered at Goodyear or at General Motors.

The very existence, method of operation, and regular functioning of the Special Conference Committee throughout two decades are evidence of the high degree of collaboration on labor relations matters by key corporations. The committee urged its members to become active with local and regional employer associations and to set up miniature Special Conference Committee groups in local areas. In view of the size of the member companies and their very great influence in quite a number of communities across the country, the effect of this small committee was very substantial. There was a good deal of inbreeding among the labor relations executives of these companies. The honorary chairman of the group until 1934 was Clarence J. Hicks, who prior to 1915 had been head of International Harvester's industrial relations work. In 1915 he went to the Rockefeller-owned Colorado Fuel and Iron Company to aid in the difficult situation that resulted from the Ludlow strike of 1914. By 1919 Hicks was head of industrial relations at the Rockefeller-controlled Standard Oil Company of New Jersey. Arthur H. Young went from the Colorado Fuel and Iron Company to International Harvester in 1918 as director of industrial relations. During the war he had served the government as a safety expert. In 1924 he became head of Industrial Relations Counselors, a management consulting group with close ties to the Rockefeller enterprises. Even after he left International Harvester he continued to attend the Special Conference meetings, but he represented no particular company. When in 1934 he became vice president of U. S. Steel, he brought that company into membership in the committee. E. S. Cowdrick, the executive secretary of the committee, like Hicks and Young had served at Colorado Fuel and Iron, where he had been assistant to the president.

The La Follette committee's investigation did not put an end to the Special Conference Committee. In fact it is still in existence, though considerably modified in purpose and membership. Upon the death of Conference Secretary Cowdrick, Industrial Relations Counselors took over the responsibility for arranging a suitable agenda for the group in the light of changed conditions. Membership is no longer restricted to the original companies.

8

Harvester's Industrial Relations Department —Origin and Evolution

Many years of conflict between the early personnel officials, called "welfare" workers, and manufacturing executives preceded the establishment of today's industrial relations departments. All welfare officials as representatives of a new and seemingly superfluous department in a corporation had to face the antagonism of the older, more powerful, revenue-producing departments. In most companies the first "welfare" official was cut to ribbons in a matter of months by the plant superintendent.

At McCormick's both the initial success of the welfare program and the rivalries it created were greater than the small size of the department would seem to merit. This was in part because of the special relationship between the welfare department and the McCormick family. The first welfare department was sponsored directly by President Cyrus McCormick II. His brothers Harold and Stanley both had a hand in its formation; his mother, Nettie Fowler McCormick, took a keen interest in its creation. Consequently, the welfare department officials received far more attention and support from the owning family than their responsibilities entitled them to. Moreover, because of the public interest in labor relations and welfare work, welfare officials received more favorable newspaper and magazine publicity than major department heads with ten times their salaries and responsibilities. These circumstances enabled Gertrude Beeks, the first welfare worker at McCormick's, to retain her job while openly disagreeing with her immediate superior, the plant superintendent at the McCormick Works, and to instigate substantial reforms. This high-level support by the members of the McCormick family also increased the antagonism of plant-level executives toward her work.

TABLE 3

Stages of Development, Harvester Department of Industrial Relations

Date	Nature of Department	Principal Officer
1901–3	Welfare secretary and plant staff.	Gertrude Beeks
1903–4	Recreation committee and plant staff.	S. M. Darling
1904–5	Sociological committee and plant staff.	Frank Ericsson S. M. Darling
1905–11	Welfare department, manager, assistant in charge of women's work.	C. W. Price
1911–15	Titles abolished but department manager and assistant continued.	Clarence J. Hicks
1915–18	No separate department, director; but labor relations activities carried on by general manager, other activities under manufacturing.	G. A. Ranney
1918–24	Modern autonomous industrial relations department, director, assistant in charge of women's work. Staff: labor relations, research, medical department. Major activity administering works councils in all plants.	Arthur H. Young
1924–33	Same department and titles as 1918–24 but complete loss of autonomy to manufacturing.	George J. Kelday
1933–36	No change in departmental structure and titles, but great increase in importance and work load of labor relations.	George J. Kelday
1936–41	Same departmental structure and titles but labor relations policy kicked up to a high-level, cross-departmental committee headed by Fowler McCormick, who in 1937 was vice president in charge of foreign sales. Other members of the committee represented the legal department, public relations, manufacturing and industrial relations.	George J. Kelday
1941–44	Labor relations pulled out from industrial relations and set up under a manager of labor relations reporting to Fowler McCormick, who was now vice president of manufacturing. Title of industrial relations changed to personnel department.	George Hodge for labor relations George J. Kelday for personnel
1944–60	Industrial relations now raised to vice presidential status, though the vice president, Ivan Willis, not selected until 1947. Decentralized divisional labor relations staffs established simultaneously with great increase in power and importance of companywide manager of labor relations, George Hodge, in 1946, and William J. Reilly in 1952. Subdepartments: wage and salary administration, employment, education, labor relations.	Ivan Willis (1947–61)

As her betterment program grew, Miss Beeks became increasingly concerned with centralizing the work under a special department instead of having the program continually at the mercy of production officials. In her mid-1903 survey she emphasized strongly the need to centralize all labor relations and welfare work in a labor bureau under a full-time official. Surprisingly she urged the company to hire a labor leader for the post: "Such a man as Mr. George A. Schilling who, while a Union man understands the manufacturer's standpoint thoroughly and is absolutely fair to that side . . . ."[1]

When she left in 1903, Miss Beeks was replaced not by a full-time director of a new labor department but by a part-time committee of International Harvester third-line executives organized directly under General Manager E. A. S. Clarke, who reported on welfare matters to Vice President Harold McCormick. One committee member came from each of the three Chicago plants and one from the central office. However, this part-time committee, called the recreation committee, showed remarkable energy, chiefly because its chairman, S. M. Darling, the representative from the central office, was a man of unusual talent. Darling was an assistant to President McCormick and thus able to devote much time to the committee with the full blessing of his boss. Though his welfare work was nominally under the unsympathetic Clarke, Darling's daily contact with Cyrus McCormick gave him a certain degree of independence. By 1904 the recreation committee was recommending a full-blown welfare program, including profit sharing, cooperative purchasing, plant newspapers, and clubhouses with educational, recreational, and luncheon facilities. Company aid for nearby churches and establishment of athletic fields near each plant were envisioned. Symptomatic of the committee's expanding outlook was its recommendation that the name recreation committee be changed to sociological department of the International Harvester Company.[2] The thinking which led to this was explained in a letter of Darling's to the company's attorney:

> We beg to thank you for your kind words. Your reference to the formidableness of our name gives us an opportunity to state one of our perplexities and to ask your opinion. Several names have been suggested: Welfare, Industrial Betterment, Cooperative, Sociological. I do not think "Welfare" has the true ring, but rather has a patronizing sound; and it hardly covers the scope of our work. "Industrial Betterment" is too long and might suggest to some

people that we have started out to reform the world. "Cooperative" it is felt might bring undesirable notoriety. "Sociological" it is true sounds rather academic, but its meaning is definite. It may be urged that it is too broad a term. On the other hand this Company is bound to do a large share of the world's work and why should it not have a sociological committee,—a group of students engaged in a work worthy of the name Sociological?[3]

A last significant act of the recreation committee was the submission of a constitution for an employees' association "within the company" which might carry out all welfare activities. The committee's stated purpose was to help the employees help themselves and to abandon any notion of the company donating anything directly to the employees. However, with unionism an imminent danger, the employees' association was never established, and the company retained absolute control over all its welfare activities.

Early in 1904 C. U. Carpenter, labor department director at the National Cash Register Company and one of Miss Beeks's favorite candidates to head a labor department at Harvester, wrote President McCormick that he was available to consider a position as welfare manager.[4] His interest prompted Harold McCormick to ask General Manager Clarke for recommendations on the future organization of the company's welfare program. Clarke opposed any independent welfare director or department: ". . . in view of the newness of our organization, I have felt for some time that it would be unwise to consider employing an outsider—a special expert in this line—who would be given the authority and freedom that such a man would expect because I have felt there would be some danger of upsetting . . . the authority of the superintendents at their plants and also causing them possibly to lack interest in the scheme."[5]

Instead he recommended continuation of the existing part-time interplant committee under a new chairman: "These secretaries would constitute an investigating and advisory committee, . . . and they would report to Mr. Ericsson [assistant to General Superintendent Flather], . . . who would be the permanent chairman of this committee, and through Mr. Ericsson the work and suggestions of the committee would come to Mr. Flather and to myself for approval." Clarke's recommendation of Ericsson as permanent chairman undoubtedly was designed to curb Darling's power in the welfare field.

Gertrude Beeks, in New York with the National Civic Federation since August 1903, was sent a copy of Clarke's recommendations. In a letter to Cyrus McCormick she continued to urge her plan of hiring an outsider and explained why welfare work could not succeed if put under the control of the line officials: "Surely, Mr. Clarke's plan of having one Welfare Secretary (as he calls it) at each plant is excellent, and I presume that would overcome any feelings that the employes might have against Mr. Erics[s]on. Personally, I think Mr. Erics[s]on is a fine fellow, but you know he has been employed for so many years in keeping down the wage scale that it would be difficult, I imagine, for the employes to regard him as really working for their benefit. He is undoubtedly very loyal to the company."[6]

Frank Ericsson in October 1903 had expressed to Superintendent Flather his own thoughts on the role of welfare work and the duties of a labor department. They reveal a view which was sophisticated for that era, of welfarism as a tool against unionism:

> One of the principal objects of this [Labor] department should be to create and promote among the employees a feeling of loyalty for and confidence in the management.
>
> It should convince the employees that they can get what they most want without the necessity of paying anyone for it.
>
> It should endeavor to secure for the employee just what he most desires from the union. It should secure for him those results which labor organizations declare are their basic objects; namely, higher wages and shorter hours.
>
> It should provide means by which employees can have their grievances heard and adjusted without the necessity of joining a union.
>
> It should keep thoroughly posted on all matters pertaining to labor organizations, keeping fully informed of the wages and hours demanded by the different trades.
>
> It should have general supervision of betterment, education and recreation work.
>
> It should strive to surround employees with conditions that will conduce to better work.
>
> It should compile statistics showing the rate of wages received and hours worked by the various crafts in all large manufacturing concerns.[7]

While Ericsson's views might be labeled "advanced paternalism" for his time, his main aim was to block unionism.

The new sociological committee was launched in June 1904 with Frank Ericsson as chairman. He was to report its work to General Superintendent Flather and General Manager Clarke. Thus an assuredly antiunion sociological committee was securely tied to the manufacturing line executives. The members of this new committee were the former members of the recreation committee. At the sociological committee's initial meeting Flather bluntly made it aware of its limited scope and the company's tight purse strings on welfare expenditures. In a memorandum to the general manager he reported: "I have asked them [the sociological committee] to work on the matters suggested by you and have told them that those things which took the smallest expenditure would have the quickest approval. I have suggested to Mr. Darling that his entire recommendation had better come up at one time, as the entire matter is so problematical and some portions of it so expensive that it would hardly receive quick consideration, ..."[8]

Still another restriction was about to fall on the hapless sociological committee. Elderly William Deering, founder of the former Deering Company, learned of the committee's plan to acquire a park for outings for the Deering workers. His Methodist respect for the Sabbath was aroused, and he wrote a long complaint to President Cyrus McCormick:

> Other and permanent public parks are as accessible or more so to most of these people—and the only reason why this park is to be more attractive than the public parks would seem to be that dancing, games and drinking facilities are to be specially provided on the Sabbath Day—and perhaps some of the summer evenings—mostly at the expense of the employers. The Electric Park is three or four miles distant from the shops and I am informed has never had a good reputation, but the contrary—that of being much frequented by a doubtful class.
>
> Now, can the International Harvester Company, or that part of it designated the Deering Division, afford to disregard the sanctity of the Sabbath Day and promote, encourage and pay for its desecration by establishing and paying for dancing and beer (or perhaps other intoxicating beverages stronger than beer) and thus afford to their numerous employees amusements and dissipation common to beer gardens and dance halls?
>
> . . . . .
>
> Not a few of the employees of the Deering establishment are members of Protestant or Catholic Churches—especially of the latter. These good Catholics respect Sunday, especially Sunday forenoons, as sacred to their church services. This scheme, if put in practice, would make some persons (for instance, your good mother and those of her religious profession and character) unwilling participants in the establishing and financial support of amusements and liquor drinking or selling on Sunday, that would not only be distasteful, but very offensive to them.[9]

The park and Sunday outings were abandoned.

In spite of the limitations imposed by the company's fear of unionism, the budget cuts due to the recession of 1904, the jealousy of the line manufacturing executives, and the Sabbath observance views of a founder, the sociological committee—or at least S. M. Darling, its secretary—was a dynamo of activity. From June 1904 when it superseded the recreation committee through February 1905 when it in turn was superseded by a full-time welfare official, the sociological committee built an impressive list of accomplishments and a still more impressive list of items under consideration. The accomplishments encompassed employment of a woman to establish plant restaurants at cost, milk sales to employees to discourage beer at lunch, an employee magazine subscription club, lodging and transportation arrangements for employees visiting the St. Louis World's Fair, improved athletic fields, arrangement with public libraries for book-lending at the plants; and company sale of coal, waste wood, and ice to employees, despite opposition of local merchants. The items considered but not adopted included a mutual benefit association for sickness and accidents, a savings bank, a vacation camp, a house newspaper for employees, life insurance, a full-time welfare director, an apprenticeship system, and suggestion system. These accomplishments and recommendations corresponded quite closely to the activities which Chairman Ericsson had prescribed earlier.

To broaden the committee's outlook Secretary Darling carried on a wide correspondence with other companies engaged in similar work and even with several university professors. Illustrative of Darling's viewpoint is a letter to John R. Commons at the University of Wisconsin. Commons, at Darling's request, had sent an article from the *Quarterly Journal of Economics,* November 1904, entitled "Labor Conditions in Meat Packing and the Recent Strike." Darling concluded his thank you letter, "I had made a memorandum to get your book for my library, and will use the copy that is being sent me for missionary purposes."[10]

This energetic missionary spirit was finally Darling's undoing. Even with Darling as secretary instead of chairman, the sociological committee, which was to have been a conservative, subservient committee, had continued to be an aggressive, crusading force. By 1905 a new general manager, G. F. Steele, recommended that the committee be replaced by a single full-time welfare manager to be promoted from within the company and paid a modest salary. Of course Darling, who had been devoting all his time and interest to the company's welfare work, desperately wanted this new position of welfare manager. However, Steele saw Darling only as an obstacle and a troublemaker. He wrote to Harold McCormick:

> If anything can be done to call off Mr. Darling on this welfare work I think it would be advisable. We have ascertained we think to our satisfaction that the reason Mr. Price was so reluctant to make terms with us and so dead set to get fifteen hundred dollars per annum was on account of information which had been given him by Mr. Darling, . . . I feel satisfied that if Mr. Darling had kept out of it we could have made arrangements with Mr. Price. . . . I am also of the opinion that Mr. Darling has given Miss Beeks information regarding our plans, for I do not know where else she would have got the information if not from him.[11]

Though C. W. Price, an incumbent employee of International Harvester, had at first refused the job because the company would not raise his salary from $1,080 to $1,500 (the amount paid Gertrude Beeks three years earlier), he did become the new welfare manager.[12] He was a former minister and a man with a forceful personality. He believed that "In factories similar to ours, where the great majority of the men are humble foreigners . . . the leadership must come . . . from someone acting in the capacity of social secretary."[13] Price served from 1905 to 1911. During his tenure bold new welfare experiments, classes for welfare department workers, pensions, profit sharing, sickness and accident benefit programs, were begun, though he was not always their initiator.

One of the most interesting new activities was the Harvester Company's participation in the pioneering welfare training program of Graham Taylor. From his experience with the West Side settlement house, Chicago Commons, Taylor soon saw the need for training welfare workers of all varieties, and attached an educational branch to Chicago Commons. In 1906 he offered a course of twelve lecture-discussions for industrial welfare workers. Students were welfare workers from such plants as International Harvester, Sears, Roebuck, and Marshall Field. In response to a letter from Professor Taylor, Stanley McCormick interested Price in these lectures. The result was that four representatives of Harvester's Chicago plants—two men and two women—

attended the weekly course. When the course was repeated in 1907 Harvester attendance fell to one person. Top Harvester management kept a close record of the content of the course. Elaborate notes of each session were taken by a Harvester secretary and copies were sent to eighteen management personnel in various plants and to Gertrude Beeks in New York.[14]

Speakers and topics of the course included Professor Graham Taylor on the history of labor relations; General Manager Scott of Sears, Roebuck on his company's welfare and personnel experience; C. W. Price on Harvester welfare experience; a Mr. Becker on factory education; Mr. Thomas on the welfare work and philosophy of the National Cash Register Company; University of Chicago professor Charles Zebelin on municipal and industrial betterment; Mrs. Raymond Robins, former president of the Trade Union League for Women of New York City, on trade unionism and welfare work; Professor Charles Henderson of the University of Chicago on thrift, consumer cooperatives, workmen's compensation, and sickness insurance. Other subjects were child labor, housing and industrial efficiency, and immigration.[15]

At the 1907 welfare training course the single Harvester employee in attendance was Miss Mary Goss, welfare manager Price's chief assistant in charge of women's welfare activities. Indeed, in this year, except for one meeting, attendance at the course was entirely female; in 1906 it had been 50 percent male. For the lecture on safety and safety legislation several of the Harvester male employees turned out, but an evaluation by one of them gave it a low rating:

> No suggestions which could possibly be of any immediate benefit to the I.H.Co. were made either in the address or in the discussion which followed. The entire discussion was of a theoretical nature and dealt with the necessity of educating the public to understand the needs of the law under consideration so that the force of public opinion might cause its passage in the next legislature, as it is evident that in all probability it will not be passed at this session owing to the opposition of the Manufacturers Association. As a means of educating the general public, and of putting such matters before the people, a conference of this character may be a success, but I should say that it was absolutely valueless to practical men seeking concrete suggestions for betterments and for provisions for safeguarding employees.[16]

Despite Taylor's training course, the welfare department at Harvester was gradually purged of its social worker outlook during Price's tenure. The idealists like Beeks, Bruere, and Darling were gone. Stanley McCormick, the most liberal and welfare-minded of the McCormick brothers, had permanently left the company because of illness. Welfare department contact with outside influences declined as the department became more occupied with purely practical, bread-and-butter benefits for employee and employer alike: safety, medical care, sickness and accident benefits, profit sharing, pensions. Mary Goss approvingly described this change as follows: "There has been too little education in some places, too much in others—education of the wrong kind; too much devotion to purely esthetic attempts, things that don't make for bread-winning. Technical training is of the first importance. Much of the work that the settlements are doing I am afraid of. They merely promote social unrest without giving the means of satisfying the desires they create. We are looking only for practical benefits."[17]

After 1908 Price himself turned more to safety work, as the Harvester Company distinguished itself in this field. In 1910 he lost even his original title. The Welfare Board of Harvester manufacturing executives passed a resolution downgrading his title from superintendent of welfare to inspector of protection and sanitation.[18] At the invitation of John R. Commons, Price left within a year to take charge of the safety program for the newly created Industrial Commission of the State of Wisconsin. Miss Goss stayed on but in 1913 was reminded that she was to confine her work to the women.

Clarence J. Hicks, a YMCA secretary, took Price's place; but the welfare position by then was so de-emphasized by the other executives that Hicks had no title at all. According to Hicks, his salary was less than he had been receiving from the YMCA. His work at Harvester appears to have been largely safety work rather than labor relations or welfare activities. There were at this time no permanent trade unions among Harvester employees. The records do not indicate that Hicks was even consulted in the big labor relations crises that occurred during his tenure, including the Auburn, New York, strike of 1913. The weak position of the welfare department in the company structure at this time is even more evident when one realizes that this period was when the spectacular welfare programs of profit sharing, health and accident insurance, and pensions were instituted—initiated by Morgan partner George W. Perkins.

These new welfare programs gave International Harvester a justly deserved national reputation as a leader in welfare work and, in spite of the deterioration of the welfare department, made its head, Hicks, a national authority on labor relations. John D. Rockefeller, Jr., asked Cyrus McCormick II and Hicks for assistance during the labor troubles following the Ludlow massacre of 1914. First Hicks was loaned for a month to Rockefeller; then he was released to become assistant to the president at Colorado Fuel and Iron Company. In releasing him, Cyrus McCormick explained his feelings to Harold:

> I am sending you a letter from J. D. R., Jr., which discloses a very interesting conference that Mr. Hicks has had with them. In the midst of their troubles, which have been many and serious, John D. Jr., wrote me, asking me if we could lend them Mr. Hicks to make a month's investigation of their situation. I told him we would be glad to do so. The result of the month's investigation is that they want him to take an executive position with them in welfare work. Mr. Hicks is to go this week.
>
> I feel that our close relations with Mr. Rockefeller and their interests make it in every way desirable that we should help them as much as we can.[19]

Cyrus McCormick felt little loss at the departure of a welfare secretary. "In this instance," he wrote Harold, "it is not apparent that it will be to the detriment of our Company's interests, as our work is well organized and will go on without deterioration." This statement only seven months before the outbreak of the 1916 strike indicates a substantial overestimate of the contribution of the company's welfare program to industrial relations. In the light of Mr. Hicks's career with Jersey Standard Oil it would appear that Mr. McCormick grossly underestimated his potentialities.

Hicks's departure in 1915 marked the end of an era in industrial relations at International Harvester. From the time of Gertrude Beeks through that of Clarence Hicks, welfare officials had dealt with factory betterment and welfare programs, not with wages, hours, or union relations. When industrial relations was reinstituted as a new move in 1918, supervision of a company union, studies of wages and hours, and surveillance of union activity across the country were the new department's major responsibilities. This evolution of industrial relations from welfarism to labor relations was mirrored in the change in the industrial relations personnel. A marked feature of the early betterment years was the prominence of women in the welfare positions. In an era when business generally recognized women only on the worker and clerical level, women were chosen for the top welfare jobs. Social workers, clerical workers with strong personalities, and schoolteachers with reputations as disciplinarians were considered especially qualified to clean up the factories and institute welfare programs. The men in welfare work came from the YMCA, the ministry and from schoolteaching. When the Harvester industrial relations department began to deal with wages, hours, and union relations, not only were women bypassed for the top positions but the men were recruited directly from production departments, such as timekeeping and safety.

Miss Beeks was the only woman to hold the top welfare position at Harvester, but over the years women played a prominent role in the company's welfare work. Mary Goss's appointment in 1905 as assistant to welfare manager Price reveals the qualifications, or lack of them, which were thought necessary for these early welfare workers. The assistant comptroller wanted to get Miss Goss out of the accounting department, so he proposed her for the head of the welfare department:

> I would also suggest your consideration of the case of Miss Goss. She has been working during the past year on foreign accounting matters, but . . . this work will be done during the season 1905 by the regular foreign accounting division. . . . This will relieve Miss Goss of all current work in the Accounting Department; and before assigning any new work to her (which, perhaps, could be done at less expense through regular channels), I would like to have your advice in the matter. We can employ her in looking after the liquidation affairs of the old Companies, but it would probably be more satisfactory to all concerned if her abilities could be employed in some other direction than the Accounting Department. It occurred to me that the Company might consider her for the position of Business Agent of its sociological work, etc., ...[20]

Miss Goss, though lacking to some extent the broad outlook of Gertrude Beeks, was a talented women, a former secretary to the president of the Plano Company. Like Miss Beeks, she interested Nettie Fowler McCormick in the work of the welfare department. When Miss Goss threatened to resign over a minor frustration Mrs. McCormick personally offered her $500 to remain in the department.

By 1909 the company had welfare representatives in many of its nineteen plants. Women headed the work at the twine mills, which employed women. The welfare worker at the St. Paul Twine Works was Nesta Edwards. Her qualifications were that she had been the Chicago office secretary assigned to take notes at the Graham Taylor welfare training course. Miss Edwards' laughing explanation of her promotion to welfare work was that the company considered her incompetent as a clerical worker. With this background at Harvester she went on to a distinguished career as a welfare consultant and practitioner with a number of other corporations, including Kimberly-Clark, and with the Wisconsin Industrial Commission. Later she entered the industrial department of the YWCA.[21]

Another women to hold an influential executive position in International Harvester's industrial relations department was Sara Southall. A social worker living at Hull House, Miss Southall learned of the Harvester position from another Hull House resident, the Harvester medical director, Dr. Britton. She was at first reluctant to work for a large corporation, but Jane Addams advised her that by intelligent working together labor and management could make a contribution "far beyond mere production and distribution."[22] Miss Southall began working for Harvester in 1920 in the women's section of the industrial relations department, and after rising to the directorship of women's activities in the early 'twenties, moved over into personnel and employment work. Because of her social work background and interests she was selected, during World War II, to play a key role in initiating one of International Harvester's most significant reforms, the employment integration of whites and Negroes in all plants of the company, both North and South. During her experience at Harvester—she retired in 1948—Miss Southall bridged the change from the early social worker–welfare concept of industrial relations represented by Miss Beeks to the modern labor relations–efficiency concept.

The Harvester Company went through World War I with no full-time director of welfare or labor policies. However, just as in 1903 International Harvester had enlarged betterment work to counter increased union activities, so in 1918 it established its first autonomous industrial relations department in response to the labor unrest of World War I. This new department was a separate entity in charge of all labor relations, personnel, and medical service.

Arthur H. Young, as we have seen, became the department's first director. Young, like Hicks, was destined for a notable career with Rockefeller enterprises. After working as a laborer at Joliet Steel and at the Minnequa steel plant of the Colorado Fuel and Iron Company, he had risen to management level in the latter company as a safety expert. One of the pioneers in labor relations work, he had served as a director of the American Museum of Safety and as a safety expert with the government during World War I.

The new and independent industrial relations department he headed reawakened the second-level executives' antagonism to welfare work. Whenever superintendents were pressed to cut costs, they recommended abolition of industrial relations and other professional services. For example, at the end of 1923 the McCormick Works superintendent proposed reducing the number of doctors to the 1913 level, reducing safety work, abolishing time study (not a part of the industrial relations department), and reducing the number of managment representatives on the works councils to one or two men. Ironically, the West Pullman Works superintendent wished simultaneously to eliminate time studies and establish 100 percent piecework departments.[23] Another instance of this conflict between manufacturing executives and the industrial relations department occurred when in 1923 a superintendent demoted an employment official at one of the plants without first checking with the department. This violation of the department's rights led Vice President Cyrus McCormick III personally to restate the policy that no discharge or change of position should be made without knowledge of the industrial relations director. McCormick then listed the following occupations for which dismissals could not be made without the knowledge of the interested general office department head (not all of the following were under the jurisdiction of the industrial relations department): doctors, inspectors, power plant men, metallurgists, chemists, firemen and watchmen, buyers, clerical help, storekeepers.[24]

But the superintendents were too powerful in the 1920's to be curbed for long. They cut the industrial relations department down to size just as they had repeatedly done with the old welfare department from 1901 on. By 1925 even Vice President McCormick had joined the superintendents in the opposition to independent power for the industrial relations department. At a meeting of the American Management Association he explained:

> In 1919, when we set up our new Industrial Relations Department, gathering into it our existing welfare and medical activities, we followed the usual practice and started to organize it alongside the manufacturing department. . . . We have found we can progress far more quickly, far more soundly, if the industrial relations department is considered not as standing alongside the manufacturing department, but as part of it.
>
> . . . while industry needs specialists in industrial relations . . . these specialists will be most effective when their daily contact is with men who think and live production. Believing this, we have torn down every barrier until

today the industrial relations department is a separate agency in name only.[25]

With the decline of the department's autonomy, Arthur Young resigned the directorship and went to head up the Rockefellers' new Industrial Relations Counselors. His successor was George J. Kelday. In selecting Kelday, Harvester broke its usual pattern of bringing welfare and industrial relations directors from outside. Kelday came to his position by the route of head timekeeper and wage specialist at the Harvester Ontario plant (which he had entered in 1904) and then to the central office as assistant.

While the industrial relations department lost its independence and power at this time, it retained its major function of keeping unionism out of the Harvester plants. In some respects the department's antiunion and antiradical activities were so farfetched as to make one wonder if it might not have been nurturing a bogeyman to justify its existence. The unions had been defeated in the Chicago implement strikes of July and August 1919 and in the September–December national steel strike of the same year. Union leadership had been eliminated from the Harvester plants at that time. This purging process could be expected to protect the plants from unionism for some years. Nevertheless, the industrial relations department busied itself with a host of windmill-tilting activities. For example, each May Day through 1925 it ran a careful check of absences in principal plants to learn if Harvester employees were participating in Communist activities. The results were always negative. The 1925 report even showed a better attendance record on May 1 than on the preceding two days.[26]

Another absence study was carried out at the time of the execution of Sacco and Vanzetti on Tuesday, August 23, 1927. The average number of employees absent at each principal plant that Monday and Tuesday was compared with the average number absent on other Mondays and Tuesdays. Again the result was negative.[27]

Any union organizing activity in any part of the country served as an occasion for the industrial relations director to alert Harvester manufacturing executives. Thus in September 1925, a warning letter was sent to each Harvester plant on the innocuous fact that the AF of L was launching an intensive campaign for new members. Nothing happened at Harvester.[28] In November 1926 the director reported to works managers that the AF of L was raising money for a propaganda distribution campaign and that union activity in the East was in full swing. Labor trouble was expected in the spring. In Akron the AF of L was reported as making an attack on works councils and stock ownership plans in particular. Thirteen thousand rubber workers were reported to be AF of L members in Akron.

Only two or three cases of suspected outside union activity at Harvester plants were reported by the department between 1920 and 1933. In March 1929 several union men were reported working in Harvester toolrooms for purposes of organization. In September the director informed the work managers that the AF of L in Springfield, Ohio, was pushing for a five-day week and that this idea had been raised by a committee of one of the Harvester works councils but had been withdrawn before reaching the council floor.[29] In February 1930 the works managers discussed the unionization problems of the firm's truckdrivers. The McCormick Works drivers, it was reported, were organized and were receiving the union scale; union officials periodically called on the Deering Works superintendent for permission to organize the drivers. The company refused but decided to raise Deering rates to the union scale.[30]

In the 1920's, as we have seen, the industrial relations department's major contribution to antiunionism at Harvester, and its primary responsibility, was administration of the works councils. This called for a staff of three to five able professionals who traveled a circuit, chairing regular monthly and special meetings of twenty-five works councils, and for a department large enough to gather and analyze information pertinent to all problems which might come before the councils. The department's information appears to have come from many sources. One was the Special Conference Committee; a second, the National Industrial Conference Board; a third, the U. S. Bureau of Labor Statistics. In addition the department made wage surveys of its own of neighboring plants and cooperated with local employers and employer groups such as the Chicago Metal Trades Association in exchanging local wage and labor information. It kept close tabs on union wage rates and hours and presented the latest information on this subject to manufacturing officials.

Besides bringing in outside information, the industrial relations department had a big task merely communicating and interpreting wage information and industrial relations practices among the Harvester plants themselves. Harvester plants producing similar products in the same city, Chicago, often had quite differing policies, since superintendents interpreted central office directives differently. The department discovered that the West Pullman plant in 1922 was paying substantially higher piecework prices than other Chicago plants; that in 1923 the Deering plant had exceeded the common labor rates established by management and paid in other Chicago plants; and that overtime and night premium policies differed even in Chicago plants.[31]

Though the industrial relations department had been established in 1918 to block unionism for Harvester, it really came into its own when the government entered the field of industrial relations through the National Industrial Recovery Act and the Wagner Act. During the 'twenties and up to 1933, antiunionism had been quite effectively executed by plant superintendents with the help of foremen—except for the administration of the works councils, which required professional personnel leadership. The major antiunion weapon was simply nonrecognition of union representatives and dismissal of union employees by the superintendent. At the May 24, 1926, meeting of the works managers, the industrial relations director presented a 1903 document which showed that company labor policy had changed very little in twenty-three years.

Section 7A of the NIRA and subsequent labor legislation outlawed these crude old intimidating practices of the foremen and superintendents. To oppose unionism legally under the New Deal took knowledge of the law and finesse. New antiunion techniques were needed. For the first time Harvester superintendents, bewildered by Section 7A and by the Wagner Act, recognized their need for the know-how of the industrial relations department. Consequently the department was substantially enlarged by the addition of labor relations men at each plant, and superintendents were regularly briefed on union matters by the central industrial relations department. After the Wagner Act the superintendents asked that letters from the company president on the company's attitude toward unions be put in pay envelopes. This was rejected in favor of having foremen personally pass the word to the men—lest any written document play into the hands of the union organizers.[32] From 1933 through 1937 hardly a meeting of the works managers occurred without the subject of combating unionism arising. In these discussions the director of industrial relations was the sought-after authority. Through these years only the constant coaching of the superintendents by the department kept the company out of the tangles of the Wagner Act.

In spite of this expertise the industrial relations department could not save the company from censure. The NLRB held International Harvester Company in flagrant violation of the Wagner Act in 1936 for its domination of the works councils, and in 1941 for its domination of the "independent" unions at six plants and intimidation and interference with the right of employees to self-organization. In its antiunionism the Harvester industrial relations department of the 1930's must be regarded as fairly successful. Harvester's key plants, except for the Chicago Tractor Works and an ore mine at Hibbing, Minnesota, were not unionized until 1941, four years later than most of the basic mass-production industries.

The recognition of unions by International Harvester in 1941 posed a serious challenge for the industrial relations department, eliminating what had heretofore been its major assignment. Men who had spent their professional lives trying to avoid unions found themselves sitting down with union representatives to bargain.

Following the CIO victories at key Harvester plants in June 1941, the industrial relations department was split up into labor relations and personnel. George Hodge, an assistant director of the department, was made manager of labor relations. George J. Kelday, the former director of industrial relations, was in charge of the remainder of the department, which for three years became the personnel department. The reasons for this split were personal rather than theoretical; apparently the company thought that Hodge was particularly knowledgeable or gifted in dealing face to face with union bargaining committees.

The split was only temporary. In 1944 International Harvester began a fundamental management reorganization. The new setup was called a divisional structure. Instead of the traditional corporate structure based on sales, manufacturing, accounting, advertising, etc., the new structure followed product lines: motor trucks, agricultural implements, construction machinery. Industrial relations did not fit neatly into the divisional structure. Though each division after the reorganization had its own labor relations manager and staff, and each plant had a local staff, major union contracts had to be negotiated companywide with a union which encompassed all divisions. Under these circumstances there could be no real decentralization of labor relations. Therefore Harvester retained a companywide labor relations manager and staff reporting to the newly created vice president of industrial relations. Labor relations was so important that for practical purposes it continued to serve as an almost autonomous department, reporting in crisis times directly to the president of the company. In addition to labor relations, the industrial relations department took charge of employment, wage and salary administration, pensions, sickness and accident benefit programs, and such new or expanded activities as education and training.

Upon George Kelday's retirement an outsider, Ivan Willis, became in 1947 the first vice president in charge of industrial relations under the new divisional structure. Originally a schoolteacher, Willis learned the personnel profession at Humble Oil, one of the Rockefeller companies. At Humble during Willis' tenure personnel policies still reflected the labor-management holocaust in another Rockefeller company, at Ludlow, fifteen years earlier. According to Willis, Humble Oil personnel were told that the company could easily afford a million dollar error in drilling for oil but could not afford one personnel blunder such as an unfair discharge of a worker.[33] Willis went to Harvester from the Curtis Wright Aircraft Company, where he had directed labor relations during World War II.

Besides the men holding the top industrial relations post, two men within the department have greatly influenced Harvester labor relations policies in recent years. The first is George Hodge, who held the title of manager of labor relations from 1941 to 1952. Hodge like Kelday was an insider, coming to the central industrial relations staff in 1922 from a post at the Harvester plant in Richmond, Indiana. Like Kelday again, he spent much of his professional career administering the works councils. The second man to hold the post of manager of labor relations was William J. Reilly, who succeeded Hodge in 1952. Without question Reilly has been the most influential management representative in Harvester labor relations from the postwar period into the present decade. He entered the Wisconsin Steel Works as an electrician in 1926. In the early 'thirties he was elected an employee representative to the works council and soon became chairman of the employee delegation. In 1937, when the works councils were disbanded, he took leave of absence from the company, borrowed money from the employee credit union, and established a new unaffiliated union of which he became the president. After brief service in labor relations departments at Harvester plants in Springfield, Ohio, and Milwaukee, Wisconsin, he was promoted to the Harvester central industrial relations staff.

Scientific Management

What has been the impact on Harvester industrial relations of such movements as "scientific management," the industrial psychology of the 1920's, and the human relations school of Elton Mayo?

A great deal has been written about these movements and their influence on American industry; their impact at International Harvester, however, has been minimal. From 1902 to 1919 Harvester's immersion in betterment work and welfarism seemed to crowd out any interest in scientific management—although Miss Beeks in 1902 strongly recommended the employment of a production engineer, J. U. Gunn, who had been employed by Bethlehem Steel to change its day rates to piece rates.[34] She had been shocked by the ruthless cutting of piece rates and felt that her betterment work was being hampered by lack of a fair wage scale. Her advice was not followed. International Harvester offered profit sharing to all employees through stock ownership instead of Taylor's "scientific" setting of piece rates. At the McCormick Works straight piecework had been widely used since the 1860's. By 1896, 65 percent of McCormick employees were paid by the piece. Piece-rate prices were set by the foremen without the use of stopwatch studies and were kept in line by annual adjustments, which usually meant cutting rates that yielded earnings above the expected level.

While not espousing scientific management in the manner of Taylor, the McCormick Harvesting Machine Company and the International Harvester companies seem to have been technologically very progressive. In the late 'eighties and 'nineties skilled crafts were broken down into a series of simple, repetitive operations to be performed by unskilled or semiskilled workers with the aid of improved machinery. As indicated in Chapter 1, the introduction of labor-saving techniques had profound effects on wages and union organization.

Piecework prices have continued to be a chronic problem. In the early 'twenties two outside engineering consultants were brought in to survey piece-rate practices. Their work was deemed so important that several time study men were employed for each plant; the McCormick

Works alone had three in 1923; there were twenty-seven in the entire company. This innovation was fought by the superintendents and foremen just as they had fought the early welfare workers and the industrial relations department. In 1923, superintendents at the McCormick, Plano, and Rock Falls, Illinois, plants recommended the abolition of all time study men in order to save money.[35]

While the opposition of the plant superintendents to the growth of professionals in time study and labor relations was successful in the 'twenties, they were fighting a losing battle. The difficult labor relations of the 'thirties brought a multiplication of specialists, each whittling away some part of the superintendent's once absolute authority. The 1964 Harvester rates and methods department included 273 men at the local plant level who were concerned with setting piece rates. In the central office six professionals were engaged in research on standards and methods and in supervision of standard-setting procedures.

The company's decision to set its piece rates "scientifically" after World War II was one contributing cause of the most difficult period of labor relations in the company's history.

Harvester never used any of the elaborate counseling techniques of the Elton Mayo school. During the 'twenties and 'thirties the company put all its energies behind the employee representation plan and felt it was a successful program.

Though the welfare department was begun largely as a deterrent to unionism, unionism profoundly influenced the size and character of the developing department. In fact, the status and strength of the industrial relations department were directly proportional to the strength of the outside unions. From 1905 to World War I, when Harvester felt comparatively safe from union attack, the welfare department failed to hold its own against the sniping of hostile line manufacturing executives. The rise of unions during World War I transformed the dying welfare department into an active industrial relations department which supervised the Harvester counterunion force, the works councils, for twenty-two years. As unions weakened again in the mid-'twenties, the industrial relations department remained active but its independence in the company hierarchy was again destroyed. When the federal labor legislation of the 1930's gave unions lasting protection and strength, the department grew steadily in size and function, finally achieving in 1947 vice presidential status.

Equal Employment Opportunity Program

The motives for the early welfare programs—the stock gifts, sickness and accident insurance, pensions, profit sharing—were mixtures of altruism and insurance against trade unionism and trust busting. The end of the antitrust suit in 1927, the serious industrial depression of the 'thirties, and Harvester's recognition of trade unions in 1941 put a virtual end to new forms of welfarism. The major exception was the launching of an equal employment opportunity program at the close of World War II. This reform now appears the most significant and far-reaching industrial relations reform originated by International Harvester in its entire history. While far from achieving its ultimate goals in this area the company has made steady progress under a well-conceived plan.

The inventor of the reaper, Cyrus H. McCormick I, was a Virginia farmer and owner of four slaves. When he moved to Chicago in 1847 he retained his Southern viewpoint toward the question of slavery. Before and during the Civil War McCormick became almost a fanatical opponent of any use of force to end slavery. He purchased newspapers, and even imported a Presbyterian minister to further his views. He broke early with Stephen Douglas, the advocate of compromise. So strong were his feelings that he spent most of the Civil War in England, returning in 1864 to run for Congress on the Democratic stop-the-war platform.[36]

There is no reason, however, to believe that the founder's views on slavery had any influence on the employment policy of the firm. The question of Negro employment at the Chicago factory did not arise for many years, probably not until the labor shortages of World War I and the early 1920's. Many firms began using Negroes as strikebreakers at this time, but there is no evidence that Harvester did in the strikes of 1916 or 1919.

The first written statement of company policy on equal employment opportunity appeared in March 1919 in the constitution of the newly established Harvester Industrial Council Plan. Article XVIII declared: "There shall be no discrimination under this plan against any employee because of race, sex, political or religious affiliation, or membership in any labor or other organization."[37] This statement presumably became official company policy after an employee vote of adoption. The constitution was widely distributed to Harvester management, to employees, and to the public. But to assign the origin of the current Harvester equal opportunity policy to this early period, as the company did in a 1962 statement,[38] is to misinterpret the original purpose of the article.

In line with the purpose of the Harvester Industrial Council Plan to block trade unionism, Article XVIII, properly read, was a backhanded statement of the company's open shop policy. The insertion of "race, sex, political or religious affiliation" was a subterfuge to give a liberal coloration to the antiunion policy of the company. In fact, no sooner was the plan adopted than its coauthor, Arthur H. Young, was pressuring the manufacturing executives to cut down on the proportion of Negro employees. This cloaking of the open shop policy with the philosophy of the Declaration of Independence was a common practice and abounds in open shop literature, especially since the big open shop campaigns of 1903–4.

During World War I and throughout the 1920's, conflicting pressures governed Negro employment at International Harvester. Labor shortages encouraged the hiring of Negroes, while the industrial relations department fretted over the increase and repeatedly urged that the number of Negroes be reduced. The actual employment policy, however, was left to the discretion of the individual plant superintendents. Some hired large numbers of Negroes; some hired none. In the twine mills and foundries, areas of the greatest labor shortages, Negro employment rose substantially. In certain other works, the superintendents hired no Negroes.

After World War I the industrial relations department compiled regular reports on nationality, race, and citizenship of Harvester employees. From time to time Industrial Relations Director Arthur Young discussed the growing proportion of Negro employees with the manufacturing executives. He reported to the works managers in October 1922 that the Illinois Steel Company boarded 400 Negroes but that tenure among them was only three days. At the Chicago stockyards, he added, the Negro quota was held at 20 percent of the work force, and the packers considered Negro workers of poor quality. The Deering and McCormick twine mills employed 15 percent Negroes at that time.[39]

The superintendents themselves were reluctant to hire "too many" Negroes, probably because they regarded them as much the same as a nationality group. Harvester experience showed that the cohesivensss of nationality groups worked against the company in strike situations.

Nevertheless, with the increasing labor shortage Negro employment increased. By January 1923 the Negroes at the McCormick twine mills had increased to 20 percent. Even so, spindles were idle for lack of labor. By April the McCormick malleable core room was employing 50 percent Negro girls. Wisconsin Steel, employing no Negroes, had gone as far as Kansas City to import Mexicans.[40]

In May 1923 Arthur Young presented to the works managers a comprehensive survey on Negro employment at all Chicago Harvester plants. The McCormick Works employed 18 percent, Deering 11 percent, and Tractor 9 percent. The minutes of works managers' meetings at this time reported, ". . . Webber [Works; in Chicago] has the worst showing with 21 per cent quite generally distributed through the various departments."[41] Wisconsin Steel, the Deering Rolling Mill, and the West Pullman Works employed no Negroes. The Chicago meat packers, according to Young, still drew the line at 20 percent; and Western Electric, with 30,000 employees, used no Negro help at all. It was suggested that Harvester try to get English, Swedish, and German immigrants.

Still the proportion of Negroes continued to rise. By April 1924, even after a slight decline, it was 35 percent at the Tractor foundry, 29 percent at the McCormick foundry,[42] and 24 percent at the twine mills. Young called this decline "an improvement over previous months," and warned the manufacturing executives that Negro help should not exceed 20 percent of the total number employed. Two superintendents explained that Negro help was never taken in preference to white help but that satisfactory Negro employees were not released merely because they were not white. Works managers were in agreement that the best way to stay within the quota was by restraint at the time of hiring.[43]

Comparative studies of Negro and white performance made by the Harvester industrial relations department challenged the prejudice against Negroes. The first study made was of turnover and absenteeism at two Chicago plants for the period February to August 1924. The results indicated that McCormick Works Negroes had less turnover and absenteeism than whites, while at the Deering plant the reverse was true. The report explained the poor Negro showing at the Deering Works as due to poor housing.[44]

Company policy toward minority employment was obliquely challenged in 1925 by a Negro leader who sent a letter to Industrial Relations Director Kelday asking for an opportunity to sell the idea of employing more Negroes. The request prompted Kelday to warn the works managers that the Negroes were working through the AF of L to promote the idea of employing more Negroes. He agreed, however, to meet the man and tell him of the company employment of Negroes in the foundries. At this point Cyrus McCormick III proposed a special study of Negro employment in the Chicago plants to see if Harvester could not further increase its Negro employment. This expression by Mr. McCormick in 1925 appears to be the first indication that Harvester executives were concerned about the discrimination against Negroes.[45]

The industrial relations department undertook the study but did little more than survey the opinions of the various superintendents. The report, though shot through with unsupported generalizations, revealed that the superintendents, after added experience, were raising sharply their assessment of Negro performance:

Kelday Report on Minority Employment[46]

1. That the works are not receiving applications for common labor jobs from American born white persons.

2. That there are very few if any European immigrants applying for common labor but the Negro is considered equally efficient as the foreign born whites. In some instances the Negro is held to be suitable for semi-skilled work. In one instance a superintendent found that Colored help in his foundry resulted in better costs and better quality than formerly was the case with foreign immigrant employees. The large number of Negro applicants permits of a good selection. Colored employees understand the English language and endeavor to comply with instructions. They are considered more loyal than foreigners. Steel mills are more satisfied with Mexicans for common and semi-skilled labor.

3. No racial trouble between Mexicans, Colored, and white is being experienced.

4. Colored employees do not develop into skilled mechanics. One or two superintendents felt that if employed for a period of years a few might become skilled. The Mexicans at the steel mills are developing into semi-skilled tradesmen but none are employed in mechanical or electrical trades.

5. All superintendents believe that Negroes and Mexicans indulge less in intoxicating liquor than do white employees.

6. The Colored and Mexican employee is less troublesome on the wage and labor question than is the white immigrant.

7. As concerns absenteeism and tardiness the Negro is found no worse a violator than the white employee, American or foreign. Mexicans are seldom absent and are considered more stable than whites.

8. At the Deering Works it has been found that Colored employees suffer fewer injuries than a proportionate number of whites. Similar information was not obtainable from other works.

9. Negroes and Mexicans are no worse trouble makers than other employees.

10. No racial distinction is made in handling Mexican and Colored employees as far as washroom, locker room, job preference, etc. are concerned.

11. The careful selection that the present large number of Colored applicants permits of is resulting in securing an intelligent class, probably of higher intelligence than the white immigrant who does not speak English.

12. When asked whether Negroes or Mexicans were preferred the superintendents were not ready to answer because of limited experience with Mexicans. They liked Negroes, however, because of being able to speak English and being larger in stature. The steel mills have not tried Colored help but are of the opinion that Mexicans will more readily develop into semiskilled employees.

13. Negroes and Mexicans work in all departments excepting the strictly skilled mechanical trade departments. Generally, however, they fit into semiskilled or common labor jobs.

14. The superintendents did not desire too many employees of one nationality, preferring a mixture of nationalities unless American employees are largely American born.

The results of this 1925 company study would appear to have removed the grounds for any discrimination in hiring Negroes; in fact to have encouraged Negro preference. But Cyrus McCormick III did not follow up his interest in Negro employment, and no policy change was forthcoming. By 1928 there were still no Negroes at the Deering Rolling Mill, West Pullman Works, Wisconsin Steel, or the Rock Falls or Hamilton, Ontario, plants. Mexican employment at Wisconsin Steel had risen to 20 percent. By December 1929 Negro employment at the McCormick Twine Mill had risen above the 24 percent of the 1925 survey to 27.5 percent. This proportion was assumed to be too high, and an assistant director in the industrial relations department informed the works managers that he had "ordered the situation corrected, which is gradually being done."[47]

However, in the Harvester plants that hired Negroes, the end of the labor shortage in the 1930's proved more effective than industrial relations department directives in "correcting" the percentage of Negro employees. In the McCormick Twine Mill, for example, Negro employment had declined to 18.75 percent by 1940; in the McCormick Works it dropped from the 18 percent of 1923 to 10 percent.[48] This decline temporarily halted company concern with this matter.

When returning labor shortages in World War II again brought the problem, the policy at International Harvester was markedly different. Table 4 gives plant-by-plant and companywide figures that indicate the switch from a negative to a positive approach toward Negro employment. One reason for the change was the national policy of fair employment set by President Roosevelt. Executive Order 8802 of June 1941 required a no-discrimination employment clause in all defense contracts and established a Fair Employment Practices Committee. The company's initial response was to terminate the plant superintendents' traditional autonomy in hiring. Consequently, Wisconsin Steel, which had never hired Negroes under the autonomy policy, employed 640 Negroes, 13 percent of its work force, by 1943; and West Pullman, in a similar about-face, had 10 percent.[49] Table 4 indicates that these changes were the beginning of a program of nondiscrimination in employment at Harvester which extended far beyond the dictates of the President's order and the World War II labor shortage.

Two people gave Harvester's commitment to fair employment an intensity and endurance which were unique in American industry at this time. One was Sara Southall, a member of the Harvester industrial relations staff. For some years after she joined Harvester she worked as a volunteer with the industrial department of the YWCA and with the Chicago Urban League, where her efforts were directed toward fair employment. Because of her knowledge and experience in this field she was asked to serve on President Roosevelt's Fair Employment Practices Committee. The Harvester Company granted her leave for this assignment. Awareness of Miss Southall's work on the FEPC inevitably tended to focus more interest of Harvester executives on the company's own performance in this area. However, no compelling, companywide program for fair employment would have been possible without the interest and vigorous leadership of Fowler McCormick, who became president of International Harvester in 1941. McCormick held a deep conviction that people should be dealt with as individuals, not as groups. He vitalized this belief by insisting on a fair employment policy in all Harvester plants throughout the country.

Under Miss Southall's planning and guidance and Fowler McCormick's personal attention the company quietly developed a comprehensive plan for equal employment opportunity at the end of World War II. At this time Harvester was opening new plants in Memphis, Tennessee; Louisville, Kentucky; and Evansville, Indiana.[50] Carrying out a policy of nondiscrimination in these Southern plants was a task of substantial magnitude in comparison to the integration of the plants in Chicago under the impetus of wartime pressures. It required determined and creative leadership from a broad range of Harvester management. President Fowler McCormick set the tone at a Chamber of Commerce banquet celebrating the opening of the Memphis plant, where he told the assembled political, civic, and business leaders: "It is our belief, in our company, that all of us have a responsibility to hire colored people, ... We must give them an opportunity to earn a living. It is our company policy." Negroes would be given "the same wages for the same work" as the white employees.[51]

Wise use of the unique opportunity of hiring an entire factory force at one time was an important factor in Harvester's success with nondiscrimination in these plants. All who applied for work were informed of the company policy and accepted it as a condition of employment. Negroes were hired for many jobs outside the traditionally Negro common labor jobs and were dispersed throughout the plants. They were carefully selected so that the first Negroes working in any department were "superior both in qualifications and personality"[52] to the white workers in the department. Negroes at these Southern Harvester plants were working "in jobs that were probably the best they had ever had or could aspire to in their communities at that time, ..."[53] In 1946, the first year of operation of the Louisville plant, 4.2 percent of the employees were Negroes; in the Memphis plant's first year, 1947, 12.2 percent of the employees were Negroes.

The company gained valuable allies, for the most part, and useful tools for carrying on the nondiscrimination policy, when unions were certified and nondiscrimination clauses were included in the union contracts. For example, the UAW contract read: "Neither the Company nor the Union, in carrying out their obligations under this contract, shall discriminate in any manner whatsoever against any employee because of race, sect, political or religious affiliation, or nationality."[54] Discrimination became a violation of the contract, and questions of discrimination were handled under the regular grievance procedure specified in the contract. Thus these grievances could not be avoided and had to be decided upon the objective basis of "Does the act in question violate the contract?" The seniority provisions of the contracts were especially important in ensuring Negroes equal opportunity for advancement in the plant. Among the bidders for an open job, the worker with the highest seniority who could qualify for the job was entitled to it. Because of the company's hiring of Negroes when the plant opened, there were Negroes with sufficient seniority to claim the open jobs. These advancement opportunities were greatly increased by the worker's right to bid on job openings in departments other than his own. In many Southern plants strict departmental seniority held the Negroes within a few departments.

For the most part the company itself had to give the Negroes the training they needed to qualify for advancement. In his study of community training opportunities, such as high school and vocational school courses, John Hope found that "Almost invariably the subjects available to Negro students had limited transfer value to Harvester operations, while those taken by White students were concentrated in the mechanical, metal-working and electrical trades characteristic of modern factory processes . . . ."[55]

"The Harvester plants in the cities studied are virtually the only places where Negroes can obtain even the basic machine-shop training necessary for semiskilled jobs."[56] By 1959, 72.4 percent of the Negro employees in the Memphis plant and 65.7 percent in the Louisville plant were in semiskilled jobs.[57]

The conscientiousness of the local plant managers in carrying out this companywide policy of nondiscrimination was enhanced by the company requirement that reports of each plant's progress in this integration program be submitted regularly to the executive committee.

Strong contracts and earnest leadership have not produced integrated factories automatically or painlessly. Adamant opposition from some craft unionists, work stoppages, and wildcat strikes have slowed and sometimes temporarily halted the drive toward integration. The intensity of the prosegregation feeling with which both the company and the unions have had to cope is evident in the struggle within Local 988 of the UAW at the Memphis plant.

At the time of this conflict, 1956–60, about 500 of the approximately 1,800 local union members were Negroes. As required by the national union, the union meetings were integrated, though the Negro members tended to sit together. The UAW policy of integration was being challenged repeatedly at union meetings by segregationists under the leadership of a union steward who was formerly a vice president of Local 988. The steward's motions were continually ruled out of order by the local president. On an appeal of these rulings Herschel Davis, administrative assistant to UAW Vice President Pat Greathouse, came from Detroit to Memphis. At a union meeting he warned that Local 988 might lose its UAW membership by segregationist activity. He was jeered with shouts of "Go back up North." The leader of the segregationists told Davis: "We belong to Reuther's union but we don't believe in Reuther's integration. . . . . We may have to choose between CIO and segregation. For my part, I'll take segregation. The time will come when workers of the South will decide whether we want your union with desegregation or our own union with segregation. When the showdown comes, we'll take segregation and leave you guys up in Detroit."[58] Davis warned that loss of UAW membership would mean loss of the contract with the company while leaving the racial problem unsolved.

In 1956 Local 988 planned a new union building. The number of restrooms indicated in the drawings aroused suspicions that segregated facilities were planned. The national union approved a special dues assessment for the building fund only after being assured that no segregation would be permitted. When the building was completed, signs "White" and "Colored" appeared over restrooms and drinking fountains. Thus began a two-year battle between Local 988 and the national union. After trying to persuade the local to remove the signs, UAW Vice President Greathouse went to Memphis and ordered the signs painted out. When he left Memphis the local ordered new signs painted on. A labor columnist, Jack Crellin, told the story of Pat Greathouse's return to Memphis: "It was late this last Monday night when a car, headlights out, glided up to the curb in front of Local 988 UAW in Memphis, Tenn. Three men, one carrying a brush and a can of paint, climbed out and scurried across the sidewalk to the main entrance of the darkened building."[59] They painted out the signs, changed the building's locks, and were in physical control of Local 988 when the local's officers returned the next morning.

In describing a subsequent meeting with the local membership Douglas Fraser, member of the UAW Executive Board, said "I have never been called such filthy names in my life. They said they were going to throw both Pat and I into the Mississippi and for a time we thought they were."[60]

The strength of the segregationist attitude in Local 988 was further demonstrated by a contribution of $325 made by white members of the local to the Little Rock, Arkansas, Private School Corporation, for

TABLE 4

Percentage of Negroes Employed at International Harvester

Year	*West Pullman*	*Wisconsin Steel*	*McCormick*	*Tractor*	*McCormick Twine*	*Melrose Park*	*Louisville*	*Memphis*	*Company Total*
1940	*	*	10.3	6.5	18.8	†	†	†	4.5
1941	*	*	*	*	*	†	†	†	*
1942	0.5	11.2	11.2	7.3	29.9	†	†	†	5.9
1943	9.7	13.4	19.3	12.9	51.9	†	†	†	9.5
1944	10.2	11.1	24.8	18.9	62.1	†	†	†	11.6
1945	7.4	13.3	25.3	17.5	63.6	†	†	†	11.7
1946	6.4	10.0	26.0	18.5	67.0	4.0	4.2	†	11.0
1947	8.4	13.2	30.3	18.6	70.4	8.5	6.5	12.2	11.5
1948	8.6	17.2	31.5	19.4	59.6	10.1	5.9	19.6	11.9
1949	7.9	14.4	19.3	19.3	52.7	10.5	9.5	23.2	10.6
1950	8.9	17.0	28.5	22.4	64.8	12.8	14.1	23.1	12.8
1951	9.8	18.6	20.5	23.6	75.6	13.5	14.3	21.1	12.7
1952	12.7	19.7	31.4	24.1	42.4	14.1	16.9	20.5	13.8
1953	5.5	14.4	13.6	16.2	†	11.8	11.2	26.1	9.8
1954	10.7	17.3	24.1	17.5	†	14.4	13.2	24.8	11.3
1955	12.0	19.1	33.0	19.3	†	16.6	20.9	23.0	14.5
1956	10.7	18.3	25.7	22.1	†	18.1	20.1	23.8	14.1
1957	12.4	17.4	32.6	18.5	†	14.5	16.7	23.3	13.0
1958	11.5	18.6	34.5	17.9	†	16.0	15.4	21.6	13.5
1959	12.3	16.9	37.1	25.8	†	18.4	14.4	23.5	13.8
1960	9.4	13.4	28.7	13.3	†	9.3	11.9	19.3	9.3

Source: I. H. Co. Files, Chicago.
* Figures not available.
† Plant not yet built, or closed.

the education of white children. The acting chairman of the local directed the solicitation of funds.[61]

Perfect integration has not been achieved, but the company has moved forward, reaching a companywide percentage of Negro employment of 13.8 in 1959 compared to 4.5 in 1940 (Table 4). In most plants the ratio of Negro to white employees is about equal to the ratio in the community. There is still a higher level of Negro employment in plants that have foundries, and a higher percentage of Negroes in unskilled work; but large numbers of Negroes are employed in semiskilled work.[62] In 1959, 207 Negroes were in skilled apprenticeable occupations throughout the Harvester plants.[63] Gradually a few Negroes have been put in salaried jobs and clerical jobs, even in the Southern plants. In the general office in Chicago in 1959 thirteen Negroes were in positions of clerk or above.[64] Locker rooms, toilets, and eating facilities have all been integrated.

A by-product of Harvester's equal opportunity program was that in implementing it the company found itself working hand in glove with the unions. This experience occurred during the very period, 1946–55, when collective bargaining relationships were so bitter. Whites who walked off the job when Negroes were promoted found their own union officers breaking up their wildcat picket lines and separating fighting groups of whites and Negroes. The firm stand of unions and company together successfully protected the Negroes' contract rights and minimized the disruptive and at times violent protests of the segregationists.

In 1963 International Harvester jointly with the President's Committee on Equal Employment Opportunity put out a "Plan for Progress." This is a very specific and progressive plan for further implementation of the equal opportunity program. Chiefly it is a reaffirmation of the company policy of welcoming minority members to its employment and of providing them with equal opportunities for training and advancement in the Harvester plants. In 1963 the equal employment opportunities program of International Harvester was one of the most advanced in the nation. Like other programs it has some distance to go, but its progress toward the goal has been steady and consistent since its origin in World War II.

9

Permanent Unionism

Phases of Labor-Management Relations

In his book *Labor and Industrial Relations* Richard Lester has outlined four common stages in the evolution of management's labor relations policy, from hostility to cooperation with unions.[1] The first stage he calls the policy of union exclusion: management seeks to discourage organization among its employees. The next he labels containment: the union is considered an alien or outside agency, to be dealt with at arm's length; management lives up to legal requirements in terms of recognition of the union and collective bargaining but goes no further. The third stage is acceptance and accommodation. Here the union is used as a two-way channel of communication. Management endeavors to live with the union and to make collective bargaining a constructive force; it seeks the union's aid in speedy, harmonious settlement of grievances and in collective bargaining negotiations. The fourth stage of management policy is union-management cooperation. This, according to Lester, is extremely rare and frequently involves some form of profit sharing and/or union responsibility toward production. He of course recognized that there was "no pattern of inevitable evolution" of management's labor relations policies.[2]

The evolutionary acceptance of unionism described by Lester has clearly occurred in the United States since 1933. But Harvester's pre-1933 experience with unionism indicated a different pattern. The twenty-three years of collective bargaining, 1862–86, ended with expulsion of the union in a series of violent strikes. The additional experience of the 1903–4 contractual relationship brought not company acceptance of unionism but another determined and prolonged rejection.

Before 1935 Harvester history was typical of the experience of American industry. Unionism made great strides in the 1880's, only to be thrown back by successive employer offensives and economic recessions. Similarly the spectacular resurgence of unionism in 1900–3 and 1916–20 was obliterated by the management open shop drives of 1904 and 1921.

The union advances after 1933 might well have met the same fate as earlier ones but for the Wagner Act, the Supreme Court decision in the Jones-Laughlin case, and sympathetic national and state administrations. Only for the post-1935 period does Lester's view of management's progressive acceptance of unionism with increasing union contacts seem valid.

General Motors is typical of the many corporations which have followed the Lester pattern in the post-1935 era. As late as the mid-'thirties it was using labor spies to ferret out union officers and members systematically. From 1937 to 1950 General Motors progressed slowly through the normal stages listed by Lester to at least the third stage, acceptance and accommodation. International Harvester, however, did not move normally through these stages. It did not move from exclusion to containment until 1941, four years behind General Motors and U. S. Steel. The transition from containment to acceptance and accommodation was particularly prolonged and was not accomplished until the late 1950's, almost ten years behind the norm as represented by the majority of the large firms.

The CIO Comes to Harvester

By the beginning of 1941 the Harvester Company was one of the few large companies still holding outside unionism at bay. In only three of twenty-three plants and in the company's iron ore mines at Hibbing, Minnesota, had an outside union been recognized. The first unions to gain recognition—both in 1938—were the Farm Equipment branch of the Steelworkers Organizing Committee (soon to become the Farm Equipment Workers Organizing Committee) at the Chicago Tractor Works and the United Steelworkers at the iron ore mines. At the Tractor Works the FE had gained control of the Works Council in early 1937 and achieved formal recognition a year later. Yet it was unable to negotiate even a first wage increase by January 1941 in spite of signing two contracts. The United Steelworkers at Hibbing signed a contract in 1938. The next Harvester plants to be unionized were the Richmond, Indiana, plant and the Fort Wayne Truck Works, both through NLRB elections. Having lost an Automobile Labor Board proportional representation election at Fort Wayne in 1935, UAW Local 57 after a prolonged struggle won an NLRB election on March 21, 1940, and was certified as the bargaining agent at this plant. Nine months later no contract had been signed and the union called a strike for New Year's Day, 1941. By communicating directly with the workers, the company was successful in getting the strike called off after only eight hours.

The slow pace of the CIO's organizing at Harvester resulted from several factors: the existence of long established and functioning company unions, company opposition to outside unionism, and the fact that the severe recession of late 1937 and 1938 nipped the CIO drive before it got moving.

Early in 1937, at the peak of the auto and steel drives, an organizer from the SWOC's Chicago office, Joseph Webber, began recruiting International Harvester employees. Progress was slow. Through April 21, 1937, every Harvester plant had a works council which met regularly. The older Harvester employees, who predominated in the leadership of the works councils, showed an almost feudal obsequiousness toward management. At the councils of the McCormick Works requests for improvements or mild criticism of management tended to be preceded with expressions such as, "I don't feel there is any doubt in the minds of management about our being real loyal employees of the Harvester Company."[3] CIO unionism at this period was quite a wrench from this type of thinking. During the time of the CIO successes in steel and autos, International Harvester passed out comparable wage increases: two weeks' pay, labeled extra compensation, in October 1936; five cents per hour in December 1936; and five cents in April 1937.

When the company abolished the works councils following the Jones-Laughlin decision, the creation of "independent" successors to them in April 1937 gave their officers an ever greater stake in blocking the CIO, except where Webber had already captured the works council leadership for the SWOC. Thereafter the insecurity attendant on heavy layoffs in the sharp economic recession that began in August 1937 severely checked the rising tide of unionism. Even so, if Webber had been able to start six months earlier he would probably have toppled the key plants of the Harvester empire. Besides capturing the Tractor Works Council, Webber in 1937 recruited a young McCormick Works councilman, Gerald Fielde, who was to become the Farm Equipment Workers' most talented leader. Fielde was put on the SWOC staff in the summer of 1937 along with four non-Harvester employees. Grant Oakes, formerly of the Tractor Works Council, followed Fielde onto the staff of the SWOC in 1938.

In mid-1937 Van Bittner, organizing director of the SWOC, conducted a purge of left-wing staff members. Probably Webber would have been eliminated but for his key role in the farm equipment organizing drive. Max Kampelman reports that Webber was a Communist party member who had had a training period in Moscow.[4] Webber's position was strengthened when in 1938 the Farm Equipment branch was spun off as a separate union, the Farm Equipment Workers Organizing Committee.

Webber, Fielde, Oakes, and the other staff members of the Farm Equipment Works Organizing Committee worked with only modest success on the Harvester farm equipment plants from 1937 to January 1941. There were FE members at many plants; but at the key plants the FE did not have the confidence that it could win elections. The greatest stumbling block was Fielde's own plant, the huge McCormick Works, where by January 1941 the FE had fewer than 200 members out of 6,000 employees.[5]

Meanwhile, finding the International Harvester plants too tough to crack by direct organizing assault, the FE was proceeding through the legal procedures of the NLRB to get the "independent" unions outlawed as company-dominated. In 1938 it filed charges of company domination against independent unions in six Harvester plants; McCormick, West Pullman (Chicago), East Moline, Farmall (Rock Island), Rock Falls (Illinois), and Milwaukee. The outcome of the case was probably never in doubt, but the sheer volume of the legal work and the maneuvers of the company attorneys took over three years to complete. The decision branding the six unions "company dominated" and ordering their dissolution came on February 8, 1941. The union through its attorneys and its informal connections within the NLRB may have known the probable outcome and the approximate timing of the decision. The company too may have anticipated the outcome. As the time of the decision approached, the hour of decision for the four-year union organizing drive arrived. The FE believed it could not win an election in the key plants, such as the McCormick Works, and the alternative was to force recognition through a strike. Even if the strike failed to gain company recognition, if it achieved a substantial wage concession, it would make possible a victory in a subsequent election. This in fact had been the successful pattern at General Motors in 1937, where sitdowns in selected plants by a minority of employees won concessions which aided the union in the subsequent NLRB election.

At this critical juncture the CIO quietly loaned to the FE Robert Travis, the man who with Wyndham Mortimer had engineered the General Motors sitdown. Travis had cut his teeth on the rough strikes at the Toledo Chevrolet plant in 1935. In this period before NLRB election procedures were readily available, open discrimination by employers was common and unions called minority strikes and organized afterwards.

When the NLRB decision of February 8 was announced, the Tractor plant workers were already on strike as of January 29. The Rock Falls plant had been closed since January 19; the Richmond plant was struck February 18. But in the other key plants—Milwaukee, Farmall, East Moline, West Pullman, and McCormick, the FE was weak. Worst of all from the FE point of view, after the NLRB decision outlawed the independent unions, the officers of these unions began recruiting their former members into AF of L federal unions. At the McCormick Works the AF of L was strong enough to circulate petitions for an NLRB election. An AF of L election victory would rob the FE of the gain from four years of organizing effort.

Travis proved equal to the occasion. Undeterred by having a mere handful of union members in the McCormick Works, he went ahead with plans to shut down the heart of the Harvester empire. His aim was to demand recognition as the price of reopening the plants, and thus avoid a representation election. At noon sharp on Friday, February 28, Travis had sealed letters delivered to eight key FE members located in strategic departments in various sections of the McCormick Works. One or two FE millwrights with plantwide access could easily have made the deliveries. Each letter instructed the reader to walk, one-half hour hence, to the main switch of the department and shut it off; he was to announce to all workers that they were to go home because the plant was on strike and was being shut down. Each of these eight men was then to proceed to the successive departments listed in the letter and to shut them down in a similar manner, picking up as he went along the few FE reliables in the department.[6]

On the whole the shutdown operated like clockwork. In a few cases foremen turned the switch back on and reassembled their work forces. Some departments had to be shut down two or three times, with accompanying threats to foremen not to start up again. The only violence occurred in the malleable foundry, which was an AF of L stronghold. By the time the FE minutemen arrived to shut it down they numbered several dozen. A bitter clash occurred when foundrymen, who substantially outnumbered the FE, resisted the shutdown. Tractor wheels were rolled down upon the invaders. Bricks and tools were thrown. Several persons were injured. Police finally entered, stopped the fighting, and expelled both factions. Over the weekend the company notified workers that the plant would not reopen on Monday.

Irving Brown, an AF of L organizer, claimed that the shutdown was carried out by a small minority of 200 men from the inside aided by 150 outsiders who climbed over the fence. Before a National Defense Mediation Board panel Brown described how the minority went from department to department armed with monkey wrenches and other tools and drove the workers out of the factory. "Then," Brown continued, "the company closed the gates and even permitted pickets to build shacks on company property. This in my experience is a new style strike."[7]

Four Harvester plants with 15,000 employees were now closed by FE strikes: Tractor, McCormick, Richmond, and Rock Falls.

At this point Secretary of Labor Frances Perkins intervened, telegraphing the parties to attend a special conciliation meeting in Washington on March 3. The AF of L promptly notified Miss Perkins that it represented workers at the McCormick Works and did not see how there could be mediation without first picking a bargaining agent. It demanded an NLRB election.

The meetings, headed by John Roy Steelman, director of the U. S. Conciliation Service, lasted four days and one full night. The FE delegation, headed by FE President Grant Oakes, included DeWitt Gilpin, Powers Hapgood, and Alan Haywood, the last two representing the CIO. Vice President Fowler McCormick headed the International Harvester delegation. The FE at first demanded recognition at the

McCormick and the Rock Falls Works, wage increases of 12½ cents an hour, and return of strikers to jobs without discrimination. Fowler McCormick was adamant in refusing any recognition for the FE at either of these Works and in refusing a wage increase at any of the four plants. At one point William Knudsen, director of the Office of Production Management and former president of General Motors, was brought in. After listening to the company's statement of its inability to meet the FE's request to raise the hiring rate from 62½ to 75 cents, Knudsen bluntly asked Fowler McCormick if the company couldn't go to 70 cents, as it had recently done in its Fort Wayne Truck Works. When McCormick refused, Mr. Knudsen asked about a five-cent raise and then a two-cent raise. Each time the answer was the same.[8]

Unable to budge the company and unable to offer the FE anything, Steelman could only recess the meetings indefinitely. Publicity, probably useful, was all the FE got from the Washington conclave. With government help, however, it had brought a McCormick to the bargaining table for the first time since 1885. Though the delegation left Washington empty-handed, the FE prospects were still good. Plants with 15,000 Harvester employees were tightly closed. If the FE could just keep them shut, the defense crisis would bring added pressure on the company for concessions or perhaps arbitration.

But rival unionism and an adamant employer tipped the scales against the FE. The AF of L leaders on March 7, 1941, filed a petition for an NLRB election at the McCormick Works and publicly demanded that the company reopen the plant and the city of Chicago provide police protection. Frank P. Fenton, AF of L director of organization, and organizers Harry O'Reilly and Irving Brown were on the scene with assistance from the Chicago Federation of Labor.

An AF of L mass meeting in Chicago for Harvester employees, attended by 2,900, encouraged the company to attempt to reopen the plant.

The CIO picket lines at McCormick were reinforced from neighboring steel mills and the Tractor Works. It was difficult to see how the McCormick Works could be reopened without a pitched battle of the 1886 variety.

At this point AF of L President William Green joined the effort to break the FE strike by announcing on March 11 that the AF of L was chartering federal locals at various International Harvester plants; he predicted that 47,000 Harvester employees would shortly come into the

AF of L. On the same day Fenton disclosed that the AF of L had followed up its filing for an election at the McCormick Works with filings at other Harvester plants.[9]

Encouraged by the AF of L and the knowledge that the FE strike had been carried out by a small minority, the company completed plans to reopen the McCormick Works. The reopening was made definite, for March 23, when Judge John C. Lewe granted a company request for an injunction limiting pickets to ten per gate and forbidding the FE to use violence.

Grant Oakes, as FE president, sent the following message (refused by Postal Telegraph) to President Roosevelt: "Thousands of Harvester Workers have sweated and toiled for many years in these plants to pile up profits for the McCormick family. If these workers line the morgue tomorrow, with their blood on Chicago streets, responsibility for such mass murder shall lie solely and heavily on the heads of this greedy family which will do anything to gain its enormous profits."[10]

Irving Brown, AF of L organizer, announced that 4,000 employees of the plant were members of the AF of L union there and added, "These men will go into the plant and nothing will stop them."[11]

The community and the country sensed the danger. Memory of the brutal Chicago police action in the 1937 Memorial Day massacre was still vivid. CIO leaders across the country telegraphed President Roosevelt and Secretary of Labor Perkins to intervene. Joe Curran, National Maritime president, warned of a repetition of Haymarket. Mayor Kelly and Governor Dwight Green made personal appeals to Fowler McCormick to delay the opening. The night before the opening Anita McCormick Blaine arranged a meeting at her home between Powers Hapgood, Harvard-educated CIO leader, and her nephew Fowler McCormick.[12] In vain. Nor was there any response to the Roosevelt and Perkins telegrams.

In 1886 Police Inspector Bonfield had turned out 400 police to protect access to the McCormick Works. This time Captain John Prendergast, canceling all leaves, had 1,386 police, a quarter of the entire force, on hand at the reopening of the same plant. The next day the *Chicago Daily Times* headlined on March 24: "3000 AFL Workers Nip Harvester Strike—No Violence." Five days later the Richmond, Indiana, plant was reopened, but not without a pitched battle between citizen back-to-workers and deputies and pickets.

By the end of the first week at the McCormick Works 4,870 men were back at work out of nearly 6,000 employees. It became apparent to the 200 discouraged FE partisans that the Travis strategy had backfired, revealing their weakness.

CIO pressure on Roosevelt and Perkins for government intervention continued as the only hope for the dispirited FE. Four days after the plant's reopening Secretary Perkins certified the dispute to the new National Defense Mediation Board. The following day, March 28, William H. Davis, vice chairman of the NDMB, sent telegrams to FE and Harvester officials asking them on the basis of the executive order of the President to call off the strike, resume production, and come to a meeting in Washington on March 31. An NDMB panel would hear the case, study the facts, and make recommendations for settlement.

To the FE this intervention was a godsend, a face saving way to get its few members back into the McCormick Works. The AF of L again vigorously protested any mediation until after an election.

What basis was there for sending this case to the NDMB? Little, so far as the McCormick Works was concerned. The Navy, following a World War I pattern, had decided to expand domestic hemp production. The McCormick Works had the only patterns and blueprints for the hemp binder. The Office of Production Management complained that it could not get drawings out of the McCormick Works during the shutdown.[13] But by the time the NDMB got around to intervening, that plant had been successfully reopened. The Tractor Works, however, where several million dollars of army tractors were on order, was still tightly closed.

The NDMB panel met in Washington separately with each of the various parties from March 31 through April 2, 1941. Its deliberations are revealing of FE and company attitudes in the formative period of establishing a bargaining relationship. This dispute case which began with the Conciliation Service in January 1941 was not ended until the War Labor Board decision of April 15, 1942.

On the NDMB panel were, as public members, Chairman C. A. Dykstra, president of the University of Wisconsin; Frank P. Graham, University of North Carolina, Eugene Meyer, publisher of the *Washington Post;* as employer members, Roger Lapham and Walter Teagle; as employee members, Robert Watt, AF of L; Philip Murray, CIO. Mr. Murray was absent much of the time and was unofficially represented by Alan Haywood.

The FE representatives were Gerald Fielde, secretary-treasurer,

Herbert March, DeWitt Gilpin, Ben Meyers, attorney, and six local officers; Powers Hapgood and Alan Haywood represented the CIO on the FE delegation. The International Harvester delegation was headed by Fowler McCormick, vice president of production, two attorneys, and two representatives of the industrial relations department. An AF of L delegation composed of Frank P. Fenton, Harry O'Reilly, and Irving Brown was given a hearing.

The panel met first with the FE. Powers Hapgood stated the FE demands, which were mostly a repetition of those made at the meetings of March 3–6 with Steelman: (1) abolition of piecework; (2) minimum wage raise from 62½ to 75 cents; (3) an end to wage inequalities; (4) financial help to conscripted employees and retention of their seniority; (5) recognition of the FE as the bargaining agent for its members at the McCormick and Rock Falls plants. The FE requested the panel to arbitrate these issues, claiming the union had put 15,000 men back to work to aid national defense.

The company's position was very effectively presented by Vice President Fowler McCormick. He began slowly and moderately. The only CIO representative, Philip Murray, left during the evening recess. Thereupon McCormick talked frankly to the panel and went off the record on several occasions. He expressed the view that this was an organizational strike, and that the case should be heard not by the NDMB but by the NLRB, which had AF of L petitions before it and was the proper agency to settle matters of representation. The Harvester Company, he declared, was not antiunion. It dealt with many unions. "We want to know who the majority of our employees want to represent them. . . . Just tell us the name and we will bargain with them."[14] He explained that at the McCormick Works the CIO had not filed for an NLRB election but took "the other course, the course of a strike for recognition." ". . . to my mind," he declaimed, "the greatest mistake that I or any of us could make today would be to encourage organizational strikes these days. We are dealing with two issues here, whether organizational strikes in the time of defense are the things to do and second, whether violent minority shall control majority, and I mean if we have taken this stand here, it isn't only that we believe it right for the Harvester Co., it is that we believe it right for American citizens."[15]

Both Fowler McCormick and George Hodge, Harvester manager of labor relations, described for the panel the left-wing nature of FE leadership. Hodge continued,

I can name you fellows that are fired from the SWOC and from the UAW that came right over and because they are the kind of fellows that they are they found a ready berth all made up for them in the FEW. We first had Joe Webber; he was too tough for Van Bittner and he was an out and out Communist. Dies has been hunting him for a long time; that's what we had to deal with in the Tractor Works until they finally [fired him out of the CIO], when Dies came to town.

. . . . .

After Webber leaves in comes Travis, but he is just as bad.

For the most part the board appears to have been convinced by the company's argument. Perhaps it was natural for the new board, which was just getting on its feet, to bypass this difficult case if possible. McCormick had presented a convincing argument for the board's keeping its hands off at least until after the imminent NLRB election. After that, he assured the board, the Harvester Company would come to an agreement with the winner (presumably the AF of L).

An important influence on the board's thinking was the viewpoint of the third party, the AF of L. On grounds that the McCormick Works strike was a minority strike, the AF of L representatives urged that the panel do nothing except press the NLRB to expedite the elections in Harvester plants. The AF of L's reassuring view was that this was no dispute between labor and management, only a difficulty between the AF of L and the CIO. As Frank Fenton expressed it, "We are working in the McCormick plant today. We have no dispute."

The panel's recommendation was: (1) The board would appoint an investigator to study the FE's wage requests and complaints of employer discrimination. (Professor Don Lescohier of the University of Wisconsin Department of Economics was immediately picked by Mr. Dykstra.) (2) The board would ask the NLRB to expedite the representation elections at Harvester plants. (3) All employees were to be rehired without loss of seniority. (4) To avoid possibility of discrimination in the weeks immediately ahead, the company should agree to pay all workers the average earnings of the prestrike period. (5) The employees should agree that good order and shop discipline will be maintained.

The AF of L and the company approved the panel recommendation. The FE was outraged. Its position was that this settlement did nothing at all for the workers at Tractor and Richmond who already were recognized as bargaining agents by the company. The FE further insisted that the board should order the company to give each union, FE and AF of L, representation for its members at the McCormick Works and at Rock Falls in discrimination cases prior to the NLRB election. Lastly, the board should within 30 days render an arbitration decision on the wage question which was one of the main causes of the strike at Tractor and Richmond.

The decision was released on April 3, 1941. Chairman Dykstra was firm in the board's position. "You can't come before this Board and ask us to participate in a struggle between two unions."[15]

It would appear that the board's position was strongest applied to the situation at the McCormick plant, weak on the others. The board, however, was convinced that as things stood the AF of L would win the election in the big McCormick Works and it didn't want to be accused of upsetting this project. If the board had recommended wage increases at the Tractor and Richmond plants, the FE would have used this to urge workers at McCormick Works to vote FE in order to share in the increase. However, by turning down all requests for wage increases the board was playing into the hands of the company and the AF of L, since it was demonstrating that FE strikes could get the employees nothing.

While Professor Lescohier was studying the wage and discrimination questions, the company made a mockery of the board's position by unilaterally announcing on April 14 a five-cent across-the-board wage increase at all plants.

Lescohier's report, which the board unsuccessfully endeavored to keep out of the AF of L–CIO election campaign, supported the company on major points. It did not recommend a wage increase, in part because of the company's having already granted the five-cent raise—which Lescohier averred was not the correct amount. The discrimination cases which he carefully heard were primarily cases at the McCormick Works, where, after the strike, bands of AF of L workers seized CIO members and tore off their CIO buttons. On these charges Lescohier exonerated the company, attributing the actions to natural partisanship as a result of the strike. He apparently gave little weight to the argument that such flagrant violations of shop discipline would never have been committed unless the perpetrators knew they had company sympathy. There were no reported cases of disciplining by the company for such violations. Lescohier reinforced the board's expectation that the AF of L would win the forthcoming NLRB election in the

McCormick Works by privately predicting a 3–1 margin of victory.[16]

The election on June 18 was a surprise to all and not the least to the FE. The results showed FE victories in three of the six Harvester plants it contested. In a fourth, the controversial McCormick Works, the FE led the AF of L by an 11-vote margin out of almost 6,000 votes. Since neither union had a majority of votes cast, because of a handful of "no union" votes, a runoff was set for July 30, 1941, at the McCormick Works.

Between the primary and the runoff election the FE again pressed the NDMB to act on its wage request, but the board refused on the ground that the FE wanted the wage recommendations for election purposes. The board was unwilling to take any action which might influence the outcome unfavorably for the AF of L.[17] As before the first election, the company did not feel so constrained, and, a week before the runoff, made another unilateral wage increase of 5 cents an hour to 55,000 hourly employees.

The reactions of two of the parties to the NDMB's handling of the case are known as expressed shortly before the runoff. The Harvester Company's appreciation was voiced by George Hodge to Dykstra: "We take this opportunity of expressing our management's appreciation of the time spent by the Board on this case and the patience and courtesy accorded the representatives of our Company."[18] Frank Sliva, chairman of the Tractor Works shop stewards, protested because the AF of L in election leaflets was quoting portions of the Lescohier report which rejected the FE position. Sliva's telegram declared: "This dastardly piece of business completes the sordid picture of collaboration between Lescohier, his alter ego, Dr. Dykstra, the AFL and the Harvester Company which has marked the 90 day period in which the board has been sitting on the issues of our strike. . . . Who wrote the report, Lescohier or Harvester's Industrial Relations Department?"[19]

Although the attack on Lescohier was unjustified, the Tractor employees and their union, FE Local 104, had good cause for complaint at the board's handling of their case. They alone had the bargaining power to force wage adjustments in their favor. They called off their two-month strike at the NDMB's request. Yet the board refused to make any determination of the justice of their wage request lest the FE reap the benefit in the impending runoff.

On July 30, 1941, over four years after the original organizing drive had begun, the FE defeated the AF of L in the McCormick Works by a vote of 2,806 to 2,565. The FE had won four of the six plants contested with the AF of L.

Robert Travis had led the Farm Equipment Workers' election campaign with extraordinary effectiveness. Somehow he had galvanized the defeated FE remnant which returned to work at the end of the strike into successful propagandists who were able to capitalize on a latent pro-CIO feeling prevalent among industrial workers across the country. McCormick Works employees who hitherto had been unwilling to join an outside union or to remain out on the FE's strike now voted CIO.

The only solace the company might find in the NLRB elections of mid-1941 was that, of its major implement and truck plants, two—Milwaukee and Farmall (Rock Island)—had selected AF of L federal labor unions, some of whose officers had been leaders of the works councils which preceded them. Two major plants, Springfield and Fort Wayne, were represented by United Auto Workers (CIO). But the heart of the Harvester empire with the largest number of employees was represented by the allegedly Communist-led[20] Farm Equipment Workers (CIO), an ironic outcome to the company's 55-year campaign to avoid unionism.

Following the FE election victories in June and July 1941 the company and the FE began collective bargaining over the issues which had been before the Steelman panel, March 3–6, 1941, and the Dykstra NDMB panel, March 31–April 2. Five months later the bargaining had reached an impasse and the cases were back with the NDMB. An executive order of January 12, 1942, transferred all NDMB cases to the newly created National War Labor Board. The NWLB appointed a new mediation officer, who failed to settle the dispute but recommended a new panel to hear the case and make recommendations to the board. This new panel had two employer members, two union members, and one public member, Professor I. L. Sharfman of the University of Michigan. The FE after its election victories was now demanding a union shop, company payment for grievance time for stewards, penalty pay for Saturday and Sunday work, and a general wage increase.

The Sharfman panel recommended to the NWLB denial of the union shop, on the ground that antiunion activity of the company had ceased; granting of grievance pay for stewards; refusing Saturday and Sunday pay as such; and approval of a 4½ cent general wage increase.

In the meantime the NWLB had appointed a special investigator, Stanley P. Farwell, to gather information and to aid it in final resolution of the case. Because Professor Lescohier had intensively worked on this case, investigator Farwell privately consulted with him on all phases of his study. The FE had been extremely bitter about Lescohier's earlier recommendations, but on the new issue of union security his turned out to be the only staff voice urging that the union be granted the outright union shop.[21] In the NWLB's final settlement of the case as of April 15, 1942, it moved in this direction, reversing the Sharfman panel on this one issue and granting the FE a maintenance of membership.

In granting the maintenance of membership the NWLB used such language as "The facts developed in this case indicate that the company has not developed a sound labor relations program with the unions; . . . . Long standing frictions between the company and the union and antagonisms to the union on the part of some representatives of management are part of the industrial relations picture presented by this case."[22]

The FE and the AF of L accepted the NWLB decision without delay. The company went through a great deal of soul searching before it accepted the maintenance of membership. On April 30, 1942, it accepted all points of the NWLB order except this provision, asking for a ten-day extension to consider it. On May 2 Fowler McCormick had a talk with NWLB chairman William H. Davis. Davis then assigned Thomas Neblett to go to Chicago to talk with McCormick and get his compliance. In their lengthy interview McCormick proposed five changes in the maintenance-of-membership provision. Neblett accepted only one. On May 10 International Harvester's Board of Directors, under the duress of wartime, voted to accept an award to which it would never have acceded in peacetime.[23]

Postwar Labor Relations

The years from 1945 through 1958 witnessed more prolonged labor-management strife than had any other period. With the exception of 1949 every contract negotiation of his period was accompanied by strikes, in 1946, 1947, 1948, 1950, 1952, 1955, 1958. The signing of the agreements signified little, as the unresolved conflict raged unabated through the media of the grievance procedure and local work stoppages in Harvester plants.[24] From 1954 through 1959 more than 48,000 grievances went to the last stage of the grievance procedure. At one time during the 1955–58 agreement, 12,000 grievances were awaiting arbitration.[25]

So marked was this conflict that within fifteen years three special studies have been published describing these very contentious union-management relations at the International Harvester Company.[26]

What have been the reasons for the abnormal and prolonged conflict at International Harvester? The company attributes the bulk of its difficulties to the twin causes of radical and rival unionism. The unions blame chiefly the tardiness of the company in fully accepting unionism. Both company and unions agree that the large number of piece-rate jobs has accentuated the bad relationship.

By the end of the war the labor relations situation faced by International Harvester had changed markedly from the prewar period. Employees in all its major plants except the Wisconsin Steel Works had replaced their works councils and unaffiliated local unions with powerful international unions. The largest of these was the Farm Equipment Workers (CIO), with approximately 30,000 members in eleven Harvester plants. The second major union selected by Harvester employees was the United Auto Workers, with 17,000 employees in six plants. One major plant, Milwaukee, was represented by an AF of L federal labor union; and a newly purchased foundry at Waukesha, Wisconsin, was represented by the United Steelworkers. Powerful AF of L craft unions represented maintenance and other skilled employees in many plants. Free collective bargaining with a minimum of government intervention was now being tried on a large scale for the first time in the memory of company and union officials.

For a while following the NWLB's decision of April 1942 there had been almost an era of good feeling between the company and the FE. Both sides were interested in war production. Wage controversies were settled by government boards.

In early October 1945 International Harvester, in order to forestall postwar labor troubles, offered a 10 percent raise to all employees retroactive to October 1. This offer was announced to all union officers. No strings were attached; and the question of wages could be reopened at any time, presumably as wage patterns emerged in other industries. The UAW and the AF of L accepted the company's proposal; the FE turned it down.

The company's offer can be taken at face value as an effort to avoid labor strife. Yet it was reasonable for the FE to refuse it until an entire package was negotiated. Any union leader knows that putting contract gains into effect piecemeal progressively weakens the membership's will to strike. If at the tail end of negotiations company and union had not reached agreement on, for example, union security, the membership would probably not strike.

As it happened, the union's suspicions were confirmed. In the first postwar negotiations in 1945–46 the company refused to renew the maintenance of membership which the NWLB had granted in 1942. It further proposed cutting in half the wage payments to stewards for handling grievances; and in line with its historic opposition to arbitration, insisted on a very limited arbitration clause compared to the one in effect under NWLB procedures.

Bargaining during January and February 1946 took place before a special government fact-finding panel headed by Milwaukee attorney Philip Marshall. Expressing his views on union security, FE leader Gerald Fielde, back from the Merchant Marine, made it clear that not one iota of the bitterness of the prewar organizational period had been forgotten by the union.

> What fears does the union hold, that if they [the Company] even want to withdraw the maintenance of membership which was ordered by the [War Labor] Board after fair consideration, for which it had a trial period of four years and knowing the background of the company, we can arrive at but one conclusion, that there are some grand plans being laid in high places to take advantage of certain situations economically that may take place in this country, to for once and for all get rid of this so called nuisance, the union.
>
> Incidentally, we have some of the same executives who are steering the course of industrial and labor relations for this company with us today, who were with the company back in 1937.
>
> . . . . .
>
> Naturally, our fears have not diminished for we believe they have not changed their spots. . .
>
> . . . . .
>
> No, their record is consistent that they have been intimidating and coercing to prevent, first, the formation of a union; secondly to prevent the strengthening of a union; and thirdly, the plans that they lay, with the expiration, to actually get rid of the union.
>
> . . . . .
>
> This company has been cited that they have engaged in anti-union activi-

ty. They have been cited officially on the record that they have engaged in acts of intimidation and coercion, and, therefore in our request for a union shop, it certainly is well founded, based upon the fears we possess.[27]

For the company, Assistant Labor Relations Manager William Reilly brought out that under the maintenance-of-membership clause since 1942 the company had had to discharge 200 employees for failure to pay dues, and that the union had demanded that the company fire 20 employees for other reasons.[28]

In support of its demand for union security the FE presented the results of the NWLB's 1942 secret ballot on the question of maintenance of membership. At the McCormick Works 94.5 percent of ballots were cast in favor of union security, a figure far above a majority of eligible voters. Results were similar at other Harvester plants.

Hardly had the panel met in mid-January when the FE took its 30,000 members in Harvester plants out on strike. Thus was the die cast on the postwar FE-Harvester relationship. The law had brought the parties to the bargaining table but it had failed to produce constructive collective bargaining. That the union was stronger now served only to escalate the conflict. On both sides the same men, with the same prewar philosophies, set the tone for labor-management relations in the postwar period.

On February 18, 1946, the Marshall panel made public its recommendations for settling the strike: continuance of the NWLB maintenance-of-membership provision, checkoff, a wage increase of 18 cents an hour, broad, binding arbitration for the final step of the grievance procedure. The FE voted to accept the panel's recommendations. The company refused to accept the same points it had objected to before but had acceded to under wartime duress. As the strike continued into its second month, national concern over its consequences mounted because of a serious shortage of farm machinery.

Simultaneous with the strike at International Harvester were prolonged strikes by the UAW in two other large implement companies, Allis-Chalmers and J. I. Case. In all three strikes management's withdrawal of wartime union security was the major issue.

The concurrent shutdowns of these three large companies greatly enhanced management's bargaining power, since the few producing companies could not take away the market of the struck firms. As the strikes dragged on, the union members were relatively "hurting" worse than the companies. Management showed no signs of weakening.

Eventually it became imperative for the FE to extricate itself without total defeat.

Fortunately for the union there was a friendly Administration in Washington. An unusual weapon, threat of government seizure and operation of the plants, was brought up. To avert public and company opposition to such government intervention in favor of labor, a case had to be built on grounds acceptable to the public and the courts. For instance, the Secretary of Agriculture might demand government action because of a critical food shortage. In early March Secretary of Agriculture Clinton Anderson sent a stern warning letter to Secretary of Labor L. B. Schwellenbach, which of course was released to the press: "Each day the strikes are allowed to continue brings us closer to a national emergency . . . ."[29] Not publicized was a handwritten note—"Dear Lew" from "Clint"—accompanying Secretary Anderson's letter. It assured Schwellenbach that he wasn't trying to "talk 'tough' to you—I merely want you to have a letter to 'show cause'" for the intervention.[30] This letter was cause enough for Schwellenbach to ask the President for an executive order seizing the farm equipment plants.

What was there to justify Secretary Anderson's letter? Presumably he had received from farmers a dozen letters demanding government action to remedy the farm machinery shortage. As it happened, the complaining farmers were all local or state officers of the Farmers' Union,[31] the farm organization which at that time cooperated closely with the labor movement. An executive order seizing the farm machinery companies was actually drafted. Another Cabinet official, Henry Morgenthau, Jr., publicly urged government seizure of the struck plants.[32]

Telegrams were then sent from Schwellenbach and Anderson summoning to a Washington meeting at the office of the Secretary of Agriculture the top officials of the three firms, Fowler McCormick for International Harvester, Walter Geist for Allis-Chalmers, and Leon R. Clausen for J. I. Case. The companies were reluctant attendants at the meeting. Both McCormick and Geist were "en route" to various destinations and could not be reached, but sent subordinates. Clausen was on the West Coast, could not leave, and sent no substitute.

No agreements were reached at the conference, but shortly thereafter the FE and International Harvester arrived at a contract settlement. FE Secretary Gerald Fielde sent a letter of congratulations to the Department of Labor's John Gibson for his fine assistance in settling the strike.[33] The strikes at Allis-Chalmers and Case, both of UAW unions, continued; but the Harvester–FE settlement ended the critical farm machinery shortage and cut the ground from under the government's seizure argument.

In the settlement on April 9, almost three months after the beginning of the strike, the company was victorious on the union security issue, replacing maintenance of membership with a voluntary checkoff. The union won a continuation of grievance pay for stewards. The wage package was settled at 18 cents, whereas the company had offered 17 cents. The arbitration clause finally written was restrictive along the lines of the company's views, but inclusion of final binding arbitration was a concession over company prewar thinking. The FE was victorious in negotiating the first companywide wage agreement. The issue of piece rates remained unresolved.

How Radical Were the Unions?

Reflecting the influence of its founder Joseph Webber, the FE to its demise in 1954–55 retained its left-wing ties. Its newspaper regularly pushed the Communist foreign policy line. It followed all the twists of Soviet foreign policy. It cooperated with the Communist elements in the UAW prior to 1947 and fought with the anti-Communist Reuther faction. Along with other leftist-led unions, it supported Henry Wallace for president in 1948. As with other leftist-led unions, the Communist party membership did not penetrate deeply. At various FE Harvester plants, small cells of ten to thirty persons, among them some of the top local union leadership, belonged to or cooperated with the Communist party.[34]

The United Auto Workers was non-Communist and anti-Communist after the Reuther faction's victories in 1947. Before 1947 there was a Communist minority in the UAW but none of the UAW locals at Harvester plants was part of this faction.

The Harvester Company takes the position that a large share of the enormous volume of grievances, the many work stoppages, and the frequent strikes at contract expirations were the result of FE's alleged Communist leadership.[35] Presumably Communist philosophy called for constant strife and conflict and did not desire peaceful relationships.

This argument has some truth to it though it can explain only a portion of the turbulent labor relations since 1935. Lending some support to this view, Milton Burns—an influential FE leader prior to 1954, when he switched to the UAW—offered the opinion that the harmonious "new look" grievance procedure evolved by International Harvester and the UAW after 1958 could probably not have been achieved with the FE. "The philosophy of our union," he declared, "was that management had no right to exist. Therefore our policy was to offer no quarter and no compromise on grievances."[36] Here Burns clearly implies that the FE's militant handling of grievances, frequently enforced by work stoppages, stemmed from its political philosophy. In practice the FE was, of course, not quite as militant as Burns's "no compromise" philosophy implies. Though rightfully known as a "tough union," like all unions it compromised on grievance settlements as on contract terms.

A case for bargaining militance as the exclusive attribute of leftist-led unionism is not very well sustained by a comparison of FE and UAW bargaining patterns in Harvester. The non-Communist UAW had almost equally turbulent grievance and collective bargaining relations. While the FE had many more work stoppages than the UAW (1,035 to 197 from 1945 through October 1, 1954[37]), some UAW plants such as that at Springfield in 1946–47 had more stoppages than many FE plants.[38] In 1952 the UAW at Harvester's Melrose Park plant in Chicago struck for months, presumably over time study grievances, thus surpassing in hours lost the work stoppage record of the FE's most militant plant, East Moline. If we total all the wages lost in work stoppages from October 1945 through October 1951 for Harvester plants controlled by each union, and then divide each figure by the average number of workers in each union in Harvester employ, we get what might be called a work-stoppage wage loss per union member. In this tabulation the six-year wage loss per member in UAW plants was $1,189 to $893 per member in FE plants. If we extend the dubious comparison another year to include the big FE strike of 1952, the FE leads with a $1,454 loss to $1,356 for the UAW.[39]

By these measures the two unions, one allegedly Communist-led and one anti-Communist, appear about equally militant. The greater reputation of the FE for work stoppage was based on a larger number of short intracontract stoppages; the UAW made fewer but longer ones. A study of work stoppages plant by plant might indicate more correlation with distance from Chicago than with the political radicalism of the union. Even after the demise of the FE, the UAW in 1954–58 found itself in a morass of grievances, with strikes occurring regularly at every contract expiration.

One could argue that although the UAW was non-Communist it was a radical class-conscious union, itself interested in fomenting class discord. However, such a characterization of UAW goals would be unwarranted.

There is no evidence that a leftist philosophy in trade union leadership results in more militant and disruptive collective bargaining relationships, while there is much experience of stormy bargaining relationships with various non-Communist unions. Political radicalism of union leadership is no more synonymous with militant or disruptive collective bargaining than politically conservative union leadership is synonymous with harmonious labor-management relations. If the union leaders of Harvester locals, both FE and UAW, were militant and radical, the cause is more likely to be found in the working conditions and labor relations policies of the company than in the political philosophy of the union leaders.

It is ironic that the very triumph of radical, aggressive leadership among Harvester workers was in part a consequence of the company's assiduous antiunion policy pursued relentlessly after 1885. Harvester history in the late 'thirties appears to support the thesis of Philip Taft that American employers who successfully frustrated their employees' attempts at unionization over long periods of time left a leadership vacuum which tended to be filled by more radical leadership.[40]

For many years the Harvester Company dismissed or harried out of the plant the spontaneous conservative worker leadership such as that which led the unions through 1885. In September 1904 Ralph Easley of the National Civic Federation pleaded in vain with the McCormicks: "I am such a firm believer in conferences that I cannot help feeling it would be a mistake on your part not to talk this matter out with the [union] committee which signed your contract, especially as it is signed by several very conservative men."[41] In 1913, 1916, and 1919 union leadership was pushed aside in the same ruthless manner it had been earlier.

During the 'twenties and early 'thirties the company so manipulated the works councils as to dominate their leadership. Council officers, with a few notable exceptions, were not top leadership material. By the late 'thirties many had become so dependent upon management as to be incapable of standing on their own feet. In addition the older works council leaders carried the double onus of a do-nothing policy during the prosperous 'twenties and meek acquiescence to the wage cuts of the depression. Perhaps by 1920, and certainly by 1936, the company had passed up its last chance to deal with genuinely independent, conservative union leaders.

When after 1933 Harvester workers turned to unions, the indigenous conservative trade union leadership had long since been destroyed, replaced by the more docile works council leadership. In the late 'thirties a handful of young men, able, radical, frustrated by the depression, men with little to lose, arose to challenge the "company union" leadership. To these men, who had observed the helplessness of the works councils, the program of a Joseph Webber and a Robert Travis made sense. As the McCormick strike of 1941 demonstrated, it was not numerical strength that enabled the FE partisans to shut the plant, but the complete vacuum of leadership in the opposition. The strike collapsed completely after a few days for lack of rank-and-file support. The FE leaders had returned to the plant deserted and impotent. Yet forty-five days later they triumphed in the NLRB election. There was no one else to vote for except the discredited works council leaders. The fact that the works councils, phantom-like, transformed themselves into "independent" unions in 1937 and into AF of L unions in 1941 was insufficient in most contests to enable their leaders to escape the kiss of death which company support had unwittingly bestowed upon them.

The Nature of FE–UAW Rivalry and Its Impact on Harvester Labor Relations

The impact of FE–UAW rivalry on Harvester labor relations is difficult to assess because it had counterbalancing effects. The rivalry began at least as early as February 1939. In that month the UAW director of the Chicago-Midwest area and Philip Murray, president of the SWOC, protested to the CIO and FEWOC's employment of Emil Costello as a staff representative in the Milwaukee area.[42] Costello was known as an extreme left-winger. The protests indicate that even at this early date the FE–UAW rivalry was not merely over jurisdiction, bitter as that can be, but over ideology, trade union vs. Communist, as well.

During 1940 UAW President R. J. Thomas urged that the FE be transferred to the UAW. A conference on merger was held, and the CIO exerted heavy pressure on the FE to accept the terms. In 1941 Powers Hapgood and Philip Murray urged the FE to join the UAW in order to get enough money to conduct the impending NLRB representation election at International Harvester and to free the FE members still in jail as a result of the strike at Harvester's Richmond, Indiana, plant.[43]

One of the unacceptable UAW conditions for merger was that the FE fire Robert Travis and DeWitt Gilpin. The reason the FE gave for rejecting the merger was that it would lead to confusion in the elections.[44]

During World War II jurisdictional conflicts between the two unions increased as they strove to organize the same plants. Early in 1945 the CIO again recommended immediate merger. The FE leaders refused and won support in a membership referendum. At this point the UAW took the offensive by attempting to raid the FE membership in the McCormick Works. Both on this occasion and on subsequent UAW raids FE partisans attacked and injured UAW staff representatives. CIO "goon" activity was hitherto unheard of and not understood by the public, which was shocked. In 1947 the FE, in order to strengthen the anti-Reuther forces in the UAW, reversed its position and proposed joining the UAW. UAW President Reuther, elected with a paper-thin majority and faced with a hostile executive board, likewise reversed his position and by carrying the FE merger to a UAW membership referendum was able to defeat it. Reuther's smashing election victory in 1948 brought another reversal of position on merger and resulted in the FE's ouster from the CIO in 1949 for failure to merge. Thereupon the FE merged with the left-wing United Electrical Workers, which was shortly thereafter expelled from the CIO on grounds of Communist domination. The FE hereafter became the "UE–FE."

Between 1945 and 1953 the UAW made several rounds of raids on FE members in NLRB elections in International Harvester plants. All were unsuccessful. After Harvester had broken the UE–FE strike of 1952, the UAW deliberately picked out the plants where the back-to-work movement had been most successful to petition for new NLRB representation elections. Even here the UE–FE emerged victorious, winning 2–1 at Richmond and 3–1 at West Pullman. The UAW quietly withdrew at Farmall two days before the election. This internecine warfare, however, had at least some repercussions on union-company relationships.

The major impact on collective bargaining of the deep union split was to prevent a united front against the company and to weaken union bargaining power. In 1946 the UAW Harvester plants worked throughout the long FE strike. In 1950 both unions began their strike together, but the UE–FE broke ranks after two weeks while the UAW stayed out for eleven weeks. In 1952 the UAW worked while the UE–FE went out on a disastrous thirteen-week strike. Prior to 1955 in all the strikes the Harvester Company was able to count on roughly half its plants operating, as first one union and then the other went on strike.

Yet a weakening of union bargaining power did not mean peaceful union-management relations. The frequent UAW raids on FE plants perhaps increased the FE need for aggressive grievance handling and spectacular contract gains. The company's abrogation of union security in 1946 put a premium on union militance as a method of winning a maximum of rank-and-file support. A disgruntled worker whose grievance had been dropped by the incumbent union was presumably a potential defector to the raiding union. Thus a small part of the large grievance load may have been attributable to a supermilitance resulting from the union rivalry.

The election wars between UAW and the FE could not be won solely on ideological grounds, which workers understood but dimly. Each union therefore had an incentive to talk the worker's language by claiming more militance toward the company in grievance handling and contract negotiations. From 1946 through 1952 the growing union rivalry, though founded on ideological conflict, gradually began to find its expression in bargaining militance. In the immediate postwar years the FE dominated the bargaining. But as the UAW membership in International Harvester grew through capture of new plants, the UAW became a real threat to the UE–FE's existence. The UE–FE strike of 1952 was in one sense partly a result of rival unionism. In its 1950 strike settlement the UE–FE had agreed to a two-year contract; the UAW had a five-year one. In view of the frequent UAW raids, it was imperative in 1952 for the UE–FE to make some gains above the UAW five-year agreement. Since the UE–FE had more members in Harvester plants than the UAW, it was imperative from the company's standpoint not to strengthen the UE–FE further by giving it one iota more than the UAW was receiving.

In addition to this rivalry with the UAW, there is some evidence that FE strong man Gerald Fielde was dissatisfied with "soft" UE collective bargaining tactics and hoped that success in the 1952 strike would validate his militant views and his position within the UE–FE. Although Harvester officials repeatedly accused FE leaders of Communism both in 1947 and during the 1952 strike, they were of the opinion in 1964 that the Communist UE leadership had been opposed to Gerald Fielde and the FE leadership on the question of calling the strike in 1952.[45]

With its flank presumably protected by the operation of the UAW plants, the Harvester Company went into an all-out battle with the UE–FE in 1952. The UAW's five-year agreement had no contract reopening provision but did provide for the right to strike over production standards. To the company's dismay, in the midst of the UE–FE strike the UAW local at the Melrose Park plant went out on a strike of several months. During the UE–FE's thirteen-week strike, which was marked by considerable violence, the company successfully reopened its UE–FE plants, sent foremen to workers' homes to urge them to return to work, and hired replacements. When about 65 percent of the workers had deserted the strike, the UE–FE officials capitulated.

The strike settlement proved eventually to be a death blow to the UE–FE, which was forced to accept terms substantially less favorable than those before the strike began and, what was more important, less favorable than what the UAW was receiving in Harvester plants. Within two years after the UE–FE settlement two of the company-dictated contract terms destroyed the union. They were (1) union members must sign new individual checkoff requests to have their UE–FE dues deduction continued; (2) stewards were no longer free to leave their jobs at company expense while doing grievance work. Only 50 percent of the employees signed the new dues deduction requests. This undermined the union financially and inclined UE–FE staff members to look favorably on joining the UAW. Loss of company-paid grievance time so alienated stewards and local officers that they too looked longingly toward the greater privileges then available under the UAW contract.

Hence the end of the long, bitter FE–UAW rivalry came in 1954. FE locals, beginning in the East Moline and Farmall plants, voted to join the UAW. The movement spread to the Chicago plants and then to all UE–FE Harvester plants. Obviously a deal had been made, with the UAW agreeing to hire the former FE staff representatives—except Grant Oakes and Gerald Fielde—in return for their "delivering" the locals to the UAW. The new UAW locals demanded recognition from International Harvester. With dispatch UE–FE national officers suspended the disloyal local officers and appointed new ones, reminding the company that UE–FE was the certified exclusive bargaining agent. In this crisis the company, which had publicly urged the FE membership to get new leaders, not only continued to recognize the UE–FE but used the occasion to fire precipitously several staff representatives who were serving as full-time local union officers on leave from jobs at Harvester plants. In the subsequent NLRB elections between the UE–FE and the UAW the company maintained a strict neutrality. The UAW won all elections. Thus in the 1955 collective bargaining negotiations the company, in all but three plants, faced a work force united in one union.

While the differing ideologies of their respective leaders were a cornerstone of UAW and FE rivalry at International Harvester, normal predatory union rivalry, Gerald Fielde's differences with UE leadership, and the company's widespread piece-rate cuts (to be discussed in the following section), all played a part in the disastrous strike of 1952.

The radicalism of FE leadership was not a direct cause of the 1952 strike, though once the strike had started this stiffened the company. Harvester's all-out challenge to the UE–FE was probably based on three factors. First, it was sound collective bargaining not to permit the UE–FE to whipsaw the company into granting more to it than to the UAW. Second, the company recognized that the alleged Communism of the UE–FE leaders was an Achilles' heel for the union and that the political climate in December 1952 was ripe for exploiting this: during the strike the House Committee on Un-American Activities held a hearing in Chicago on alleged Communist activities in the UE–FE. Third, company officials had a greater emotional antagonism toward FE leadership, based partly on bargaining behavior and partly on alleged political beliefs. No doubt the Communist issue somewhat weakened membership support of the strike and was responsible for employees' reluctance to sign the dues deduction authorizations after it.

Rival unionism created some bad feeling toward Harvester in the minds of both FE and UAW leaders. Each side felt sure that the company was favoring the other. It was certainly to the company's short-run advantage to play one union off against the other. Whether or not management did so deliberately, the suspicions were inevitable so long as Harvester reaped the bargaining advantage of facing rival unions. Rival unionism delayed the day of reckoning when the firm would be forced to face a united work force which could shut down substantially all its operations. After the UAW absorbed Harvester's UE–FE unions during 1954 and early 1955, the company had a greater incentive to work out harmonious union relationships. The union security which came with the abolition of rivalry also permitted union leadership to act more responsibly.

The Grievance Rut

During the year after the FE's death at Harvester, unsettled grievances were at an all-time high, the bulk of them from the long-time UAW plants. Several factors made their settlement particularly difficult.

One factor was the high proportion of incentive workers in Harvester plants. In 1959, 56 percent of the employees at the McCormick Works were on piece rates. In the entire Harvester Company the proportion of pieceworkers was 45 percent. By contrast the auto companies had no pieceworkers. During World War II it had been normal for incentive plans to permit considerable looseness to develop so that wages might be raised above those permitted by the National War Labor Board and employee turnover be thus cut down. Consequently, in the late 'forties and well into the 'fifties Harvester was engaged in a wide-scale effort to tighten up what it felt were loose incentives. This tightening-up process had a real bite. Company sources estimate that earnings of piece-rate workers in some plants were cut an average of 3 percent. Union membership and leadership—FE, UAW, and AF of L—resisted these piece-rate cuts vigorously. The resulting incentive grievances were the single largest cause of the overwhelming grievance load in the 1950's and frequently involved large sums of money for many workers.

A serious fault in the grievance procedure was the tradition of settling grievances by production stoppages rather than by arbitration. The company's opposition to binding arbitration as the final step in the grievance procedure prior to 1946 encouraged this tradition. But most importantly, the prolonged delays in grievance settlements goaded rank-and-file workers, no doubt encouraged in some cases by union staff representatives, to lead work stoppages as the only way of breaking through the deadlocked grievance procedure.

There were numerous causes of the grievance bottleneck. At first the centralization of the procedure contributed to the difficulty. Settlement of grievances at the local plant level inevitably resulted in inconsistencies among plants. Alert unions naturally demanded extension of the most favorable local settlements to the rest of the company's plants. The full companywide implications of grievances are frequently not evident at the plant level. To avoid this whipsawing, local plant managers were restrained from making final grievance settlements without clearance from the central administration. Such delays were particularly serious in the many incentive grievances, since retroactivity enabled workers to accumulate claims amounting to thousands of dollars during these delays. Nor could the union afford to permit stewards to make precedent-setting decisions. A somewhat comparable centralization and delay began to develop on the union side.

Moreover, centralization of grievance procedure encouraged passing every doubtful case to higher authorities. Foremen were fearful of settling first-level grievances; union members preferred "kicking them upstairs." Once this was started, few grievances were handled at the more expeditious, initial stages. A worker who came to a foreman with an oral grievance was frequently told, "Don't bother me with your grievance, write it. Let's not argue."

As of 1946, a contract clause which limited retroactivity in grievance cases to the date of filing a written grievance also tended to drive some grievance cases to the more cumbersome stages of the grievance procedure. It increased the actual number of grievance cases as well. Workers who suspected that they might have a grievance were encouraged, because of limited retroactivity, to write it up and file it immediately. There were some exceptions to the retroactivity rule, but a worker was not likely to want to take a chance. In one case known to the author a diligent UAW steward at the Memphis plant filed 1,800 written complaints over only one real grievance that affected nine workers. If he had not done so, he felt, retroactivity might have been jeopardized. In addition, writing grievances on company time was less onerous than machine-tending. Even more important in motivating the plethora of written grievances was the company's restrictive policy in applying grievance settlements to other similar cases. Thus if nine workers had presumably similar grievances all nine might end up on the arbitration docket.

Only after the grievance was at the fourth step could the international union representative represent the worker. This regulation again discouraged the workers' reliance on the early stages of the grievance procedure. Before long the easiest path for the local union leadership as well as for the labor relations department was to send all grievances up to the arbitrator. Once a litigious spirit had been built up among workers and union and company officials, the delays and the enormous backlog of grievances merely fed an ever-increasing volume of new filings.

The lack of union security has already been suggested as a cause of grievance difficulties in the early stages of the process. For proper functioning of a grievance system a union must be willing to drop the weak cases of many workers. This is particularly true in incentive grievances. But to do so a union must have security. At Harvester prior to 1955 neither union, as we have seen, had adequate security, primarily because of rivalry and secondarily because of the company's delay in granting full union shop.

The final step in the grievance procedure was arbitration. Through 1945 Harvester clung to its typical preunion attitude of not accepting arbitration even of contract enforcement. In 1946 the company successfully resisted FE's demand for a very broad arbitration clause, finally settling for a highly limiting provision. Some of the UAW plants still had no arbitration provisions. The large number of wildcat stoppages brought the company to favor arbitration; and from 1946 on all contracts included an arbitration clause, but with severe restrictions on the arbitrator's powers and freedom in conducting the proceeding. This restrictive contract language is indicative of the reluctance with which the company gave up its right to make final decisions on grievance matters. Harvester arbitrations were highly contentious, compared to those of other companies. With batteries of company lawyers and scores of witnesses, they were inevitably cumbersome and time-consuming. At first no single umpire could be trusted with so much power so several were used. When the single-umpire system was established in 1948, the company took the lead in firing umpires after relatively short service because the decisions were unacceptable.

The frustrations aroused spilled over into the contract negotiations. As one union representative has described the situation to the author,

"Harvester workers are the only ones I have ever seen who at a contract ratification meeting will get up and scream 'To hell with the contract terms, did you get my grievance settled?' " At contract negotiation time such workers were willing to strike not for new contract terms but merely in hope of either getting a favorable grievance settlement or punishing the company for its seeming intransigence.

At the expiration of the 1955 contract the grievance war had reached its peak. The company had continued its downward revision of what it considered loose piece rates. The unions had fought these revisions vigorously. Another source of irritation was the fact that, unlike General Motors and Ford, Harvester had publicly rejected the "living document" approach of Walter Reuther, who in 1953 attempted to get some revisions of the 1950 five-year contract. The inevitable Harvester strike of 1955 was fought through four weeks to a draw.

This strike demonstrated on the one hand that despite the success of the back-to-work movement in 1952 which broke the UE–FE, Harvester workers were still fiercely loyal to unionism and had not lost their will to strike. There were several occasions in which the principal negotiators appeared ready to settle but the rank and file refused to concur.

Role of Company Antiunionism in the Post-1935 Labor Strife

The FE attributed its difficulties at Harvester to the company's long antiunion history dating back to Haymarket;[46] the UAW is somewhat less harsh in its criticism, merely feeling that until 1955 the company had not fully accepted unionism. Our study of Harvester labor relations supports the view of the company's long opposition to unionism until well after World War II.

Harvester antiunionism of the 'thirties took the form of a series of attempts to preserve the only type of labor relations which the company executives of that period understood: employee representation. This effort to avoid outside unionism was pursued with vigor and in pretty clear violation of the Wagner Act; as we have noted, the company was convicted of fostering and dominating labor organizations on two occasions, November 1936 and February 1941. Harvester antiunionism was not, however, the virulent antiunionism which was revealed as common industrial practice by the Senate subcommittee headed by Robert La Follette, Jr. That Harvester did not in the 'thirties use professional labor spies or dismiss workers for union activity may have been due to the gradually moderating influence of the works councils.

Harvester executives of the 1930's and early 1940's did not forget that under the works councils there were no strikes after 1919. The company's success in avoiding strikes during the first CIO surge of 1936–37 further sold them on the merits of "company" unionism. Harvester's key labor relations decision-makers of 1936–41 had not even witnessed the strikes of 1919, to say nothing of those of 1916, 1913, or 1904. They knew absolutely nothing of the long period of union-company collective bargaining which ended with Haymarket.

Since World War II International Harvester has gone along pretty closely with the automobile bargaining pattern including adoption of a modified union shop in 1950 and full union shop in 1955. Is there, then, anything to the accusation of antiunionism in this period? The indications lie not so much in the actual terms of contracts as in the balky and reluctant way the contracts have been arrived at. In 1946 the company not only withdrew union security but made it a noisy issue of principle. The company's arm's-length legalistic handling of grievances and its insistence on a very limited form of arbitration demonstrate less than full acceptance of unionism. But long and frequent strikes at contract termination do not yield to any simple interpretation. They may have been due to company stubbornness in refusing to grant pattern conditions, to well-founded reasons for not following auto patterns, or to special Harvester problems such as incentives.

By 1947 Harvester had built a long record of tough, dogged opposition to the demands of its principal union, the FE. There still appeared a possibility, however, that the bitterness would wear off with increasing experience. As soon as the Taft-Hartley Act was passed, the company, taking maximum advantage of the "employer free speech" provision, declared open war on the FE. These attacks were unleashed in direct mailings to all employees in plants represented by the FE. Harvester President John McCaffrey's letter of October 20, 1947 to FE members recited a long string of strikes and work stoppages.

What causes these difficulties?

. . . . .

We say it is because in dealing with the FE we are dealing with an international union many of whose officers are irresponsible radicals, who have no respect for their contracts and who are more interested in disruption than in labor-management peace.

. . . . .

Not only does FE have more strikes, it also has longer and bigger ones.[47]

McCaffrey then made a direct appeal to FE members to oust the union leadership: "Attend union meetings, stay until the end, make your voice heard. . . . If either your local or your international officers are not properly representing you, see that they change their policies—or get yourself some new leaders. The company wants good relations with responsible unions. . . . We think we can have them, if you want them enough to act."

The smashing of the UE–FE strike in 1952 was viewed by the company less as a necessary but distasteful job than as a moral crusade against Communism.[48] When the UAW asked Harvester for contract revision in 1953, at the time of the "living document" appeal, Harvester President McCaffrey used the occasion of his rejection of the request to make a pronouncement publicly chastising the union.[49]

To what extent were Harvester labor relations after 1935 influenced by family management? Any hypotheses on this must be highly speculative. For the most part a family-managed corporation the size of International Harvester behaved much like any other corporation, since it faced the same competitive market forces in the consumer and factor marketplaces.

Fowler McCormick's opposition to the CIO's "taking over" Harvester, as he expressed it to the National Defense Mediation Board panel in 1941, was probably stronger and more personal than William Knudsen's fear of having General Motors captured by the UAW or Myron Taylor's fear of U. S. Steel being captured by John L. Lewis. Family management at Harvester was a secure management. It was not rapacious for dividends. It could afford to make substantial wage concessions when threatened by unionism or to resist union demands firmly for the sake of company "principles" such as the open shop, though this meant prolonged strikes.

One maverick member of the McCormick family, and a substantial stockholder, Anita McCormick Blaine, did urge, on the occasion of the reopening of the McCormick Works in 1941, that the plant be kept closed.[50] Mrs. Blaine made financial contributions to FE strike relief.[51] She appears to have had no impact on management thinking.

As Chapter 7 indicates, the works councils were mercilessly manipulated by Harvester management. This practice was continued during the period of "independent" unions from 1937 through February 1941. The formation and rapid growth of AF of L federal unions in 1941 was abetted by what by then was a management habit of manipulating employee organizations. The division in the labor movement, AF of L vs. CIO, of course invited such manipulation. If this policy had succeeded, management might have faced less militant unions. At International Harvester during 1937–41 the policy of favoring the AF of L over the FE and the UAW backfired. The CIO unions established themselves through NLRB elections in spite of the company's antagonistic behavior. Company antagonism to outside unionism during the late 'thirties and early 'forties merely increased the militance of FE and UAW leadership.

Yet the serious deterioration of Harvester-union relations from 1945 to 1955 does not necessarily indicate any strong antiunion pattern by the company or any monumental irresponsibility of the union. Once deterioration in labor relations sets in it can feed upon itself. Delays in grievance handling beget more grievances, unsettled grievances snowball into strikes; strikes bring still more grievances. The momentum of one or two unfortunate situations can set a trend in motion. Good labor-management relations involve recognizing such trends and breaking out of them.

It is always possible that what appears to the unions as antiunionism may be lack of ability to communicate with the unions or some inability of the management of a big organization to reach decisions in a timely fashion. The published studies on recent Harvester labor relations[52] have stressed the unsettling effect of the FE–UAW union rivalry, a rivalry which of course received much publicity. On management's side there have also been divisions and even rivalries, which, though different from the inter- and intraunion divisions, have been real roadblocks to harmonious labor relations.

In the first place the Harvester industrial relations department prior to 1955 generally did not have enough power vis-à-vis manufacturing to carry out a centrally directed companywide labor relations policy. As a small staff department rather than a line department, it has had difficulty in the long run in getting its policies carried out by the many division managers, plant managers, and supervisors.

Secondly, the structure of the department has not always been well suited to the job of labor relations. During the 1930's when labor relations activities grew rapidly, the director of industrial relations personally administered labor relations along with all his other duties in employment, pensions, insurance, medical services, recreation. In the early 'forties the functions were divided, labor relations being set up within industrial relations as a semi-autonomous department under a manager of labor relations. The director of industrial relations then became a director of personnel services. The separation was judged unsatisfactory, so in 1947 the directorship of industrial relations was raised to a vice presidency, with theoretical authority over labor relations and all other personnel functions. Despite this nominal unification labor relations remained relatively autonomous. Even within the labor relations subdepartment coordination was difficult. Some company officials worked with the FE, some with the UAW. Grievance handling required close teamwork among top plant management, foremen, all segments of labor relations, time study, and the legal department—teamwork which staff rivalries might seriously interfere with.

When one adds to the above internal problems the very size of the company, twenty to thirty plants in many locations, and the number of its employees (see Table 5) it is not surprising that it has been difficult to formulate and execute a workable labor relations policy in the rapidly changing situation since 1933.

TABLE 5

Employment and Profits, International Harvester Company, 1948–60

Year	*Employment (thousands of workers)*	*Net Profits (millions of dollars)*
1948	96.6	55.7
1950	90.5	66.7
1952	87.2	55.7
1954	70.7	36.3
1956	74.0	49.6
1958	63.2	42.9
1960	68.2	53.7

Source: International Harvester, *Annual Reports.*

Union-Management Harmony: The "New Look"

The grievance load reached its peak in 1955. By this time forces were at work that helped bring the parties to their senses. Declining employment, disappointing profits, and a national reputation for bad labor relations put pressure on both company and union to develop a more constructive relationship. An important high-level meeting between Harvester, UAW, and the contract umpires occurred early that year. The company team was headed by President McCaffrey, the union team by Pat Greathouse. The contract umpires were David L. Cole and Willard Wirtz. The olive branch tone of the meeting was set by McCaffrey, who asked what could be done to develop more stable relations. This attitude was an about-face for one who in the FE days had taken the lead in fomenting attacks on union leadership. The key person in this meeting and subsequent ones was David Cole, who not only had persuaded both sides of the necessity for the meeting but was able to guide them to constructive joint action.

Joint union-management committees were set up to ride circuit of the plants and expedite grievance settlements. This significant turning point in the union-management relationship did not come soon enough to prevent a strike that year but it pointed the way to the future.

It was evidence of the success of the conference that the understandings reached were not destroyed by the four-week strike of 1955. During the negotiations the company offered to go back and pick up some of the fringe changes made by General Motors and Ford two years earlier as a result of the union's "living document" appeal. Union-management relations slowly improved, and by the end of the strike Harvester and the UAW were moving gingerly toward rapprochement.

Between 1955 and 1958 the company made greater efforts to expedite and broaden the application of arbitration decisions. The union began earnest attempts to discourage the filing of unnecessary and harassing grievances. Arbitrators Cole and Wirtz showed the way to streamlining the grievance procedure. Fewer witnesses, fewer pre and post briefs were used. No longer could a local union decision send a case to arbitration; cases must be reviewed by the strengthened UAW-Harvester Council.

Serious efforts were made by both sides to reduce the grievance backlog, especially before the 1950 contract negotiations. Progress was made but not enough to avoid the usual strike. The 1958 negotiations were prolonged and complicated by the company's presentation of a long list of demands for contract changes. One of these demands was revision of the night shift bonus, which had become much higher than at other firms because it was stated in percentage terms. On this item the company was successful; but this unconventional company maneuver, together with the still considerable backlog of grievances and the union's insistence on equaling or bettering the settlement reached in the more profitable auto industry, made agreement impossible before expiration of the contract. The strike this time lasted nine weeks.

In the attempts to reach settlements in both 1955 and 1958 a new bargaining technique was used, that of employing the permanent umpire as mediator. Traditional practice had been to separate contract negotiation completely from contract enforcement. Use of the umpire as mediator, without violating this underlying principle, permitted focusing the skill of the umpire who was intimately familiar with both parties on the most difficult contract problems. In this new role David Cole made a very significant contribution to the resolution of some of these problems. Contract mediation came naturally to Cole, since his informal approach to contract enforcement at Harvester had at times included as much mediation as arbitration.

The joint circuit-riding teams, originated to expedite grievance settlements, gradually brought about something much more significant: a wary but nonetheless real feeling of mutual union-management trust. The successful settlement of grievances became a by-product of this new relationship. The new spirit led to what company and union in 1960 would jointly report, with elaborate fanfare, as the "New Look, Story of a Revolution,"[50] the innovation of speedy oral grievance settlement.

Though not uncommon in other labor-management relationships, the "new look" was indeed a revolution for Harvester management and workers. Its essence was the responsibility of leaders on both sides to abandon weak cases and make quick settlement of strong cases so as to avoid the delays of arbitration.

While the origin of the "new look" went back to the high-level conference of 1955, results at first were not spectacular. The improved and speeded-up arbitration procedures were negated by the continued high filing rate of new grievances, despite the combined efforts of umpire Cole, Labor Relations Manager William Reilly, and Arthur Shy, assistant director of the UAW's Harvester department. Not until 1958 did an experiment at the Memphis plant point the way to a breakthrough of the grievance impasse.

Both Reilly and Shy were in Memphis in 1958 on a troubleshooting expedition to a plant that was sending 8,000–10,000 cases a year to arbitration. After several days the problem seemed as hopeless as ever. Then the two men agreed to the following procedural changes on an experimental basis at the Memphis plant only: (1) The company agreed to waive the retroactivity clause, which denied back pay until the grievance was put in writing. Thus grievances would now be retroactive to the date of their occurrence. (2) The company agreed to permit the union to skip the former intermediate steps in the grievance procedure, including referral to in-plant union officers, and go directly to the stage involving the union's international representative and the plant labor relations director. (3) The union agreed not to write a grievance until both union and company had agreed on the facts.

These simple procedural changes worked miracles. Waiver of the written grievance prerequisite for retroactivity ended the workers' rush to file written grievances. Skipping the intermediate stages gave the worker prompt top-level consideration. The written grievance load plummeted from 450 to three a month. Gradually the experiment was extended to the other Harvester plants, with similar results. The 1961 contract negotiations were entered with no backlog and, for the first time since the war, concluded without a strike.

This commonsense method of grievance settlement was of course not as simple as this brief description implies. It meant the reversal of well-established traditions of behavior by both parties. Both had to be willing to modify the occasional errors of quick settlement and not try to exploit them throughout the system. It meant serious risks, particularly of blame for union officers who withdrew weak grievances. It meant cost risks for the company, since the compromises of quick settlements might give up more than an arbitrated settlement would have.

The "new look" was a real wrench to local plant management and supervisors, who for years had been taught to handle grievances strictly in accord with company policies. When it was extended from Memphis to other plants, local management was ordered to settle grievances before they got to the written stage and under no circumstances to let them go to arbitration. One way to avoid written grievances was to give each case top-level consideration at the first stage. Time study men who had formerly refused to take a fresh look at the job now restudied each grievance. A considerable number turned out to have some justification, and the company made appropriate concessions. In other cases management simply made minor concessions over and above past company practice in order to avoid written grievances. Foremen who had been diligent in maintaining management's policies sometimes felt let down by the "new look" order. Old rules had to be relaxed. Some supervisors reacted by making too many concessions. The difficulty of adapting to the new requirements brought some replacements among local plant management and supervison.

On the union side additional powers were given to the UAW Harvester Council, a body representing UAW members from all Harvester plants. No longer did a local union have the sole power to decide whether or not a grievance went to arbitration. Now the council screened cases and selected only a few for submission to arbitration. The union urged its members to accept compromise settlements rather than go through the delays of arbitration. In a number of cases local officers and stewards who openly balked at the new conciliatory policy were defeated in local elections.

It is to be expected that International Harvester and the UAW have overstated the accomplishments of the "new look." However, stripped of Madison Avenue verbiage and examined impartially, it is still a substantial achievement. Its uniqueness, if any, seems to be in the speed with which complaints are settled without being pushed to the formality of writing. Most plants in the Harvester chain have reached the point of no written grievances whatsoever. Like the reformed alcoholic who dares not take a sip, today both company and union make a point of not permitting a grievance to reach the stage of writing. According to spokesmen for the union, workers on balance net more on grievance settlements than previously, since cases are generally settled promptly; and the company finds the cost of grievance administration less and gets better production from more satisfied employees.

Do the new success in oral grievance handling and the peaceful contract settlement of 1961 mean that the Harvester Company truly accepts and believes in collective bargaining? Or is the "new look" primarily a gimmick to pacify a costly and aggressive union? Certainly there is a greater degree of confidence between union and management at Harvester than ever existed in the earlier history of the company. The company-union relationship is today fairly typical of that in other large manufacturing firms, most of which fit Lester's description of the third stage of development: acceptance and accommodation.

Optimism is tempered when one notes the company's dismissal of arbitrator David Cole in 1961 because of strong objection to a decision granting compensation to workers for bargaining unit work performed by supervisors. Harvester's entire labor relations history suggests that today's apparent acceptance of and accommodation to unionism are not a reflection of an evolution of company philosophy from exclusion to acceptance of unions but a recognition of the realities of strong unions buttressed by federal law. Never, before the Wagner Act, did International Harvester or its predecessor, the McCormick Harvesting Machine Company, voluntarily follow Lester's steps toward acceptance and accommodation in union relations. The early years of labor relations at the McCormick Company, 1862–86, were ones of containment, of dealing with the unions at arm's length. During these years the company met unionism as it met other hazards of business competition, such as price wars, inflation, and depressions. Association with these early unions did not lead the company to acceptance any more than association would lead to love of price wars or depressions. The bitterness and violence of the 1885 strike convinced McCormick management that unions not only were costly but were formidable foes which had to be destroyed. After the twenty-three years of association with unions, the company used its growing economic power and new technology not to advance from containment to acceptance but to regress to exclusion of the union altogether. From the destruction of the union in 1886 to the Federal Government's intervention in 1941, International Harvester fought doggedly to remain at the exclusion stage of labor relations. For only sixteen months, following the Deering strike in 1903, was Harvester forced to grant recognition. Again the union seemed too costly, and the company deliberately destroyed it.

Instead of accepting unionism, Harvester developed highly successful substitutes for it. To the usual discrimination against union officials and members, Harvester after 1900 added elaborate welfare programs and finally, a direct substitute for unions, the works councils. These company unions proved to be the perfect union repellent. They gave the company an unprecedented twenty-one years—1920–41, including the period of the 1937 sitdowns—free of strikes. Only direct intervention by the National Labor Relations Board destroyed this defense.

Continuing government action was largely responsible for the establishment of unionism at Harvester. The 1941 strike was ended when company and unions agreed to the National Defense Mediation Board's recommendation of a union representation election. Harvester recognized the UAW and FE in consequence of this NLRB election. Union security was first given to Harvester unions by the National War Labor Board. When the government-imposed contract expired in 1946 the company withdrew union security. Association with outside unionism in 1941–46 did not lead Harvester to look forward to years of union-management cooperation. Instead, with the end of World War II the company, reverting to its traditional suspicion of unionism, set about cutting the unions down to size.

It is significant that the full union shop now stipulated in Harvester union contracts has never been philosophically approved by Harvester management. It has been wrung out of a reluctant management in prolonged strikes, in which management's position was weakened by bargaining patterns set by the auto industry.

The FE and UAW in the 1935–55 era of government protection of union rights proved to be much stronger adversaries than the unions of 1886 and 1904. After more than a decade of constant labor strife, a relationship of accommodation was established between International Harvester and the UAW. There is no past evidence to indicate that weakened, unprotected unions would not encourage Harvester—and much of American management—to regress from their present acceptance of unionism. Should the current federal legislation favoring union organization be watered down at a time when technological developments encourage the displacement of key workers by machines, a gradual weakening of unions would result.

There is on the other hand no indication that either Harvester management or the UAW is eager to upset the present mutually acceptable bargaining balance of power. Competition of stockholders and workers for corporate income will continue in the future as in the past to bring about periodic disputes, but the political and economic company-union battles of the near future will more probably be in the nature of holding actions. Management's purpose is to keep the union's bargaining power down to reasonable size yet not wage perpetual warfare which hurts production.

Thus while the "new look" in grievance handling at Harvester has been a welcome relief to both union and company, from the company's standpoint it is a desirable pragmatic compromise with a powerful and respected adversary. This does not mean that the company has philosophically accepted unionism and the union shop as a desirable system of employee relations.

From the union's standpoint the present situation, with full recognition and the security of the union shop, gives the union almost everything it wants—including, of course, the excellent prospect of achieving continuing economic gains for its members.

A possible area of union-company clash is the union's efforts to unionize Harvester's clerical, technical, and professional employees. Here the company is fighting unionism with every legal technique. To date the bitterness of these unsuccessful efforts at white-collar unionization has been contained and has not spilled over into the blue-collar relationship. If the union effort were to be stepped up, and particularly if it were to meet with some success, a new test of the current relationship might ensue.

10

The Impact of Unions on Wages and Hours at the McCormick Works

Wages

In this account of a hundred years of industrial relations we have time and again found McCormick executives testifying that they raised wages because of strike pressures or fear of unions. Do wage statistics based on McCormick and International Harvester payroll records bear out this picture of unionism as a major force in wage movement?

From 1860 through 1960 real wages and fringe benefits at McCormick Works rose an average of 2 percent a year.[1] If we eliminate from consideration the 49 years of war and major depressions in this period, and divide the remaining 51 years of "peacetime prosperity" into two groups—(*a*) years when the McCormick Works was unionized in whole or in part and (*b*) years of no union—we find a significant difference in the rates of wage growth for the two periods. In the 31 years of "peacetime prosperity" when the McCormick Works was unionized, the growth rate of real wages and fringes averaged 3.85 percent a year. In the 20 roughly comparable nonunion years it averaged only .1 percent a year. Even during the highest nonunion subperiod, the booming 'twenties (1923–29), it was but .93 percent a year, or less than a fourth of the average growth rate of real wages and fringe benefits in years of unionism.[2]

Not only the amount and frequency of the wage increases but the type of wage increase in use at the McCormick Works points up the important role of unions in wage determination. Before 1862 wage increases were seasonal: raises in the spring when the competition with building trades labor was at its height, cuts in the fall when a surplus of labor appeared because of construction layoffs. These raises and cuts were never plantwide; they were scattered among various classes of workers over a four- to six-week period.

During the Civil War the organization of the foundry by the Molders' Union brought a second type of increase, the department (foundry) increase. With departmental collective bargaining from 1862 through 1885 the Molders steadily pushed foundry wage rates further and further above those of the rest of the plant, which was generally nonunion in this period. Increases initiated in the foundry had a tendency to be passed on in part to the rest of the plant, though some groups, notably common labor, were sometimes bypassed completely. With the destruction of the Molders' Union in the great strikes of 1886, the wage advantage over the rest of the plant was rapidly eliminated both by wage cuts and by breaking the work into simpler operations that used less skilled labor.

A third type was the plantwide, companywide, or general increase. This has resulted essentially from union pressure, principally strikes. The first plantwide increase (10 percent) occurred in 1867 in settlement of the May Day "eight-hour" strike. The second, in settlement of the plantwide strike of 1885, was 10 percent for dayworkers and 15 percent for pieceworkers. The temporarily successful "eight-hour" strike of May Day, 1886, brought a 25 percent raise. The fourth and fifth general raises came in 1903 and 1904 as settlement terms of the 1903 strike.

The sixth general wage increase, which came in 1912, was not a result of union pressure but of the Harvester trust's political vulnerability and unfavorable publicity in the presidential campaign. The investigation of working conditions at one of the company's plants by the New York Senate's Wagner committee forced a general cut in weekly hours from 58½ to 55; this was accompanied by a companywide wage increase. A strike, in April and May 1916, brought a general raise in connection with a union demand for a cut in weekly hours from 55 to 50.

World War I witnessed for the first time plantwide, sometimes even companywide, wage increases, under the combined impact of labor shortages, inflation, government labor board policies, and union pressures—though the company did not bargain collectively at this time. But these increases ended with the onset of the depression.

In all the history of the McCormick Works the only clear-cut example of a broad (though not universal) raise initiated by management, for reasons that might be termed good public relations, was that of

1910. International Harvester profits zoomed from roughly $10,000,000 in 1908, the highest year to that date, to $16,500,000 in 1909. At this time the company recognized no union and there were no overt pressures on management. On the other hand, the trust was very apprehensive about public and government criticism of its monopolistic image. In January 1910, at the suggestion of Vice President Harold McCormick, President Cyrus McCormick II, in a genuine burst of good feeling over the extraordinary profit showing, had a special resolution put through the Board of Directors:

> *Wages resolution.* The spirit of this is that while we are caring for stockholders with dividends and head men with profit sharing we must not omit the workmen—laborers, piece-workers, skilled workmen, assistant foremen, and foremen—in view of the marked increase in the cost of living which has recently taken place.
>
> To this end, let the payroll be carefully examined again *now* and any adjustments recommended to put our men in their proper relation to the employees in other places.[3]

The effect of this order on the average hourly earnings of McCormick Works employees was a healthy 6 percent raise in money terms—though it amounted to only 1 percent in real terms. Moreover it was a selective raise, not received by all workmen.

The only truly companywide wage increase initiated by management without direct union or government pressure was that of February 1923, a 10 percent raise for all unskilled and semiskilled, and 15 percent for all skilled workers. On this occasion serious labor shortages were the cause. The weakness of such management-initiated raises as 1910 and 1923 was that they came so seldom. The nonunion period of the 1923–29 boom is an example of the ineffectiveness of this type of wage pressure. From 1924 through 1929 there were no general increases and no changes in rates of skilled or common labor. The McCormick Works average in money wages in 1929 was 62.6 cents an hour compared to 61.1 cents in 1924.

After a general companywide raise of July 1933, which Harvester made as a result of the National Recovery Act, companywide raises under union pressures gradually became the company's major pattern. The unionized period of 1947–60 witnessed average *annual* real increases in the McCormick Works of 3.6 percent, with regular quarterly wage adjustments beginning in 1950. The frequency of the wage increases in unionized periods accounts for the major share of the better wage showing at these times. The biggest increases too have come in these periods. Individual raises, typical of nonunion periods, were seldom widespread enough to have much impact in the plantwide or companywide wage average.

In the long history of this company the strike and the threat of strike have been the primary forces raising wages. Although labor shortages played a role during the Civil War and World Wars I and II, unions were powerful in these war periods, and their strikes and strike threats gave a significant fillip to the upward pressure of labor market forces. This explanation of wage movements does not ignore the important role played in wage levels in the long run by rising national and company productivity. But productivity has been a relatively constant factor which does not explain the widely varying wage movements. It is these short-run wage movements which vary in close relation to union activity.

Increasing experience of the company with unions has been accompanied by a growing lag between the onset of a depression and the first wage cut. In 1873 the start of the depression, the wage cut, and the month-long strike (which the union lost) were simultaneous. In the depression of 1884 the cut was delayed several months; this time the strike was successful. The depression of 1893, coming close on the heels of the terrible labor troubles of 1885 and 1886, brought a dramatic change in the company's wage-cutting tactics even though at that time there were no unions in the plant. Instead of an across-the-board cut as in 1884, the company maintained its common labor rate through three years of depression, cutting it only at the end of 1896. The skilled departments had been whittled down in a series of piecemeal cuts in 1893 and 1894.

In the depression of 1904, a sixteen-month union contract which was in effect even brought a depression raise in January of that year. The wage cut was instituted in September 1904, as soon as the contract expired. In the recessions of 1908, 1921, and 1931–32, the cuts came later and later after the onset of the depression. The cut of November 1931 was not instituted until two years after the stock crash—though unionism was no immediate threat in this depression. Since the massive growth of unions began in 1933, Harvester has not made any general wage cuts in depressions.

Hours of Work

Until recent years, reduction of weekly hours was often a more important union objective than wage increases. Such cuts in hours were usually accompanied by compensatory increases in pay. It is important, however, to note just when hours were cut and what the motivating forces were.

In today's collective bargaining the matter of shortening hours is reduced to its cents-per-hour cost and evaluated much as is any other item in the package. A union capable of negotiating a 4 percent package seldom puts it into reduced hours, since such a small increase in leisure per year is not worth foregoing a pay increase. At 4 percent per year a union would need to forego a wage increase and all other monetary improvement for three years just to move from a 40- to a 35-hour week. Instead, leisure is now negotiated in smaller units in the form of increased vacations and paid holidays.

Historically, at the McCormick Works such calculations did not impede hours changes. In fact, almost all the reductions in weekly hours made from 1848 through establishment of the current 40-hour week in 1933 were accompanied by nearly proportionate wage increases which maintained weekly pay unchanged. Weekly hours reductions (except in 1903–4) were made at one stroke rather than being spread over several years.

The work week at the inception of the McCormick Works in 1848 was 60 hours, 10 per day, Monday through Saturday. This was substantially lower than in manufacturing generally and conformed to the hours of the Chicago building trades. The first interest of workers in shorter hours culminated in the citywide strike of May Day, 1867, for an eight-hour day. At McCormick's the union was unable to swing the 25 percent raise necessary for reduction of the 60- to a 48-hour week. It therefore accepted a flat 10 percent wage raise and continuance of the 60-hour week.

In 1886 a more famous May Day strike brought the 25 percent pay increase, as the company cut hours from 60 to 48 without any reduction in weekly pay. When the citywide union power was liquidated by police repression after the Haymarket bomb, the company returned to the 60-hour week with no pay raise.

In January and in April 1903 International Harvester reduced hours in its Chicago plants from 60 to 56 with proportionate wage increases, in vain hope of forestalling a strike for a nine-hour day. The strike came anyway. According to the union agreement, hours were further shortened, to 54 (a nine-hour day), by January 1904, with no reduction in weekly pay. At the expiration of the union agreement in September 1904, the company lengthened hours to 58½ with the same weekly pay.

When Harvester cut the work week from 58½ hours to 55 in all plants, in October 1912, as a result of the publicity about long hours of work for women in twine mills, a more than proportionate general wage increase was given.

The April–May 1916 strike was settled with a weekly hours cut, 55 to 50, and a proportionate across-the-board raise. The work schedule was then nine hours on weekdays and five on Saturday. Up to this point the wage increases incident to hours reductions or attempted hours reductions (1867) were almost the only plantwide across-the-board raises ever given by Harvester. The exception was the plantwide wage restoration after the strike of 1885.

During World War I, participation in government contracts required a basic eight-hour day. In April 1918, therefore, Harvester began payment of overtime after eight hours per day. The accompanying raise in basic hourly rates was only 5 percent. This was not a real cut in the work week since there was no increase in leisure. The 50-hour week continued into peacetime and the overtime after eight hours was dropped in 1921 in the implement plants but not at Wisconsin Steel.

During the post-1929 depression the first work-week cut, 50 to 45 hours, was made without a commensurate pay raise. In 1933, with the setting up of NIRA codes, the present 40-hour week was established, along with an 11.1 percent raise, which did not quite compensate in weekly pay for the cut in hours. Since then this work week has on the surface remained intact. However, significant increases in leisure have steadily continued via the route of increased vacations, paid holidays, coffee and wash-up "breaks."

Historically, at the McCormick Works, unions were the chief force behind the reduction in the work day and week. Government pressures brought about the hours cuts in 1912 and 1933. The recent reductions in hours of work through vacations, holidays, and rest periods at the McCormick Works—and of course for all Harvester plants—are overwhelmingly due to union pressures and can be clearly traced in the labor agreements negotiated since 1941.

11

The Evolution of Labor-Management Relations: A Summary

American scholars in recent years have pondered the extent of union influence on wages and working conditions. To what degree are improvements the result of union pressure? How important have been the elements within enlightened management which have led it to share the gains of productivity directly with workers? Has there been some regulator within the economic system which automatically gives workers a share of industry's dividends?

This study of McCormick–International Harvester demonstrates the importance of the role of the union. For almost one hundred years company officials have assumed in their correspondence and shown by their actions that they believed unions capable of having major impact on corporate policies. From at least the May Day strike of 1867 on, management was aware that the union might at one blow force the company to grant as much as a 25 percent cut in weekly hours and a commensurate rise in the hourly rate. To protect the corporation from this vast economic power of the union, a huge and, as it turned out, uneconomic investment in advanced foundry mechanization was made in 1885 in order to destroy the powerful Molders' Union. Uneconomic production schedules were frequently instituted in order to weaken the union. In 1904 an otherwise uneconomic two-week shutdown of all Chicago Harvester plants was carried out in order to soften up the union so that wages could be cut and weekly hours lengthened. In 1894, during the Pullman strike, reapers were produced though they could not be sold, in order to prevent restlessness among the workers. Not only did unions influence relatively important corporate decisions, but top management examined even the minutest detail of corporate activity for its impact on unions. For example, as we have seen, in 1903 the Board of Directors of the International Harvester Company passed a ruling ending the popular interplant football games in order to prevent the commingling of the work forces.

In terms of timing, it is of course not surprising that the union's interest in labor relations preceded that of management. With management preoccupied with sales and production, the union became and remained the major force in initiating moves for better hours, wages, and working conditions. The evolution of a mature trade union philosophy among workers at the McCormick and International Harvester plants clearly preceded the evolution by management of an employee relations philosophy.

Management's education in employee relations was forced upon it piecemeal by its unpleasant experience with unions. As the mass production of reapers was developed, the production process created stresses and strains among the workers. Traditional skills were split up, common labor took over more and more of the work. Seasonal production peaks called for high employment in the spring and heavy layoffs in late summer and early autumn. Depression wage cuts and inflation brought distress to the work force, which responded by turning to unionism at least as early as 1862.

Management first learned of labor problems through inflation-born strikes during the Civil War. With prices rising, it was simple to concede the union's demands and not look deeper into the problem. This greatly strengthened the union and encouraged more strikes. McCormick Works molders were active members of the citywide Molders' local as well as active in the National Union of Iron Molders. This national union, founded in 1859, soon had in operation an elaborate national strike fund from which the Chicago local got assistance in one of its 1864 strikes. An effective membership card system gave the union members a definite advantage in employment.

In tune with national trade union ideology, McCormick workers after the Civil War joined the eight-hour movement. The plantwide and citywide strike for the eight-hour day on May Day, 1867, in which the firm compromised with a 10 percent across-the-board raise, awoke mechanically oriented Superintendent Leander McCormick to the fact that "the union is controlling our shop complete . . . ."[1]

McCormick management now joined with other Chicago executives to curb the powerful Chicago Molders' Union. Blacklists of workers from struck firms were respected by the McCormick firm. The depression of 1873 gave the firm an opportunity to strike back at its own molders with a 20 percent wage cut and dismissal of the foundry foreman, who was suspected of favoring the union. Foremen hereafter were expected to be management oriented and antiunion.

Despite successive wage cuts from 1873 through 1878, the Molders' Union survived the depression and reached the heyday of its power on the upswing of the business cycle in 1879–83.

More elaborate accounting practices now informed McCormick management that the greatest part of the rising cost of production was going to labor. Wage increases were firmly resisted. Management became actively antilabor, moving from the defensive to the offensive in its relations with unions. Union relations and wage negotiations—which heretofore had been handled by the foundry foreman both as a logical extension of his hiring and because, as a former union member, he was assumed to understand unions—were now moved up a notch to the level of the general manager. When the depression of 1884 arrived, wages were again slashed despite—in the case of the McCormick Company—the enormous profits. The ensuing strike was welcomed by management as an opportunity to teach the union a lesson.

The total management defeat in this violent struggle gave twenty-five-year-old Cyrus McCormick II a rude introduction to labor-management problems. Union relations now received top-level treatment. Young President McCormick's first encounter with unionism was so traumatic that, following a careful study of unions, he concluded that they should be ousted. He did his homework well, and in 1886 in an even more violent struggle the company succeeded in doing just that. The Haymarket bomb of that year had important national repercussions for labor-management relations. Far and wide it alerted management that had not yet experienced unionism to its dangers. It helped turn rural and middle-class America against unions. But within the McCormick Company it brought about a change only in intensity of feeling, not in policy toward unions.

The management decision to exclude unionism from the McCormick Works had already been made in 1885 as a result of the union victory in the great strike of March–April of that year. The actual expulsion came to a climax in the violent lockout strike of February–May 1886.

Thus the Haymarket bomb of May 1886 primarily confirmed the McCormick management in the righteousness of a decision previously made and executed. The bomb had two other effects. It intensified the antiunion emotions of young Cyrus H. McCormick II; and it made him more anxious to find some substitute for unionism.

With the expulsion of the unions in 1886, McCormick management's education in labor relations was temporarily arrested. But the exclusion could not be made permanent. Every few years the union reappeared, shutting down the plant. The result was the establishment in 1903 of a personnel department, not to handle union relations but to operate the various welfare measures which were evolved as substitutes for unionism. As the head of the department expressed it in 1903: "It [the personnel department] should convince the employees that they can get what they most want without the necessity of paying anyone for it. . . . without the necessity of joining a union."[2]

Thus was stated succinctly the keynote of what came to be labeled nationally "welfare capitalism." At Harvester this period was a prolonged one, starting in 1901 and lasting until about 1940. It saw the introduction of employee welfare measures such as stock gifts to employees, sickness and accident insurance programs, pensions, recreation, clubhouses, sale of coal and other commodities at wholesale prices to employees, safety, profit sharing, and in 1919 a "company union."

There are several good reasons why the trusts led smaller firms in establishing welfare programs for employees. Primarily it was their greater concern with public relations and in particular the wish to forestall antitrust legislation. Both President Cyrus McCormick II and banker-director George W. Perkins wanted to get free of the unions in 1904 but they did not want a noisy, attention-getting fight. The small manufacturer could indulge his feelings by enrolling in the class wars of the National Association of Manufacturers that began in 1903 and 1904. Though Cyrus McCormick had the same emotions, even distributing to his friends an anti-closed-shop pamphlet by a Milwaukee lawyer named Charles Quarels, he shunned the blatant antilabor approach of the NAM.

At Harvester this need for an image of the "good trust" gave a boost to welfarism particularly from 1907 to the United States entry into World War I. However, the amount of money spent on welfare in this period was never large, and certainly less than would have been spent directly in wages had the company dealt with a union.

Welfarism by itself at Harvester never satisfied workers' needs sufficiently to destroy their interest in unionism. It had at all times to be accompanied by the old-fashioned policy of discrimination against unions and flat refusal to recognize them. This essential other half of "welfare capitalism" is often overlooked. Actually, some of the welfare policies at Harvester were utilized so as to crush unionism. The stock gift plan of 1903 was withheld from union activists. Pensions were clearly advertised as rewards for "loyal" employees. The new "company" union of 1919 was given the power to exclude from re-employment activists of the 1919 strikes.

For Harvester the best approach in trust labor-relations policy appears to have been the addition in 1919 of a company union to the welfarism of the earlier period. This enabled management to advertise its benevolence and its "democratic" labor relations policies while retaining complete control of the employees. It also offered the plausible grounds for excluding outside unions that the employees had "voted" for company unionism.

A key part of the trust labor relations policy was its participation in the secret Special Conference Committee. Here the country's biggest businesses quietly discussed programs for excluding unions by means of company unions, leaving to small business the open public fight against unionism.

There was another though lesser dimension to welfare capitalism at Harvester: the altruism of the owning and managing family. Occasionally women of the family intervened, urging concessions to the workers, when they read in the press about strikes at Harvester plants. Women of the family also took special interest in the working conditions of women employees after the firm entered the twine business in 1901. The second and third generations of McCormick men have shown altruism in varying amounts. By far the most altruistic was Stanley McCormick, but he was active in management only from 1900 through 1905. Fowler McCormick in the 1940's and 1950's set in motion a far-reaching company program for equal employment opportunities. But over the century, family altruism proved to be weak and sporadic by comparison with other forces. There was a perhaps significant tendency for the spirit of altruism to burn most strongly in those members of the family who were least actively engaged in management of the enterprise.

The largest part of Harvester management's personnel policies have been defensive and negative, a reaction to the growth of unions. The company union of 1919–37 was clearly not an effort to extend democracy to employees but a move to establish a company-controlled substitute for outside unionism. Most of the hours reductions came at the insistence of unions, the remainder at the insistence of government. The very size and importance of the personnel department itself have mirrored the growth of the union or the threat of a union. In years when the union threat declined, the department atrophied, only to grow again when unionism burgeoned.

Harvester's payroll records indicate that unionism has coincided with the higher periods of real wage growth, which implies that in the absence of unions productivity gains were not automatically handed over to workers. These findings on wage growth rates are essentially what one might expect, in view of the fundamental purposes of business and unions. It would have been quite surprising had a profit-seeking enterprise like Harvester been found to have passed out the same rate of real wage gains year after year regardless of whether or not a union by striking was about to shut it off from the market.

In addition to his own harrowing experiences with unionism, Cyrus McCormick II suffered vicariously in the labor troubles of his fellow capitalists. The proximity of the Debs-led, Chicago-centered American Railway Union strike in the depression of 1894 particularly upset him, coming as it did so soon after the Haymarket affair. The 1914 labor explosion in far-off Ludlow, Colorado, bore heavily on his mind, in part because of his combined family and business involvement with the Rockefellers. These events and the consequent close cooperation with other capitalists over mutual labor problems gradually served to transform the primarily pragmatic opposition to unionism of Cyrus McCormick's early days into a more generalized class-conscious opposition. The basis of International Harvester's long opposition to unionism remained, however, not any theoretical class ideology of management but the company's extensive and unpleasant experience with unionism. This experience was in direct contrast to the pleasant and harmonious relationship with its company unions from 1919 through 1937.

Though the young men who directed the company's labor relations after the death of Cyrus H. McCormick II in 1936 had no personal experience in dealing with an outside union and had not been given the facts on the firm's past relationships with unions, they had absorbed enough of the company's attitude of opposition to unionism to be predisposed to continue it. They were, of course, intimately acquainted with the operation of the company union.

The experience of McCormick-Harvester employees gives strong support to the belief that the desire of workers for unionism was endemic to the factory system from 1860 to 1960. Shortly after the establishment of the McCormick Works, unions appeared there and conducted systematic collective bargaining for twenty-four years. Their periodic reappearance after expulsion in 1886 is clear evidence that the basic harshness and insecurity of factory life were only peripherally mitigated by the company's welfarism.

Both craft and industrial unions existed from time to time at the McCormick Works. Up to 1885 the craft union of Molders was the principal union; yet in 1867 the entire plant went out on strike with it for the eight-hour day. When in 1885 the Molders were being jeopardized by scabs, the entire plant turned out to help the Molders. In preparation for the 1886 bargaining, the Molders helped organize the rest of the plant in the United Metalworkers and the Knights of Labor; on this occasion the company defeated the combined forces of both craft and industrial unions.

Although the formation of the trust gave a psychological thrust to union organization, it did not add much, if anything, to the union's muscle. Union power was still limited to the number of weeks a worker could live without a paycheck. Nor did industrial unionism at first add much to union strength, since the unskilled lived hand-to-mouth, were poor union-dues payers, had far less understanding of trade unionism, and could be easily replaced by more recent immigrants. The craft union dominance of these early days at the McCormick Works was probably due more to the inability to organize permanent industrial unions than to the exclusiveness of the crafts. As little as one year after the successful Deering Works strike of 1903, in which the various crafts cooperated closely under the leadership of the Chicago Federation of Labor, Harvester superintendents reported that only the skilled workmen, machinists, and patternmakers remained well enough organized to carry out a strike. Management, however, through combination had acquired multiple duplicate plants, greatly enhanced financial reserves, and additional political power.

In 1919 the McCormick Works was organized for the first time as one industrial union under an AF of L federal labor charter. The union was less successful than the earlier craft unions had been. Neither craft nor industrial unionism was able to defeat the Harvester trust once the company was prepared to fight it out.

Other forces worked in the same direction, however, so that industrial unionism which could not succeed in 1919 or before did succeed in 1940. With the decline of immigration after 1920 the divisive effect on the work force of diverse national groups dwindled rapidly. The common suffering of all groups of Harvester workers during the long depression of the 1930's unified them and alienated them from management. Lastly, the Wagner Act certification of unions by means of elections rather than prolonged strikes made it easier for any form of unionism to gain a foothold.

The company union set up in 1919 was industrial in form. This experience from 1919 to 1937 gave a great boost to that type of organization as the eventual form of Harvester unionism. Both the Farm Equipment Workers and the AF of L, which fought each other for recognition at Harvester in 1940–41, were organized industrially—except for a few crafts: the Pattern Makers, for example, was recognized in 1941. The early union history at Harvester indicates that the form of unionism did not retard the growth of unions. Early craft unions were flexible so far as structure was concerned, cooperating with and helping to organize industrial unions. The industrial form arose in 1867, in 1885–86, and in 1919, but failed to survive even as well as craft unionism. With government support since the New Deal, industrial unionism has been the major form.

The term "bread-and-butter unionism" may be used for union emphasis on a short-range, job-centered program of better wages, hours, fringe benefits, and working conditions, in contrast to favoring change in the economic and political system, as do socialism or anarchism. This study indicates that bread-and-butter unionism was well tuned to the desires of McCormick-Harvester workers; throughout a century they always favored it. The bargaining demands of their unions of all periods have been very similar: job security, shorter hours, higher wages. In two periods, 1885–86 and 1938–54, some of their union leaders were more radical—anarchistic in the former and left-wing in the latter—but the bargaining demands were still bread-and-butter ones, and the variations in leadership signified no departure of the workers from this. In both cases the leftist outside leadership would not have come into power had the company not systematically destroyed or controlled the in-plant union leadership.

There is no reason to believe, from the experience of McCormick-Harvester workers, that a union with more radical political aims would have been any more successful than was the bread-and-butter unionism of the Molders in 1862–85 or of the Chicago Federation of Labor in 1903, 1916, and 1919. The bread-and-butter unions never lacked worker interest; what they lacked was the economic power to force the Harvester Company to recognize them.

One of the unions at the McCormick Works in the 1885–86 period was the United Metalworkers. Its leaders in the Chicago Central Labor Union were anarchists. There is no evidence that this leadership prior to the Haymarket explosion had any different effect on either workers or management from that of the purely bread-and-butter-oriented Molders and Knights of Labor of the same period. The bomb highlighted the philosophy of the Metalworkers but its effect on Cyrus McCormick was to increase his previously acquired dislike of all unions.

When the Farm Equipment Workers' Union arose in the late 1930's, it succeeded in gaining the workers' support by pushing an aggressive bread-and-butter program and soft-pedaling or concealing the left-wing activities of some of its leaders. There is evidence, on the basis of its changing views of foreign policy and shifts with regard to affiliation with the United Auto Workers, that the FE was following much of the Communist line. This weakened the union; yet the very effective collective bargaining of the FE held the union together through many years of employer opposition and raids by the UAW. When the FE leaders openly moved politically to the left of United States labor in 1948 with support of Henry Wallace, they met indifference and some hostility on the part of the members.

It is also true that absence of a radical philosophy among union leaders never resulted in recognition and acceptance of unionism by the McCormick-International Harvester Company. Readiness to strike and keep the plant shut was clearly the "philosophy" that most frequently brought recognition by management. The strike and the threat of a strike have been effective in bringing about improvements in wages and working conditions not only in the early years of the McCormick Works but in the period since World War II as well. By contrast, the educational approach of the National Civic Federation to labor-management relations never brought Cyrus McCormick II and George Perkins to recognize unions at the Harvester Company plants, in spite of their financial support of and close relationships with the Civic Federation.

Despite the persistent desire of McCormick Works employees for unions, after 1886 they were unable to establish any lasting form of unionism against the implacable opposition of the company until the national government put its force and sustained support behind the right of workers to organize. It took two convictions for violating the Wagner Act, as well as intervention of the National Defense Mediation Board and the War Labor Board, to bring International Harvester to sign contracts with an outside union for its major plants. Clearly, without the Federal Government's strong support for collective bargaining, even the strong unions of the New Deal era would have been no match here for big business.

The extremely high costs of labor strife to both union and Harvester management after World War II had by the late 'fifties brought both parties in desperation to willingness to forsake entrenched beliefs or modes of action and experiment with new labor relations techniques. The company at present shows a high degree of pragmatic acceptance of unionism. True philosophical acceptance of unionism is not yet in prospect, but that is not of great consequence so long as the status quo remains in governmental labor policies.

The significance of the Harvester story in the history of labor relations may be its representativeness. The records of the National Union of Iron Molders show that the McCormick foundry, in being unionized as early as the Civil War, was typical of foundries across the country. The periodic strikes that convulsed McCormick-Harvester plants were nearly always part of broad waves of labor unrest that ran state- or countrywide: witness those in 1867, 1885–86, 1903, 1916, 1919, and 1937–41. Just as the company's policies toward employees and unions were mostly borrowed from other firms, so at any time the brand of unionism—craft, industrial, conservative, radical—was generally the vogue in the community.

Welfare capitalism was a nationwide movement. First used by the railroads following strikes, in an effort to wean workers away from unions, it spread into manufacturing after the widespread labor troubles of 1886. Each labor crisis pushed a few more firms into welfare techniques. Gertrude Beeks, visiting dozens of these firms in 1902–3 in her capacity as Harvester's first welfare secretary, found antiunionism to have been the motive for most of these schemes.

Harvester joined the welfare parade as early as 1901 and stayed with it. The high visibility to the public of welfare programs made them especially attractive to trusts under governmental fire, which could easily afford the costs. By the 1920's welfarism, at least in its cheaper forms, had spread to a broad segment of American business firms.

Obviously Harvester's experience in labor relations has differed in some degree from that of other companies. Success during the 1920's and early 1930's in finding a formula which blocked unionism retarded the company's adjustment to the changed type of labor relations that came in nationally with the New Deal. All companies faced this problem, but most reached a way of living with unions well before Harvester, whose adjustment period was more rocky and prolonged than that of most firms, and lasted until close to the 1960's.

A prediction of national labor relations trends based on knowledge of the situation at International Harvester might run something like this. The present labor-management relationship is a stable one, with a balance of power between union and management. Labor has demonstrated an ability to shut down a plant or the entire company, and management an ability to "take a strike." This ability of both sides to hurt but not destroy one another puts a premium on compromise and has brought about what is a remarkably good labor-management relationship.

Several things could conceivably disturb this relationship: say that labor-saving technology advanced fast enough to enable supervisors to run the plant for a time without the blue-collar labor force, thus increasing the cost and decreasing the effectiveness of the strike; or that the unions received sufficient response to their efforts at unionizing office employees to challenge the company in a new area; or that a significant change in federal labor legislation inspired one side to take advantage of it, thus setting off a new struggle. None of the above prospects is imminent for Harvester or for American industry generally.

Reference Material

Bibliographical Note

The basic source for this study has been the papers of the McCormick family located in the McCormick Collection of the State Historical Society of Wisconsin in Madison. This magnificent collection includes personal and business papers of various members of the McCormick family as well as many business records of the McCormick Harvesting Machine Company and its predecessors prior to the merger that formed the International Harvester Company in 1902. Papers are still being added to the collection. Especially valuable have been the voluminous McCormick Works payroll records beginning with 1848 and continuing through 1940. The collection also includes original payroll records from several of the competing agricultural implement companies involved in the merger.

All the McCormick family or company materials and International Harvester materials cited in this book are in the McCormick Collection unless otherwise stated. The sections of the collection consulted are listed below. At this date only Series A and B have been catalogued. The papers of Cyrus Hall McCormick II are currently being reorganized and catalogued; materials no longer to be found in the files given in the references may be traced with the help of an index, listing letters by the name of the writer, which is also being prepared.

Cyrus Hall McCormick I Papers (Series A)

1A Correspondence File
2A Subject File
3A, 4A Letterpress Copybooks

Nettie Fowler McCormick Papers (Series B)

1A Own Writings File
2B Chronological File
3B Subject File
7B Scrapbooks

CYRUS HALL MCCORMICK II PAPERS (SERIES C)

STANLEY ROBERT MCCORMICK PAPERS

ANITA MCCORMICK BLAINE PAPERS

PRINTED MATERIAL FILE

MCCORMICK COMPANY RECORDS

INTERNATIONAL HARVESTER RECORDS

DEERING COMPANY PAYROLL BOOKS

PLANO COMPANY PAYROLL BOOKS

Materials in the files of the International Harvester Company in Chicago were consulted by special permission. These were chiefly payroll records (since 1940) and Minutes of the Works Managers' Meetings.

The George W. Perkins papers at Butler Library, Columbia University, were a very helpful supplementary source for one period.

The journal and convention proceedings of the International Union of Molders, Blacksmiths, and Allied Workers, beginning in 1863, have been essential in interpreting the nature of the early unionism at the McCormick Works. Union officials very kindly gave me access to these records and subsequently permitted the State Historical Society of Wisconsin to microfilm them.

The only secondary source used extensively was the two-volume biography *Cyrus Hall McCormick* by William T. Hutchinson (D. Appleton & Co., 1935).

Secondary sources which were helpful in certain periods were:

DAVID BRODY, *Steelworkers in America,* Cambridge, Mass.: Harvard University Press, 1960.

JOHN R. COMMONS and Associates, *History of Labor,* Vol. 4, New York: Macmillan, 1935.

HENRY DAVID, *The History of the Haymarket Affair,* New York: Farrar & Rinehart, 1936.

JOHN J. FLINN, *History of the Chicago Police from the Settlement of the Community to the Present Time, under Authority of the Mayor and Superintendent of the Force,* Chicago: Under auspices of the Police Book Fund, 1887.

JOHN A. GARRATY, *Right-hand Man: The Life of George W. Perkins,* New York: Harper & Brothers, 1960.

NICHOLAS PAINE GILMAN, *A Dividend to Labor; A Study of Employers' Welfare Institutions,* Boston: Houghton, Mifflin, 1899.

Marguerite Green, *National Civic Federation and the American Labor Movement, 1900–1925,* Washington, D.C.: Catholic University of America Press, 1956.

Frederick H. Harbison and John R. Coleman, *Goals and Strategy in Collective Bargaining,* New York: Harper & Brothers, 1951.

Clarence J. Hicks, *My Life in Industrial Relations,* New York: Harper & Brothers, 1941.

John Hope II, *Negro Employment in 3 Southern Plants of International Harvester Company,* Washington, D.C.: National Planning Association, 1953.

Max Kampelman, *The Communist Party vs. the CIO,* New York: Frederick A. Praeger, 1957.

Richard A. Lester, *Labor and Industrial Relations,* New York: Macmillan, 1951.

Henry F. Pringle, *Theodore Roosevelt,* New York: Harcourt, Brace, 1931.

Virginia Roderick, *Nettie Fowler McCormick,* West Rindge, N.H.: Richard R. Smith, 1956.

B. M. and S. K. Selekman and S. H. Fuller, *Problems in Labor Relations,* 1st ed., New York: McGraw-Hill, 1955.

Sarah E. Southall, *Industry's Unfinished Business,* New York: Harper & Brothers, 1950.

Philip Taft, *The AF of L in the Time of Gompers,* New York: Harper & Brothers, 1957.

Arnold R. Webber, *The Structure of Collective Bargaining,* Glencoe, Ill.: Free Press, 1961.

The following people kindly permitted me to interview them. The results of the interviews are found primarily in Chapter 9, to a lesser extent in Chapter 8.

Milton Burns, Staff Representative, UAW; formerly Staff Representative, FE–UE. (Deceased.)

Larry Carlstrom, International Representative, UAW.

David Cole, Arbitrator.

Jack Conway, formerly assistant to Walter Reuther, Industrial Union Department, UAW.

Jack Cudahy, President, Local 22631, Federal Labor Union.

Nesta Edwards, Welfare Department, International Harvester Co. (Retired.)

T. R. Gockel, General Supervisor of Standards and Methods Research, I.H.Co.

Gunnar Hallstrom, General President, Pattern Makers' League, AFL–CIO.

Edward Hinchley, Jr., Patternmaker, McCormick Works. (Retired.)

M. M. Homan, General Supervisor, Personnel Policies and Procedures, I.H.Co.

SEYMOUR KAHN, Staff Representative, UAW.
THOMAS KELLY, Staff Representative of UAW, formerly on FE–UE staff.
ELMORE V. KNAACK, Industrial Relations Manager, West Pullman Works, I.H.Co.
FOWLER MCCORMICK, President and Chairman of the Board, I.H.Co. (Retired.)
BERTRAM MCNAMARA, Staff Representative, United Steelworkers of America.
GEORGE E. MOREDOCK, JR., Assistant Manager of Labor Relations, I.H.Co.
PETER NEPUTY, President, Local 1301, UAW.
WILLIAM REILLY, Manager, Labor Relations, I.H.Co.
ARTHUR SHY, Assistant Director, Agricultural Implement Department, UAW; Director Harvester Department, UAW.
SARA SOUTHALL, Personnel Department, I.H.Co. (Retired.)
JOHN W. VANCE, Director of Public Relations, I.H.Co.
AL VERRI, Staff Representative, UAW; formerly on FE–UE staff.
IVAN L. WILLIS, Vice President of Industrial Relations, I.H.Co. (Retired.)

Notes

Introduction

1 A detailed account of the origin and early years of the firm as well as the life of its founder is given by William T. Hutchinson in *Cyrus Hall McCormick.*

Chapter 1 • PRELUDE TO HAYMARKET, 1862–1886

1 *Chicago Tribune,* March 15, 1863.
2 David Brody, *Steelworkers in America;* John R. Commons and associates, *History of Labor,* Vol. 4; Philip Taft, *The AF of L in the Time of Gompers;* John Fitch, "Unionism in the Iron and Steel Industry," *Political Science Quarterly,* 24, No. 1 (1909), 59–79.
3 National Union of Iron Molders, *Journal,* 1864–86, National Office, International Molders' and Allied Workers' Union, Cincinnati, Ohio.
4 L.J.McC. to C.H.McC., Dec. 6, 1863. CHMcC I papers, Corresp. File, Series 1A, Box 17.
5 The McC.Co. to G. Monser, April 11, 1864. Letterpress Copybook, McC.H.M.Co.
6 Payroll books, McC.H.M.Co.; and Clarence D. Long, "The Illusion of Wage Rigidity," *Review of Economics and Statistics,* 42 (May 1960), 150
7 This conclusion is based on reports of local unions to the National Union of Iron Molders, *Journal,* 1866–73.
8 *Chicago Times,* May 2, 1867, p. 4.
9 L.J.McC. to C.H.McC., May 25, 1867. CHMcC I papers, Corresp. File, Series 1A, Box 24.
10 Payroll books, McC.H.M.Co.
11 J. B. Taylor to C.H.McC., Nov. 6, 1876. CHMcC I papers, Corresp. File, Series 1A, Box 65.
12 C.H.McC. and L.J.McC. [by] Matthews to J. B. Taylor, Nov. 21, 1876. Letterpress Copybook, McC.H.M.Co.
13 Iron Molders, *Journal,* May 1881.

14 Report of Local 233, ibid., Nov. 1880.
15 "Many Employees" to C.H.McC. II, Jan. 1, 1883. CHMcC II papers, unindexed material.
16 C. A. Spring, Jr., to C.H.McC., Sept. 27, 1881. CHMcC I papers, Subject File, Series 2A, Box 53. Labor cost per machine was $15.065 in 1880 and $17.389 in 1881.
17 C.H.McC. II, Diary, Jan. 12, 1882.
18 Ibid., April 3, 1882.
19 C.H.McC. II to N.F.McC., April 15, 1885. NFMcC papers, Subject File, Series 3B, Box 5.
20 Financial statements, McC.H.M.Co., in NFMcC papers, Subject File, and in CHMcC II papers, unindexed material.
21 C.H.McC. II, Diary, Nov. 20, 1884.
22 Payroll books, D.H.M.Co.
23 Molders' petition to C.H.McC. II, March 16, 1885. CHMcC I papers, Corresp. File, Series 1A, Box 100.
24 E. K. Butler to C.H.McC. II, March 19, 1885. NFMcC papers, Subject File, Series 3B, Box 4.
25 E. K. Butler to N.F.McC., March 27, 1885. NFMcC papers, Subject File, Series 3B, Box 4.
26 E. K. Butler to J. F. Utley, March 24, 1885. Letterpress Copybook, McC.H.M.Co., p. 749.
27 J. C. Michele (purchasing agent) to J. B. Field, March 27, 1885. Letterpress Copybook, McC.H.M.Co., p. 809.
28 E. K. Butler to Tom Braden, April 7, 1885. Letterpress Copybook, McC.H.M.Co., p. 132.
29 E. K. Butler to J. F. Utley, April 7, 1885. Letterpress Copybook, McC.H.M.Co., p. 122.
30 Management's labor relations vocabulary and philosophy were so primitive that official company documents labeled strikebreakers as "scabs." Thus the 1885 payroll book lists "Scab" molders. The cost of the barracks to house strikebreakers is listed under the heading "Scab House." The term "loyal worker" had apparently not yet been invented.
31 *Chicago Tribune,* April 3, 1885.
32 C. A. Spring, Jr., to N.F.McC., April 17, 1885. NFMcC papers, Subject File, Series 3B, Box 5.
33 Carter H. Harrison to C.H.McC. II, April 9, 1885. CHMcC I papers, Subject File, Series 2A, Box 57.
34 C.H.McC. II to N.F.McC., April 13, 1885. NFMcC papers, Subject File, Series 3B, Box 5.
35 Ibid.
36 Ibid.
37 Ibid.
38 Idem, July 29, 1885. NFMcC papers, Subject File, Series 3B, Box 5.
39 Financial statements, McC.H.M.Co. CHMcC II papers, unindexed material.

40 C.H.McC. II to N.F.McC., April 24, 1885. NFMcC papers, Chronolog. File, Series 2B, Box 31.
41 J. C. Harris, Special Report, April 14, 1885. CHMcC I papers, Corresp. File, Series 1A, Box 98.
42 C.H.McC. II to N.F.McC., April 15, 1885. NFMcC papers, Subject File, Series 3B, Box 5.
43 N.F.McC. to C.H.McC. II, April 13, 1885. NFMcC papers, Own Writings File, Series 1B, Box 3.
44 N.F.McC. to Virginia McCormick, April 15, 1885. NFMcC papers, Own Writings File, Series 1B, Box 3.
45 C.H.McC. II to N.F.McC., April 15, 1885. NFMcC papers, Subject File, Series 3B, Box 5.
46 Frank S. Mangum in R. O. Johnson, "History of the International Harvester Company," Vol. 2. Unpublished MS CHMcC II papers, unindexed material.
47 *Chicago Telegram,* March 1, 1886.
48 *Chicago Mail,* Feb. 27, 1886. These estimates leave 71 workers not accounted for.
49 Myles McPadden, corresponding representative, Molders' Local No. 233, Iron Molders, *Journal,* March 1886, p. 2.
50 C.H.McC. II to D. M. Osborne, Feb. 18, 1886. Letterpress Copybook, McC.H.M.Co.
51 Company memorandum [undated], with names of 82 workmen who purchased revolvers. CHMcC II papers, unindexed material.
52 According to C.H.McC. II in *Evening Journal* [Chicago], March 1, 1886.
53 According to Myles McPadden in *Chicago Mail,* March 1, 1886.
54 Payroll books, McC.H.M.Co.
55 C.H.McC. II to Ralph Emerson, Rockford, Ill., March 8, 1886. Letterpress Copybook, McC.H.M.Co.
56 *Chicago Daily Telegram,* May 3, 1886.
57 Henry David, *The History of the Haymarket Affair,* p. 190.
58 *The Noon News* [Chicago], April 9, 1885, and *Morning News* [Chicago], March 3, 1886.

CHAPTER 2 • THE ORIGIN OF WELFARISM

1 Letter, E. K. Butler to N.F.McC., May 3, 1890. NFMcC papers, Subject File, Series 3B, Box 11.
2 N.F.McC. to C.H.McC. II, July 8, 1894. NFMcC papers, Own Writings File, Series 1B, Box 26, Vol. 6, p. 183.
3 C.H.McC. II to N.F.McC., July 11, 1894. CHMcC II papers, Letterpress Copybook, No. 4, p. 872.
4 C.H.McC. II to Grover Cleveland, July 9, 1894. CHMcC II papers, unindexed material.
5 C.H.McC. II to Rev. T. C. Hall, July 9, 1894. CHMcC. II papers, Letterpress Copybook, No. 4, p. 860.

6 C.H.McC. II to N.F.McC., July 11, 1894. CHMcC II papers, Letterpress Copybook, No. 4, p. 873.
7 Idem, July 13, 1894. CHMcC II papers, Letterpress Copybook, No. 4, p. 899.
8 Idem, July 23, 1894. CHMcC II papers, Letterpress Copybook, No. 4, p. 946.
9 E. K. Butler to N.F.McC., July 11, 1894. NFMcC papers, Subject File, Series 3B, Box 15.
10 C.H.McC. II, Diary, Aug. 1, 1901.
11 *Chicago Tribune,* Sept. 24, 1902.
12 Report, Gertrude Beeks on factory inspection tours, 1901–2. NFMcC papers, Subject File, Series 3B, Box 27.
13 Ibid.
14 Ibid.
15 Ibid
16 Ibid. A few years after Miss Beeks's survey National Cash Register found the unions too onerous and threw them out.
17 C.H.McC. II, Diary, March 8, 1882.
18 Gertrude Beeks to plant superintendent F. A. Flather, Dec. 2, 1902. NFMcC papers, Subject File, Series 3B, Box 30, pp. 1, 3.
19 Gertrude Beeks to S.R.McC., Dec. 2, 1902. NFMcC papers, Subject File, Series 3B, Box 30, p. 2.
20 S.R.McC. (probably to C.H.McC. II), Dec. 2, 1902. CHMcC II papers, Private File 0-20.
21 John R. Commons, "Welfare Work in a Great Industrial Plant," *American Monthly Review of Reviews* (July 1903), pp. 79–81.
22 Virginia Roderick, *Nettie Fowler McCormick* p. 227.
23 Graham Taylor, *Chicago Commons through Forty Years* (Chicago: Chicago Commons Association, 1936), p. 36.
24 The principal stockholders of the family-owned McCormick Harvesting Machine Company and the percentages of stock owned by each were: Nettie F. McCormick, 23.132%; Cyrus H. McCormick II, 21.400%; Mary Virginia McCormick, 12.152%; Harold F. McCormick, 14.136%; Stanley R. McCormick, 15.048%; Mrs. Emmons Blaine (Anita McCormick), 14.128%; Emmons Blaine, .004%. Letter from F. A. Steuert to John A. Chapman, Agent, March 2, 1914. CHMcC II papers, Private File 15.
25 Minutes of stockholders' meetings, McC.H.M.Co., Nov. 18, 1902, and March 2, 1903. AMcCB papers.
26 C.H.McC. II, Diary, April 28, 1903.
27 Ibid.
28 Ibid.
29 Payroll books, McC. Works. McC. Col., I.H.Co. records.
30 C.H.McC. II, Diary, April 30, 1903.
31 Minutes of stockholders' meeting, McC.H.M.Co., May 18, 1903. AMcCB papers.

32 S.R.McC. to George F. Perkins, Aug. 27, 1903. CHMcC II papers, File 18.
33 Frank A. Ericsson (wage specialist on I.H.Co. staff) to E. A. Hull, Dec. 5, 1904. CHMcC II papers, File 15.
34 Ibid.
35 John A. Chapman to C. and H.McC., Dec. 6, 1907. CHMcC II papers, File 15.
36 F. A. Steuert to John A. Chapman, Dec. 12, 1907. CHMcC II papers, File 15.
37 Henry Bruere to John G. Wood, general superintendent, McCormick Works (undated, but probably March 1904). CHMcC II papers, I.H.Co. Welfare papers belonging to H.F.McC.'s office, File 6.
38 Idem, March 9, 1904. NFMcC papers, Subject File, Series 3B, Box 38.
39 Ibid.
40 Henry Bruere, "Recommendations for Dealing with Social Betterment Problem at Reaper Works," June 1903. NFMcC papers, Subject File, Series 3B, Box 34, p. 1.
41 Henry Bruere, "Factory Education: A Statement of the Case," from *An Investigation of Trade and Industrial Schools Conducted for the International Harvester Company of America* (Mimeographed pamphlet; Chicago: International Harvester Co., 1904), p. 1. CHMcC II papers, File 44.
42 Bruere, "Recommendations . . . ," p. 2. Passages that follow are from pp. 6, 9, 7–8
43 John Dewey to N.F.McC., Feb. 20, 1904. NFMcC papers, Subject File, Series 3B, Box 38.
44 Gertrude Beeks to C.H.McC. II, Sept. 12, 1904. CHMcC II papers, File 508.
45 Henry Bruere to John G. Wood, Jan. 27, 1904. CHMcC II papers, I.H.Co. Welfare papers belonging to H.F.McC.'s office, File 6.
46 Gertrude Beeks to C.H.McC. II, April 11, 1905. CHMcC II papers, File 508.
47 Idem, June 12, 1905. CHMcC II papers, File 508.

CHAPTER 3 • UNION RESURGENCE

1 E. P. Weaver, manager, Manufacturing Information Bureau, to C.H.McC. II, Sept. 17, 1901, Report of Detective "Manilla." CHMcC II papers, unindexed material.
2 Report, Gertrude Beeks to E. A. S. Clarke, general manager of Deering Division, June 27, 1903. AMcCB papers, Case 3.
3 For an excellent discussion of the merger see John A. Garraty, *Right-hand Man, the Life of George W. Perkins*, ch. 7.
4 The Milwaukee Harvesting Machine Company was purchased by the McCormick Company at the time of the merger. In addition to the three plants in Chicago, the Deering-owned Wisconsin Steel Works,

and this one in Milwaukee, the merger gave International Harvester one in Springfield, Ohio, and one at Hamilton, Ontario. The firm subsequently purchased other companies both in the United States and abroad, and constructed other plants. By the 1920's it owned twenty-three plants, and today still more.

5 C.H.McC. II, Diary, Jan. 7, 1903.
6 *Chicago Record-Herald,* May 1, 1903, p. 9.
7 *Chicago Tribune,* May 4, 1903, p. 1.
8 Ibid.
9 *Chicago Record-Herald,* May 1, 1903, p. 9.
10 *Chicago Tribune,* May 1, May 15, 1903, p. 3.
11 Ibid., April 30, 1903, p. 3.
12 Ibid., May 9, 1903, p. 3.
13 *Chicago Record-Herald,* May 1, 1903, p. 9.
14 *Chicago Tribune,* May 1, 1903, p. 5.
15 Memorandum [undated], CHMcC II papers, unindexed material.
16 *Chicago Record-Herald,* May 1, 1903, p. 9.
17 *Chicago Tribune,* May 5, 1903, p. 3.
18 *Chicago Tribune,* April 30, 1903, p. 3.
19 Ibid., May 2, 1903, p. 3.
20 Ibid., April 30, 1903, p. 3.
21 Ibid.
22 C.H.McC. II, Diary, May 1, 1903.
23 *Chicago Tribune,* May 12, 1903, p. 2.
24 Agreement, International Harvester, *Eighth Annual Report of the State Board of Arbitration of Illinois,* July 1, 1903, p. 180.
25 John R. Commons, "Welfare Work in a Great Industrial Plant," *American Monthly Review of Reviews,* 28 (July 1903), 79–81.
26 G. S. Beeks to E. A. S. Clarke, June 27, 1903. AMcCB papers, Case 3.
27 G. S. Beeks to Robert Daily, July 23, 1903. CHMcC II papers, File 4.
28 From November 1902 to April 1904 the McCormick Works laid off 814 men, 29.65%. Payroll books, I.H.Co. McC. Col., I.H.Co. records.
29 U.S. Bureau of Corporations, Department of Commerce and Labor, *Report on the International Harvester Company* (Washington, D.C.: Government Printing Office, March 3, 1913), p. 234.
30 For the story of the formation of the International Harvester trust, see Garraty, *Right-hand Man, the Life of George W. Perkins.*
31 Actually the control was given to three trustees, one representing the McCormicks, one the Deerings, and one J. P. Morgan. The practical effect was to give full control to the Morgan representative, Perkins.
32 Memorandum of a conference between J. P. Morgan and C.H.McC. II, Sept. 26, 1903. CHMcC II papers, unindexed material.
33 E. A. S. Clarke to C.H.McC. II, Aug. 19, 1904, pp. 2–7. CHMcC II papers, File 44.
34 Labor conference minutes, Aug. 29, 1904, p. 15. CHMcC II papers, File 44.

35 Ibid., Aug. 27, 1904, pp. 10–11.
36 Ibid., Aug. 29, 1904, p. 11.
37 Ibid., Aug. 25, 1904, p. 1.
38 Ibid., Aug. 27, 1904, p. 8.
39 Ibid., Aug. 25, 1904, p. 1.
40 Ibid., Aug. 25, 1904, p. 2.
41 Ibid., Aug. 30, 1904, p. 4.
42 Ibid., Aug. 29, 1904, pp. 21–22.
43 Ibid., Aug. 27, 1904, pp. 7–8.
44 Ibid., Aug. 27, 1904, p. 8.
45 Ibid., Aug. 27, 1904, p. 20.
46 Ibid., Aug. 30, 1904, p. 4.
47 Ibid., Aug. 29, 1904, pp. 17–18.
48 Ibid., Aug. 29, 1904, p. 18.
49 Ibid., Aug. 29, 1904, p. 20.
50 Ibid., Aug. 30, 1904, p. 2.
51 Ibid., Aug. 29, 1904, p. 3.
52 Ibid., Aug. 27, 1904, p. 28.
53 Ibid
54 John A. Garraty, "The United States Steel Corporation versus Labor: The Early Years," *Labor History*, 1 (Winter, 1960), 6.
55 E. A. S. Clarke to C.H.McC. II, Aug. 19, 1904, p. 5. CHMcC II papers, File 44.
56 B. A. Kennedy and F. A. Flather, labor conference minutes, Aug. 27, 1904, pp. 7, 20. CHMcC II papers, File 44.
57 Report on interview with G. W. Perkins, in C.H.McC. II to James Deering, Aug. 31, 1904. CHMcC II papers, File 508.
58 Labor conference, Aug. 27, 1904, p. 17. CHMcC II papers, File 44.
59 C.H.McC. II to James Deering, Aug. 31, 1904. CHMcC II papers, File 508.
60 "Memorandum, Labor Situation," H.F.McC. to C.H.McC. II, Sept. 8, 1904. CHMcC II papers, File 508. The quotations which follow are from this memorandum.
61 H.F.McC. to C.H.McC. II, Sept. 8, 1904. CHMcC II papers, File 508.
62 Ibid.
63 The National Civic Federation brought together prominent employers and labor leaders for educational conferences on industrial relations issues. In addition, in the years before World War I it built a record of solid achievement in mediation of labor disputes. Labor leaders like Samuel Gompers who cooperated in its educational efforts were the frequent targets of more radical labor criticism because of the open shop labor policies of many of the principal supporters of the Federation such as Cyrus H. McCormick, Judge Gary of U. S. Steel, and George W. Perkins. In the present instance criticism was not justified. Certainly Easley was not a neutral here but a strong spokesman for recognition of the union.

64 CHMcC II papers, File 508.
65 Labor conferences, Aug. 30 and 29, 1904. CHMcC II papers, File 44.
66 Labor conference, Aug. 27, 1904. CHMcC II papers, File 44.
67 From clipping sent by Gertrude Beeks to C.H.McC. II, Sept. 12, 1904. CHMcC II papers, File 508.
68 H.F.McC. to C.H.McC. II, Sept. 14, 1904. CHMcC II papers, File 508.
69 Ibid
70 Telegram, H.F.McC. to C.H.McC. II, Sept. 15, 1904. CHMcC II papers, File 508.
71 E. A. S. Clarke's directive for changes in working conditions, Sept. 23, 1904. CHMcC II papers, unindexed material.
72 Gertrude Beeks to C.H.McC. II, Oct. 6, 1904. CHMcC II papers, File 508.

CHAPTER 4 • WELFARISM, THE LABOR PROGRAM OF A "GOOD TRUST"

1 G.W.P. to J. P. Morgan, April 30 and June 28, 1907. GWP papers, Box 18.
2 Henry F. Pringle, *Theodore Roosevelt,* p. 313.
3 *Collier's Weekly,* April 18, 1908.
4 Donation Book of the McC.H.M.Co., 1896 and 1898. CHMcC II papers
5 Memorandum dictated by H.F.McC. and transmitted by William Clark, May 4, 1908. CHMcC II papers, File C-508.
6 Garraty, *Right-hand Man, the Life of George W. Perkins,* p. 145.
7 "The Underlying Principle of the Profit-Sharing, Benefit and Pension Plans of the International Harvester Company," paper by G.W.P., Nov. 23, 1909. CHMcC II papers, File 523.
8 Roosevelt's Message to Congress, Dec. 3, 1907. Copy in GWP papers, Box 18.
9 Payroll books, Plano Works. McC. Col.
10 The Deering Workmen's Mutual Benefit Association, 15th Annual Report, 1903. CHMcC II papers, I.H.Co. Welfare papers belonging to H.F.McC.'s office, File 9.
11 S.R.McC. to C.H.McC. II, April 21, 1902. CHMcC II papers, I.H.Co. Welfare papers belonging to H.F.McC.'s office, File 9.
12 Relief Department, Synopsis of Organization, Regulations, Blanks, Etc., 1904. CHMcC II papers, I.H.Co. Welfare papers belonging to H.F.McC.'s office, File 9.
13 Recommendation to Cyrus Bentley (company attorney), March 24, 1904. CHMcC II papers, I.H.Co. Welfare papers belonging to H.F.McC.'s office, File 9.
14 C. E. Woods, Works Division, to F. A. Flather, manager of Works, Aug. 18, 1904. CHMcC II papers, I.H.Co. Welfare papers belonging to H.F.McC.'s office, File 9.

15 S. M. Darling to L. S. Florsheim, Dec. 28, 1904. CHMcC II papers, I.H.Co. Welfare papers belonging to H.F.McC.'s office, File 9. For the sociological committee—the name the department of industrial relations bore in 1904–5—see pp. 163–67.
16 W. Borg to I.H. Manufacturing Dept., Nov. 21, 1905. CHMcC II papers, I.H.Co. Welfare papers belonging to H.F.McC.'s office, File 9.
17 Statement of McCormick Works Relief Fund, Season 1904. CHMcC II papers, I.H.Co. Welfare papers belonging to H.F.McC.'s office, File 25.
18 Dr. W. Fisk to S. M. Darling, Jan. 17, 1905. CHMcC II papers, File 142.
19 "Report of [I.H.] Committee on Benefit Insurance," July 10, 1908. GWP papers, Box 19.
20 Gertrude Beeks to C.H.McC. II, July 18, 1908. CHMcC II papers, File W-508
21 "Report of Committee on Benefit Insurance," p. 8; Secretary of the Benefit Committee, Mary L. Goss, "Benefit or Relief Association or Workingmen's Insurance," July 13, 1908, p. 4. GWP papers, Box 19.
22 C.H.McC. II to G.W.P., July 17, 1908. GWP papers, Box 19.
23 Idem, July 27, 1908. GWP papers, Box 19.
24 G.W.P. to J. P. Morgan, July 31, 1908. GWP papers, Box 19.
25 G.W.P. to C.H.McC. II, July 20, 1908. GWP papers, Box 19.
26 C.H.McC. II to G.W.P., July 21, 1908. GWP papers, Box 19.
27 G.W.P. to Theodore Roosevelt, Oct. 7, 1908. GWP papers, Box 19.
28 Garraty, *Right-hand Man, the Life of George W. Perkins,* p. 226.
29 G.W.P. to J. P. Morgan, Nov. 10, 1908. GWP papers, Box 19.
30 Memorandum, McC.H.M.Co., Jan. 2, 1907. CHMcC II papers, Private File 16
31 I.H.Co., *Annual Reports, 1908–11.* Printed Material File.
32 Trust agreement between McC.H.M.Co. and Trustees, Jan. 2, 1907. CHMcC II papers, Private File 16.
33 *Farm Machinery,* Nov. 30, 1909, p. 28. Printed Material File.
34 Pension Regulations, I.H.Co., Jan. 1, 1919. CHMcC II papers, Private File.
35 H.F.McC., Feb. 3, 1919. CHMcC II papers, Private File.
36 Minutes, Works Council, McCormick Works, Sept. 9, 1936. Exhibits, NLRB Cases C-1561 to C-1566, National Archives.
37 A. M. Hoit to A. H. Young, manager of industrial relations, Sept. 18, 1919. CHMcC II papers, File 185.
38 Minutes, Works Council, Wisconsin Steel Works, Aug. 4, 1925, and March 8, 1932. McC. Col., I.H.Co. records.
39 Memorandum dictated by C.H.McC. II, Sept. 27, 1909. CHMcC II papers, Private File F-20.
40 See n. 7.
41 Payroll books, McCormick Works, 1910–13. McC.Co. records.
42 N. P. Gilman, *A Dividend to Labor; A Study of Employers' Welfare Institutions,* pp. 310–16.

43 Company announcement, Feb. 14, 1906. CHMcC II papers, File 508.
44 Lists of annual bonus recipients. CHMcC II papers, Private File P-20.
45 H. H. Waterman to B. A. Kennedy, Oct. 24, 1911. CHMcC II papers, Private File P-20.
46 C.H.McC. II to C.H.McC. III, May 5, 1914. CHMcC II papers, Private File 1.
47 C.H.McC. II, notes for speech at Welfare Dinner, Dec. 2, 1915. Diary.
48 C.H.McC. II to John D. Rockefeller, Jr., Jan. 20, 1916. CHMcC II papers, Private File 316.
49 *The Union Leader* [Chicago], May 6, 1916, p. 8.
50 Marguerite Green, *National Civic Federation and the American Labor Movement, 1900–1925,* p. 289.
51 C.H.McC. II to H.F.McC., Jan. 16, 1920. CHMcC II papers, Private File 2. H.F.McC. to C.H.McC. II, Feb. 18, 1920. CHMcC II papers, Private File F-20. G.W.P. to C.H.McC. II, Dec. 21, 1917. GWP papers, Box 28.
52 I.H.Co., *Annual Report, 1920,* p. 15. Printed Material File.
53 Ibid., *1921,* p. 9.
54 Payroll books, McCormick Works. McC.Co. records.
55 C.H.McC. II to David McCabe, Dec. 13, 1921. CHMcC II papers, unindexed material.
56 Minutes, Works Council, Wisconsin Steel Works, Aug. 4, 1925. McC. Col., I.H.Co. records.
57 Minutes, Works Managers' Meetings, Aug. 31, 1925. I.H.Co. files, Chicago.
58 Payroll books, McCormick Works. McC.Co. records.
59 Minutes, Works Council, Wisconsin Steel Works, July 24, 1936, pp. 37–38. McC. Col., I.H.Co. records.
60 *Harvester World,* 28 (Nos. 9–10): 5, 22–23, and I.H.Co., *Annual Reports, 1938–43.* Printed Material File.

CHAPTER 5 • HARVESTER, A POLITICAL PARIAH

1 *New York Tribune,* Aug. 22, 1912, p. 6.
2 Ibid.
3 Garraty, *Right-hand Man, the Life of George W. Perkins,* p. 277, and *Chicago Tribune,* Aug. 22, 1912.
4 *Chicago Tribune,* Aug. 22, 1912.
5 C.H.McC. II to Cyrus Bentley, Sept. 5, 1912. CHMcC II papers, Letterpress Copybook, No. 38, Series 3C, p. 448.
6 *Chicago Examiner,* Oct. 6, 1912.
7 Ibid., and also Sept. 4, 1912.
8 Louise de Koven Bowen (Mrs. Joseph T. Bowen) to C.H.McC. II, Dec. 26, 1912. CHMcC II papers, File M-508.
9 C.H.McC. II to Mrs. Joseph T. Bowen, Dec. 30, 1912. CHMcC II papers, File M-508.

10 C.H.McC. II to C.H.McC. III, Feb. 12, 1913. CHMcC II papers, File 44.
11 C.H.McC. II to C. S. Funk (general manager selected by Perkins), Jan. 21, 1913. CHMcC II papers, File M-503. C.H.McC. II to C.H.McC. III, Feb. 12, 1913. CHMcC II papers, Corresp. File, Series 1C, File 44.
12 H.F.McC. to C.H.McC. II, March 15, 1913. CHMcC II papers, Private File O-20.
13 C.H.McC. II to Miss L. A. Coston, March 24, 1913. CHMcC II papers, File M-97. Miss Coston, describing herself as a student of social economics, had written congratulating the company on improvements in working conditions for women.
14 *Chicago Tribune,* March 21, 1913, p. 10.
15 N.F.McC. to H.F.McC., April 15, 1913. NFMcC papers, Own Writings File, Series 1B, Box 14.
16 G.W.P. to E. A. Bancroft, April 17, 1913. GWP papers, Box 24.
17 [G.W.P.] Memorandum regarding Auburn Twine Plant Trouble, May 2, 1913. GWP papers, Box 24.
18 [G.W.P.] Memorandum, May 5, 1913. GWP papers, Box 24.
19 C.H.McC. II to Hon. William Sulzer, May 5, 1913. GWP papers, Box 24.

CHAPTER 6 • MANAGEMENT DIVIDED: PERKINS VS. McCORMICK

1 C.H.McC. II to G.W.P., May 2, 1916. NFMcC papers, Subject File, Series 3B, Box 84.
2 *Chicago Tribune,* April 28, 1916, p. 3.
3 Ibid.
4 Ibid., April 26, 29, May 3, 1916.
5 C.H.McC. II to G.W.P., May 2, 1916. NFMcC papers, Subject File, Series 3B, Box 84.
6 C.H.McC. II to N.F.McC., May 5, 1916. NFMcC papers, Subject File, Series 3B, Box 84.
7 C.H.McC. II to Cyrus Bentley, May 9, 1916. CHMcC II papers, Letterpress Copybook, No. 46, p. 783.
8 C.H.McC. II to Messrs. Lamont, Howe, Perkins, Saunders [directors], May 23, 1916. NFMcC papers, Subject File, Series 3B, Box 84.
9 C.H.McC. II to Messrs. Lamont, Howe, Perkins, Glessner, Saunders, May 29, 1916. NFMcC papers, Subject File, Series 3B, Box 84.
10 C.H.McC. II to Messrs. Lamont, Saunders, Glessner, and Howe, with copies to H.F.McC., N.F.McC., and Cyrus Bentley, June 15, 1916. CHMcC II papers, File 185.
11 C.H.McC. II to C.H.McC. III, Feb. 18, 1913. CHMcC II papers, Private File 1.
12 G.W.P. to C.H.McC. II, April 27, 1916. GWP papers, Box 27.
13 In 1916 the Pittsburgh area witnessed violent strikes with frustrated workers stoning plants of various companies. U. S. Steel gave an unprecedented three wage increases in that year.

14 G.W.P. to C.H.McC. II, May 4, 1916. GWP papers, Box 27.
15 Telegram, C.H.McC. II to G.W.P., May 6, 1916. GWP papers, Box 27.
16 Idem, May 9, 1916. GWP papers, Box 27.
17 G.W.P. to G. A. Ranney, May 18, 1916. GWP papers, Box 27.
18 C.H.McC. II to G.W.P., May 20, 1916. GWP papers, Box 27.
19 G.W.P. to C.H.McC. II, May 31, 1916. GWP papers, Box 27.
20 Thomas W. Lamont to C.H.McC. II, June 12, 1916. CHMcC II papers, File 185.
21 For the "line" officials, with their primary responsibility for manufacturing, labor relations was at this time only one of many duties. In later periods labor relations was handled by specialists, who spent full time on it and who were generally subordinate to the line officials.
22 C.H.McC. II to H.F.McC., March 22, 1917. CHMcC II papers, Private File 2
23 Idem, Sept. 27, 1916. CHMcC II papers, Private File 2.
24 *Chicago Tribune*, July 16, 1919.
25 *The New Majority, The* [Chicago] *Federation News*, Aug. 2, 1919, p. 5, col. 2.

CHAPTER 7 • EMPLOYEE REPRESENTATION

1 Percentage of workers involved in strikes: 1919, 20.8%; 1937, 7.2%; 1946, 14.5%. Source: U.S. Bureau of Labor Statistics, Department of Labor, *Handbook of Labor Statistics* (Washington, D.C.: Government Printing Office, 1950), p. 142.
2 *Harvester World*, March 1919, p. 11.
3 "Cooperation and Industrial Progress," a speech before the National Safety Council by C.H.McC. III, Oct. 1, 1919. CHMcC II papers, File 232.
4 A. H. Young to C.H.McC. II, Nov. 21, 1918. CHMcC II papers, File 185.
5 *Decisions and Orders of the NLRB*, 2 (July 1, 1936–July 1, 1937): 321–22. NLRB Case C-41.
6 See n. 10 below
7 Minutes, Works Managers' Meetings, Dec. 10, 1923. I.H.Co. files, Chicago.
8 Ibid.
9 "Cooperation and Industrial Progress" (n. 3 above).
10 Of the twenty-five works councils of International Harvester, complete minutes could be located for only one, that of the Wisconsin Steel Works. This account of the works councils therefore relies heavily on the reports for this one South Chicago plant. While the discussions must have differed in the various works councils, the decisions arrived at were always the same, since management held a veto on every council.

The Works Council of Wisconsin Steel appears to have had more detailed minutes than other councils. They even purport to be verbatim; yet it is clear that at crucial times the stenographer's pencil was stopped. Furthermore a publicity committee of employee and management representatives examined and sometimes censored minutes before sending them to the printer. Nevertheless these detailed minutes covering 1919 through 1936 have been the most important source for understanding and evaluating Harvester works council operations.

The Works Council at Wisconsin Steel established itself as an independent union in 1937 and is still bargaining with the company.

Wisconsin Steel's union history is paralleled by that of other unions which began as company unions, met the Wagner Act test of independence, and today represent the employees in such major industries as oil and chemicals. This background of company unionism leads to the current controversy over the quality of the collective bargaining done today by these independent, unaffiliated unions. While Leo Troy maintains that they are actually independent and carry on significant collective bargaining for their members, Philip Taft believes them characterized by employer favoritism, lack of genuine collective bargaining, and failure to support political action in the interest of labor as a class. (See Troy, "Local Independent Unions and the American Labor Movement," *Industrial and Labor Relations Review*, April 1961, and Taft, "Communication, Local Independent Unions and the American Labor Movement," ibid., Oct. 1961.) This chapter on International Harvester employee representation may throw some light on this question.

11 Minutes, Works Council, Wisconsin Steel Works, April 15, 1919. McC. Col., I.H.Co. records.
12 Ibid., May 6, 1919, p. 14.
13 Ibid., p. 8.
14 *Chicago Tribune*, July 18, 19, 1919.
15 Minutes, Works Council, Wisconsin Steel Works, Oct. 9, 1919, p. 2. McC. Col., I.H.Co. records.
16 Ibid., Sept. 23, 1919, p. 3.
17 Ibid., p. 5.
18 Ibid., Sept. 26, 1919, pp. 2–3.
19 Ibid., Sept. 25, 1919, p. 19.
20 Ibid., Oct. 7, 1919, pp. 16–17.
21 Ibid., Oct. 15, 1919, p. 2.
22 Ibid., Nov. 11, 1919, p. 19.
23 Ibid., Nov. 26, 1919, p. 13.
24 Ibid., p. 14.
25 Ibid., Oct. 12, 1920, Superintendent G. E. Rose.
26 Ibid., Sept. 7, 1920, p. 22.
27 Ibid., April 5, 1921, A. H. Young.
28 Ibid., May 9, 1921, p. 38.

29 Ibid., June 7, 1921, pp. 3–5.
30 Ibid., May 9, 1921, pp. 38–39, A. H. Young.
31 Ibid., Special Meeting of Aug. 22, 1921, pp. 16–17.
32 Ibid., p. 19.
33 Ibid., Oct. 4, 1921, pp. 29 and 33.
34 Ibid., Jan. 2, 1923.
35 Ibid., Feb. 6, 1923, p. 6.
36 Constitution of Harvester Industrial Council, Article XII, Sec. 6.
37 Minutes, Works Council, Wisconsin Steel Works, Aug. 7, 1923, pp. 16–17. McC. Col., I.H.Co. records.
38 Profits in 1924 were $13,037,395; and in 1925, $19,171,200. I.H.Co., *Annual Reports*. Printed Material File.
39 Minutes, Works Council, Wisconsin Steel Works, Nov. 12, 1929, pp. 7–8, Minutes of Employee Representatives. McC. Col., I.H.Co. records
40 C.H.McC. III, Melbourne, Australia, *Herald*, March 9, 1929, magazine section.
41 Mr. McCormick appears to be in error here. The Wisconsin Steel Works minutes show appeals to the president in 1923 and 1924: Minutes, Works Council, Feb. 6, 1923, and April 1, 1924. Article XV of the constitution provides for arbitration but only if both parties agree. Apparently no case ever went to arbitration.
42 Minutes, Works Council, Wisconsin Steel Works, May 27, 1932, pp. 17 and 23. McC. Col., I.H.Co. records.
43 Ibid., p. 33. The discrepancy ($16,759,000 and $16,758,000) appears in the documents.
44 Ibid., May 25, 1931
45 Letter, C.H.McC. III to Works Council, Minutes, Works Council, Wisconsin Steel Works, June 9, 1931, p. 15. McC. Col., I.H.Co. records.
46 Minutes, Works Managers' Meetings, May 29, Aug. 7, and Dec. 4, 1933, and Oct. 28, 1935. I.H.Co. files, Chicago.
47 Minutes, Works Council, Wisconsin Steel Works, Feb. 12, 1935, pp. 32–33. McC. Col., I.H.Co. records.
48 Ibid., March 26, 1935, p. 54.
49 Minutes, Works Managers' Meetings, July 1, 1936. I.H.Co. files, Chicago.
50 Minutes, Works Council, Wisconsin Steel Works, Feb. 3, March 10, July 24, and Nov. 30, 1936. McC. Col., I.H.Co. records.
51 Minutes, Works Managers' Meetings, Dec. 7, 1933. I.H.Co. files, Chicago.
52 Ibid., Nov. 13, 1933.
53 U.S. Senate, Committee on Education and Labor, 73d Congress, 2d session, *Hearings* (Washington, D.C.: Government Printing Office, 1934), Pt. 3, p. 912. Testifying at this same hearing was former Harvester Industrial Relations Manager Arthur H. Young, who had instituted company unionism at Harvester in 1919. Now vice president of industrial

relations of the U. S. Steel Company, he pleaded with the committee not to destroy the new "employee representation plans."

U. S. Steel's adoption of company unionism and employment of Arthur H. Young indicate first the extent to which big industry coordinated its antiunion efforts; second, how broad was the influence of International Harvester's personnel policies and the influence of Mackenzie King and John D. Rockefeller, Jr., who were the first to install company unionism on a broad scale.

54 Minutes, Works Council, Wisconsin Steel Works, July 9, 1935, pp. 35, 36, and 41. McC. Col., I.H.Co. records.

55 Ibid., p. 41. Since he had begun working at Harvester seven years after the works councils were started, it is questionable how much he knew about their origin.

56 *Decisions and Orders of the NLRB*, Vol. 2 (July 1, 1936–July 1, 1937), pp. 355–56, NLRB Case C-41.

57 Ibid., pp. 348–54 passim.

58 Ibid., p. 347.

59 Minutes, Works Managers' Meetings, June 3 and 24, 1935. I.H.Co. files, Chicago.

60 Minutes, Works Council, Wisconsin Steel Works, Dec. 8, 1936, p. 34. McC. Col., I.H.Co. records.

61 *Decisions and Orders of the NLRB*, 29 (Jan. 16–Feb. 28, 1941): 587, NLRB Cases C-1561 to C-1566, National Archives.

62 Minutes, Works Managers' Meetings, March 29, 1937. I.H.Co. files, Chicago.

63 The minutes, Works Council, McCormick Works, Feb. 10, 1937 (Exhibits, NLRB Cases C-1561 to C-1566, National Archives), indicate that a rising vote of appreciation was accorded Fowler McCormick at the conclusion of his visit.

64 Ibid., Aug. 6, 1936.

65 Ibid.

66 Remarks of Gerald Fielde, Transcript of Fact Finding Panel appointed by Secretary of Labor Schwellenbach, Feb. 5, 1946. U. S. Conciliation Service files, Strikes, International Harvester, 1946. National Archives.

67 U.S. Senate, Subcommittee of the Committee on Education and Labor [La Follette committee], 75th Cong., *Hearings*, Vol. 100 (1937); 76th Cong., Vol. 109 (1939–40). The La Follette committee's subpoena of the records of the Special Conference Committee was dated February 19, 1937, and called only for the files and minutes of meetings from January 1, 1933, on. Knowledge of the nature of activities of the Special Conference Committee during the 1920's is less detailed. International Harvester Company's minutes and files on the Conference Committee appear to have been deliberately burned at about the time that the La Follette committee sent its subpoena to the Conference Committee secretary, E. S. Cowdrick. (Interview with George More-

dock, labor relations department, International Harvester Company, June 4, 1963.) However, the Harvester representatives on the Special Conference Committee, A. H. Young, 1919–24, and G. J. Kelday thereafter, made regular oral reports on the Conference Committee meetings to the Harvester works managers from 1922 to 1937. The minutes of these meetings have been preserved in the International Harvester files at Chicago. These Minutes of Harvester Works Managers' Meetings become the major source of information on Special Conference Committee activity prior to 1933.

68 Clarence J. Hicks, *My Life in Industrial Relations*, pp. 136–37.

69 La Follette committee, *Hearings*, 109: 16,785.

70 Minutes, Works Managers' Meetings, March 30, 1931. I.H.Co. files, Chicago.

71 La Follette committee, *Hearings*, 100: 2,939–3,051, and 109: 16,651–733.

CHAPTER 8 • HARVESTER'S INDUSTRIAL RELATIONS DEPARTMENT–ORIGIN AND EVOLUTION

1 Gertrude Beeks to E. A. S. Clarke, June 27, 1903. AMcB Papers, Case 3.

2 Recreation Committee to C.H.McC. II, Feb. 20, 1904. CHMcC II papers, I.H.Co. Welfare papers belonging to H.F.McC.'s office, File 12.

3 S. M. Darling to Cyrus Bentley, general counsel, I.H.Co., Sept. 1, 1904. CHMcC II papers, File 32.

4 Memorandum from C. U. Carpenter, Jan. 24, 1904. CHMcC II papers, I.H.Co. Welfare papers belonging to H.F.McC.'s office.

5 E. A. S. Clarke to H.F.McC., April 29, 1904. CHMcC II papers, I.H.Co. Welfare papers belonging to H.F.McC.'s office, File 1.

6 Gertrude Beeks to C.H.McC. II, June 6, 1904. CHMcC II papers, File 508.

7 Frank A. Ericsson to F. A. Flather, Oct. 6, 1903. CHMcC II papers, File 508.

8 F. A. Flather to E. A. S. Clarke, June 20, 1904. CHMcC II papers, File 32.

9 William Deering to C.H.McC. II, May 23, 1904. CHMcC II papers, I.H.Co. Welfare papers belonging to H.F.McC.'s office, File 5.

10 S. M. Darling to John R. Commons, Feb. 6, 1905. CHMcC II papers, I.H.Co. Welfare papers belonging to H.F.McC.'s office, File 37.

11 G. F. Steele to H.F.McC., Feb. 25, 1905. CHMcC II papers, I.H.Co. Welfare papers belonging to H.F.McC.'s office, File 7.

12 The economy of hiring a current employee instead of an outside expert for the welfare position had appealed to Cyrus McCormick: ". . . there is much that they could do during this year and without much expense to us in the way of high-priced salaries, such as would be involved should we get a first class expert like C. U. Carpenter . . . ." C.H.McC.

II to H.F.McC., Jan. 3, 1905. CHMcC II papers, I.H.Co. Welfare papers belonging to H.F.McC.'s office, File 19.
13 C. W. Price to G. F. Steele, April 10, 1905. CHMcC II papers, I.H.Co. Welfare papers belonging to H.F.McC.'s office, File 19.
14 Conferences on Welfare Work at Chicago Commons. CHMcC II papers, I.H.Co. Welfare papers belonging to H.F.McC.'s office (no file no.).
15 Ibid.
16 F. G. Moore to M. B. Edgerton, May 8, 1907. CHMcC II papers, I.H.Co. Welfare papers belonging to H.F.McC.'s office (no file no.).
17 Mary L. Goss, quoted in J. K. Mumford, "This Land of Opportunity," *Harper's Weekly* (July 18, 1908), p. 23.
18 Minutes, Welfare Board, Jan. 21, 1910. CHMcC II papers, File 20.
19 C.H.McC. II to H.F.McC. (from Zurich, Switzerland), Sept. 13, 1915. CHMcC II papers, File O-20.
20 W. M. Reay to C.H.McC. II, Jan. 14, 1905. CHMcC II papers, I.H.Co. Welfare papers belonging to H.F.McC.'s office, File 6.
21 Interview with Nesta Edwards, Milwaukee, April 21, 1960.
22 Jane Addams in Sarah E. Southall, *Industry's Unfinished Business,* p. xv.
23 Minutes, Works Managers' Meetings, Nov. 12, 1923. I.H.Co. files, Chicago. Secretary's transcripts of oral reports, not printed.
24 Ibid., Nov. 26, 1923.
25 Address by C.H.McC. III, vice president in charge of manufacturing, I.H.Co., before the American Management Association, Kansas City, Mo., Nov. 30, 1925. CHMcC II papers, unindexed material.
26 Minutes, Works Managers' Meetings, May 11, 1925. I.H.Co. files, Chicago. The findings were: absentees, 6.7% for April 29, 6.7% for April 30, and 6.2% for May 1.
27 Ibid., Sept. 19, 1927.
28 Ibid., Sept. 8, 1925.
29 Ibid., March 25 and Sept. 9, 1929.
30 Ibid., Feb. 10, 1930.
31 Ibid., 1922–23, passim, on wage and rate variations. See, e.g., minutes for June 4, Dec. 24, 1923.
32 Ibid., Jan. 16, 1937.
33 Interview with I.H.Co. Vice President Ivan Willis, May 1960.
34 Gertrude Beeks to S.R.McC., Dec. 2, 1902. NFMcC papers, Subject File, Series 3B, Box 30.
35 Minutes, Works Managers' Meetings, Nov. 12, 1923. I.H.Co. files, Chicago.
36 William T. Hutchinson, *Cyrus Hall McCormick,* 2: 8–63.
37 Minutes, Works Council, Wisconsin Steel Works, March 1919. McC. Col., I.H.Co. records.
38 Joint Statement on "Plan for Progress," I.H.Co., p. 3. I.H.Co. files, Chicago.

39 Minutes, Works Managers' Meetings, Oct. 23, 1922. I.H.Co. files, Chicago.
40 Ibid., Oct. 23, 1922; Jan. 9, April 9 and 27, 1923.
41 Ibid., May 28, 1923.
42 These figures are for the foundries only and not comparable to those of the previous paragraph, which apply to entire plants.
43 Minutes, Works Managers' Meetings, April 21, 1924. I.H.Co. files, Chicago.
44 Ibid., March 16, 1925.
45 Ibid., Oct. 26, 1925.
46 Ibid., Nov. 16, 1925.
47 Ibid., Feb. 10, 1930.
48 International Harvester employment stability report, citizenship status of employees, March 3, 1941. I.H.Co. files, Chicago.
49 Ibid., Dec. 31, 1943.
50 The Evansville plant operated only until 1955.
51 John Hope II, "Negro Employment in Three Southern Plants of International Harvester Company," in *Selected Studies of Negro Employment in the South* (Washington, D.C.: National Planning Association, 1953), pp. 50–51.
52 Ibid., p. 98. Hope is quoting Southall, *Industry's Unfinished Business,* p. 155.
53 Ibid., p. 57.
54 Ibid., p. 59.
55 Ibid., p. 31.
56 Ibid., p. 28.
57 Report E, Negro Employees, Domestic Operations, Period Ended Dec. 27, 1959, Education and Personnel Department, I.H.Co. files, Chicago.
58 *Memphis Press-Scimitar,* March 14, 1956.
59 *Detroit Sunday Times,* Feb. 14, 1960.
60 Ibid.
61 News item from the Memphis *Commercial Appeal* supplied to the author by UAW headquarters, Detroit.
62 Arthur D. Shy, assistant director, UAW Harvester Department, to the author, Dec. 30, 1963.
63 Report E, Negro Employees, Domestic Operations, Period Ended Dec. 27, 1959, Education and Personnel Department, I.H.Co. Files, Chicago.
64 Ibid.

CHAPTER 9 • PERMANENT UNIONISM

1 Richard A. Lester, *Labor and Industrial Relations,* pp. 206–7.
2 A more detailed description of a similar conflict-cooperation continuum is given by F. H. Harbison and J. R. Coleman, *Goals and Strategy in Collective Bargaining.*

3 Minutes, Works Council, McCormick Works, Sept. 9, 1936. Exhibits, NLRB Cases C-1561 to C-1566. National Archives.
4 Max Kampelman, *The Communist Party vs. the CIO,* p. 68.
5 Statement by Thomas Kelly, an FE leader in McCormick Works in 1941, in interview with the author, Sept. 24, 1963.
6 Ibid.
7 Transcript, National Defense Mediation Board panel, March 31, 1941. NDMB file, Case 4, File 2093, No. 2. National Archives.
8 Testimony of Powers Hapgood before NDMB panel, ibid., describing Conciliation Service meeting of March 3–6.
9 AF of L Press Release. U.S. Conciliation Service files, Case 4, File 196 /4111. National Archives.
10 U.S. Conciliation Service files, Case 4, File 196/4111. National Archives.
11 *New York Times,* March 24, 1941.
12 Interview with Fowler McCormick, June 1, 1964.
13 Memorandum, E. P. Marsh to E. J. Cunningham, March 20, 1941. U.S. Conciliation Service files, Case 4, File 196/4111. National Archives.
14 Transcript, NDMB panel, March 31, 1941. NDMB file, Case 4, File 2093, No. 2. National Archives.
15 Ibid
16 Letter, D. Lescohier to Ralph T. Seward, May 16, 1941. NDMB informal files, Cases 4 and 4A. National Archives.
17 Memorandum, F. H. Harbison to Ralph T. Seward, July 9, 1941. NDMB informal files, Cases 4 and 4A. National Archives.
18 George Hodge to C. A. Dykstra, July 14, 1941. NDMB informal files, Cases 4 and 4A. National Archives.
19 Frank Sliva to Wm. H. Davis, chairman. NDMB informal files, Cases 4 and 4A. National Archives.
20 Kampelman, *The Communist Party vs. the CIO,* pp. 67–72.
21 Stanley P. Farwell, special investigator for the National War Labor Board, to Thomas Neblett, principal mediator. NWLB informal files, Cases 4, 4A, and 89. National Archives.
22 National War Labor Board Decision, April 15, 1942. NWLB files, Cases 4, 4A, and 89. National Archives.
23 Memorandum, Thomas Fair Neblett. NWLB informal files, Cases 4, 4A, and 89. National Archives.
24 B. M. and S. K. Selekman, and S. H. Fuller, *Problems in Labor Relations,* p. 623.
25 Robert B. McKersie and William W. Shropshire, Jr., "Avoiding Written Grievances: A Successful Program," *The Journal of Business,* 35 (April 1962), 137
26 U.S. Congress, Joint Committee on Labor-Management Relations, 80th Congress, 2d session, Senate Report No. 986 (Washington, D.C.: Government Printing Office, 1948), pp. 118–20; Selekman, Selekman, and Fuller, *Problems in Labor Relations,* pp. 606–23; and Robert B.

McKersie, "Structural Factors and Negotiations in the International Harvester Company," in A. R. Webber, *The Structure of Collective Bargaining*, pp. 279–303.

27 Remarks of Gerald Fielde, Transcript of Fact Finding Panel appointed by Secretary of Labor Schwellenbach, Feb. 5, 1946. U.S. Conciliation Service files, Strikes, International Harvester, 1946. National Archives.

28 Remarks of William Reilly, ibid.

29 *New York Times,* March 30, 1946.

30 Memorandum attached to letter, Clinton P. Anderson to L. B. Schwellenbach, March 8, 1946. U.S. Conciliation Service files, Strikes, International Harvester, 1946. National Archives.

31 U.S. Conciliation Service files, Strikes, International Harvester, 1946. National Archives.

32 *New York Times,* March 31, 1946, p. 11.

33 Gerald Fielde to John Gibson, April 17, 1946. U.S. Conciliation Service files, Strikes, International Harvester, 1946. National Archives.

34 U.S. House of Representatives, Committee on Un-American Activities, 82d Cong., 2d session, *Hearings,* Sept. 2, 3, 1952, *Communist Activities in the Chicago Area,* Pt. 1, Testimony of John Edward Cooke and Alcide Thomas Kratz (Washington, D.C.: Government Printing Office, 1952).

35 Letter to I.H.Co. employees from Harvester President McCaffrey, Oct. 20, 1947. I.H.Co. Files, Chicago.

36 Interview with Milton Burns, Sept. 24, 1963.

37 Selekman, Selekman, and Fuller, *Problems in Labor Relations,* p. 623.

38 Interview with Arthur D. Shy, assistant director, UAW Harvester Department, Jan. 6, 1964.

39 Based on I.H.Co. tabulations. I.H.Co. files, Chicago.

40 Statement of Philip Taft, in U.S. Senate, Subcommittee of the Committee on Labor and Public Welfare, 82d Cong., 2d session, *Hearings on Communist Domination of Unions and National Security* (Washington, D.C.: Government Printing Office, 1952), pp. 176–77.

41 R. M. Easley to H.F.McC., Sept. 11, 1904. CHMcC II papers, File 508.

42 Telegram, F. J. Michael to Walter Smethurst, assistant to John L. Lewis, Feb. 1, 1939, and telegram, Philip Murray to Smethurst, Feb. 2, 1939. SWOC–FEWOC file, CIO papers, Catholic University of America.

43 Minutes of FEWOC Executive Board, April 27, 1941. SWOC–FEWOC file, CIO papers, Catholic University of America.

44 Ibid.

45 Interview with William Reilly, May 27, 1964.

46 U.S. Congress, Joint Committee on Labor-Management Relations, 80th Cong., 2d session, Senate Report No. 986, pp. 118–20.

47 See n. 35.

48 See "The Unstoppables," a company pamphlet describing the 1952 FE strike. Printed Material File.

49 Letter to I.H.Co. employees from McCaffrey, May 28, 1953, I.H.Co. files, Chicago; and *New York Times,* June 13, 1953.
50 Interview with Fowler McCormick, June 1, 1964.
51 Interview with Thomas Kelly, Sept. 24, 1963.
52 See n. 26.
53 I.H.Co., *Today,* Vol. 11, No. 5, 1960, and interview with Arthur D. Shy, Dec. 30, 1963, Chicago.

CHAPTER 10 • THE IMPACT OF UNIONS ON WAGES AND HOURS AT THE McCORMICK WORKS

1 A detailed account of the subject matter of this chapter, with wage data upon which these percentages are based and an explanation of the statistical techniques used, has been reserved for another volume.
2 Of the years of peacetime prosperity at the McCormick Works, the 31 with unions were 1865–73, 1880–87, 1900–3, 1947–60; the 20 without unions were 1887–93, 1905–13, 1923–29.
3 Wages Resolution, January 1910, I.H.Co. CHMcC II papers, File P-20.

CHAPTER 11 • THE EVOLUTION OF LABOR-MANAGEMENT RELATIONS: A SUMMARY

1 L.J.McC. to C.H.McC., May 25, 1867. CHMcC I papers, Corresp. File, Series 1A, Box 24.
2 Frank A. Ericsson to F. A. Flather, Oct. 6, 1903. CHMcC II papers, Corresp. File, Series 1C, No. 508.

Index